Atlantic Studies on Society in Change
No. 43
Editor-in-Chief Béla K. Király
Associate Editor Peter Pastor
Assistant Editor Albert A. Nofi

To the memory of
MIHÁLY SOZÁN (1938-1987)
Anthropologist, member, Board of Directors
Atlantic Research and Publications, Inc.

WAR AND SOCIETY IN EAST CENTRAL EUROPE
Vol. XXIV

THE EAST CENTRAL EUROPEAN
OFFICER CORPS 1740-1920s: SOCIAL
ORIGINS, SELECTION, EDUCATION, AND
TRAINING

Béla K. Király and Walter Scott Dillard, Editors

Social Science Monographs, Boulder, Colorado
Atlantic Research and Publications, Inc., Highland Lakes, New Jersey
Distributed by Columbia University Press

1988

EAST EUROPEAN MONOGRAPHS NO. CCXLI

Copyright © 1987 by Atlantic Research and Publications, Inc.

All rights reserved, including the right to reproduce this book or portions thereof in any form whatsoever, without the written permission of the publisher.

Library of Congress Catalog Card Number 87-62416

ISBN 0-88033-138-0

Printed in the United States of America

TABLE OF CONTENTS

Acknowledgments *Béla K. Király*   vii
Preface to the Series *Béla K. Király*   ix

I. GENERALIZATIONS

The Persistence of Imperial Ideas and Institutions
in the Selection, Education, and Training of Officers
Theodore Ropp   3
The Impact of Military Establishment on Nationalism
Stephen Fischer-Galati   21
Military Leadership and Education in Sociopolitical
Responsibility
Richard Georg Plaschka   29

II. EXTRATERRITORIAL PATTERNS

The Selection, Education, and Training of British
Officers, 1740-1920
Robin Higham   39
The Royal Prussian Cadet Corps, 1871-1918: A
Prosopographical Approach
John Moncure   57

III. THE HABSBURG IMPERIAL SYSTEM

The Education of Habsburg Army Officers 1848-1914
István Deák   73
The Theresian Military Academy in Wiener Neustadt
Gertrud Buttler-Elberberg   99

IV. NATIONAL PATTERNS

The Training of Bulgarian Officers, 1878-1918
Ljudmil Petrov   107
The Selection and Education of Greek Officers from Independence to 1920
Thanos Veremis   125
The Ludovika Military Academy, 1802-1920
Kálmán Kéri   137
Revolutionary Army, Professional Officers: Active Imperial-and-Royal Officers in the Hungarian Army in 1848-49
Gábor Bona   155
Social Origins, Selection, and Training of the Officer Corps in Hungary After the *Ausgleich*, 1867-82
Tibor Hajdu   167
The Training of Polish Officers, 1765-1830
Jerzy Cytowski   177

V. PARAMILITARY OFFICERS' TRAINING

Maria Theresa's Noble Lifeguards and the Rise of Hungarian Enlightenment and Nationalism
László Deme   197

Biographical Index   213

List of Contributors   237

Books published in "War and Society in East Central Europe" series   239
Maps   242 ff

ACKNOWLEDGMENTS

The Program on Society in Change conducts research, organizes conferences, and publishes scholarly books. It has been encouraged and supported by Brooklyn College. The National Endowment for the Humanities awarded it a research grant for 1978-81 and renewed it for another three-year term (1981-84). Without this substantial and much appreciated support, the Program would not exist. Additional contributions helped us in completing the research, holding conferences, and covering the costs of preparation of the manuscript for publication. Financial aid was granted by the International Research and Exchanges Board, the Open Society Fund, and other institutions.

The copyediting was done by Barbara Metzger and the preparation of the manuscript for publication by Albert A. Nofi, Dorothy Meyerson, Frances Hetherington, and Maurice Leibenstern of the Brooklyn College Program on Society in Change.

To all these institutions and persons, I wish to express my most sincere appreciation and thanks.

Highland Lakes, New Jersey
August 20, 1986

Béla K. Király
Professor Emeritus of
History
Editor-in-Chief

PREFACE TO THE SERIES

The present volume is the twenty-fourth in a series that, when completed, will constitute a comprehensive survey of the many aspects of war and society in East Central Europe. The chapters of this an forthcoming volumes have been selected from papers presented at a series of international, interdisciplinary scholarly conferences conducted by the Program on Society in Change in cooperation with other institutions of higher learning.

These volumes deal with the peoples whose homelands lie between the Germans to the west, the Russians to the east and north, and the Mediterranean and Adriatic Seas to the south. They constitute a particular civilization, one that is an integral part of Europe, yet substantially different from the West. The area is characterized by rich variety in language, religion, and government, and, not surprisingly, a similar variety can also be observed in concepts of national defense, in the nature of armed forces, and in ways of waging war. The study of this complex subject demands a multidisciplinary approach, and, accordingly, our contributors represent several academic disciplines. They have been drawn from universities and other scholarly institutions in the United States, Canada, and Western Europe as well as in the East Central European socialist countries.

Our comparative investigation of military behavior and organization attempts to ascertain what is peculiar to particular nations and ethnic groups, what has been socially and culturally determined, and what has resulted from the exigencies of the moment. We try to define different patterns of military behavior, including decision-making processes, attitudes, and actions of diverse social classes and the degree of restraint (or lack thereof) typically shown in war. We endeavor to present considerable material that can help us to understand how the process of social, economic, political, and technological change as well as changes in the sciences and in international relations influenced the development of doctrines of national defense and altered actual practice in such areas as military organization, command, strategy, and tactics. We also present data on the social origins and mobility of the officer corps and the rank and file and on the differences between the officer corps of the various services and, above all, on civil-military relations and the origins of the East Central European brand of militarism. For a fuller understanding of the relationship among war, the armed forces, and society, the series also examines the economic and commercial aspects of life. The students will, we hope, deepen our understanding of the societies, governments, and politics of East Central Europe.

Our methodology takes into account the changes in the study of war and national defense systems which have occurred in the last three decades. During that period, the study of war and national defense systems has moved away from a narrow focus on battles, campaigns, and leaders and now views a country's military history in the context of the evolution of the entire society. In fact, historians, political scientists, sociologists, philosophers, and other students of war and national defense have come to recognize the interdependence of changes in society and changes in warfare; they accept the proposition that military institutions closely reflect the character of the society of which they are a part. Recognition of this fact is a keystone of our approach to the subject.

Works in Western languages now provide adequate coverage of the diplomatic, political, intellectual, social, and economic histories of the peoples of East Central Europe. In contrast, few substantial studies of their national defense systems have yet appeared in Western languages. Similarly, though some comprehensive accounts of the nonmilitary aspects of the history of the entire region have been published in the West, there is as yet no comprehensive account of the area's national defense systems in any Western language. Nor is there any study of the mutual effects of the concepts and practices of national defense in East Central Europe. Thus, this comprehensive study of war and society in East Central Europe is a pioneering work.

As Editor-in-Chief, of course, I cheerfully take full responsibility for the comprehensiveness, cohesion, internal balance, and scholarly quality of the series I have launched. I intend this work to be neither a justification nor a condemnation of the policies, attitudes, and activities of any of the nations involved. At the same time, because the contributors represent so many different disciplines, languages, interpretations, schools of thought, our policy in this, as in past and future volumes, is to present their contributions without modification.

In this sense, the volume is a sampling of the schools of thought and the standards of scholarship in the many countries to which our contributors belong.

Béla K. Király
Editor-in-Chief

I. GENERALIZATIONS

The Persistence of Imperial Ideas and Institutions in the Selection, Education, and Training of Officers

Theodore Ropp

These studies on the nationalization of imperial ideas and institutions about officer selection, education, and training link the studies earlier reported on maritime war and trade and on revolution and counterrevolution with a final look at political and military leadership. The geopolitical arena is isolated, agrarian East Central Europe during the era of the Enlightened Despots from 1740 to 1920, but the issues of expanding officer selection and education while retaining loyalty to a dynasty rather than to a nation raise new problems of methodology, definitions, and sources. Some of the resulting generalizations are too broad and hazy to be footnoted. Every schoolboy or Doctor of Philosophy knows that Periclean Athens was a democratic empire of merchants, artists, philosophers, and rhetoricians, the Spartans boorish soldiers, and Rome a larger Sparta with Athenian trimmings and that the Habsburg emperor who died without a son in 1740 was the philosopher emperor who had died in Vindobona in 180. That he might have died elsewhere in Pannonia need not be examined here. Myths are inextricably mixed with ideas and images many centuries old and culled from such scattered oral, historical, biographical, and prosopographical sources.[1]

Fergus Millar's *Emperor in the Roman World* deals with the expectations of the emperor's clients and subjects. With his household of clerics, soldiers, administrators, and lawyers, Marcus Aurelius Antonius tried to "form a more perfect union, establish justice, insure domestic tranquility, provide for the common defense, promote the general welfare, and secure the blessing of" philosophy for the whole Mediterranean world.[2] His images reflected this: the bronze horseman, a realistic column of his Dacian Wars, the aureole of Apollo, Alexander, and Augustus. But by 180 the emperor could not reward his family and clients from a static agriculture without new lands, slaves, or techniques, and experiments with a hereditary system — even with the most careful tutoring — had already produced a religious and an artistic maniac to be murdered by their bodyguards. The gladiator Commodus's murder was no great surprise, but plots against Julius, perhaps Augustus, and Tiberius Caesar had also been successful. By Roman standards the Benevolent Despots got senility, eccentricity, and weakness together only once after the accessions of Maria Theresa, Frederick II, and Elizabeth Petrovna. And between 1740 and 1914, the dynasts had expanded their families and loyal elites after their competitors had forced them to adopt to the secular commercial, democratic, and industrial revolutions.

This brings on other problems of definition to support two general hypotheses: that in officer selection, education, and training, Europe's Renaissance monarchs used the same ties of blood and soil, educational and religious conformity, and physical training as the Romans, and at the same time they devised new methods for those civic guildsmen who managed the loyalties, tribute, trade, and judicial activities for the land- and tradition-bound villagers and craftsmen who still did most of East Central Europe's work in 1740.

There was little in Europe's diet of classical literature, history, and biography on officer selection. Selection from the landed elite and, for high command, from some ruling family or faction were implied. Political education and military training were on-the-job. Long-service military companies could win glory and booty for an ambitious prince, from Alexander to the Caesars. No attention was paid to educational theory, though guild specialists might work under a gentleman with a how-to book on any subject from architecture to zoology. The Roman officer and gentleman's grammar schools were imitated by many European princes. The most popular military textbooks were Vegetius's Late Roman handbook on drill, discipline, and so forth, and collections of maxims like those of Sun Tsu in China. Insofar as officer selection, education, and training were concerned, the Empire lived on in the Habsburg, Bourbon, Hohenzollern, Romanov, and Hanoverian Empires of 1740.[3]

Modern philosophers made ever finer distinctions between apparently similar objects or situations. Their innovations, like those of villagers, craftsmen, pedlars, and artists, were regularly tested internally before entering world markets. Diplomats and generals' demand-oriented products were tested in cycles of more or less international turbulence. Their educators tended to stress fail-safe traditions and better discipline and training. By 1740 — to suggest the difficulties of definition and distinction — "academy" had five English meanings in addition to the name of the garden where Plato had taught: his system of ideas, a place where the arts and sciences were taught, a place of training and of training in a given art or science, and a society to cultivate and promote any or all of the above. Each academy also set its own guild standards. We need not research (a Latin dog circling its quarry) this here. But such Greek terms as history, philosophy, and rhetoric suggest intellectual dialogue, while the Roman terms for company, family, science, seminar, soldier, and training suggest the eclectic (Greek for borrowing) and pragmatic application of ideas by disciplined, orderly institutions.[4]

Another problem is to locate changes in military education and training on the time-scale of European international relations. After the fourteenth- and fifteenth-century developments of oceangoing sailing ships, gunpowder weapons, overseas empires, printing, and a power technology, the "new monarchs" jockeyed for power in sixty-year cycles of escalating and better-controlled violence.[5] The Habsburgs had been pulled and pushed from Germany to the Netherlands, the western Mediterranean, and the Danube without any nationalizing, secularizing, or individualizing of their imperial ideas and instructions. Robert R. Palmer's map of European civilization during the Enlightenment (with the boundaries of 1740) locates academies, publications, libraries, and imitations of Versailles as aspects of the "Spread of Science,...the Press, Deism, Tolerance, Reform." He sees it as an era of cultural diffusion, "reaching new classes of society through popularization" and extending its institutions "into northern and eastern Europe" and creole America. But educational theorists such as Jan Komensky ([Comenius] 1592-1670), John Locke (1632-1704), and Jean-Jacques Rousseau (1712-78), the Romantic or Utopian pioneers of free-form education, had yet had little effect on either education or training.[6]

Neither the educational nor the training reforms begun during the violent reign of Louis the Great ([XIV of France] sole ruler 1661-1715) were institutionalized until the quieter times and better-controlled wars of Louis the Well-Beloved ([XV] under a regent or favorite 1715-74). And even the more numerous court and military academies of the Benevolent Despots were similar to those set up to turn officers' sons into gentlemen by the mercenary captains who had taken over many of Italy's cities during the Renaissance and who wished to legitimize themselves and their families by turning themselves into real emperors.

One of the most famous of these court academies had been set up by the great humanist Vittorino da Feltre (1378-1446) for the Gonzaga tyrant of Mantua. Once the Gonzagas' usurpations had been legitimized by their distant German imperial employer, they trained some of their courtiers in the civilized arts of classical literature, mathematics, philosophy, and music, while others kept an eye on the more military and economically useful arts and sciences of mining, engineering, finance, and logistics. Those specialists had to help the prince impose his will on largely illiterate adventures and ne'er-do-wells, who had to be trained, disciplined, fed, paid, and watched to keep them from jumping to another employer. A courtly education like that outlined in Baldassare Castiglione's (1478-1529) *Book of the Courtier* — a Socratic dialogue supposedly held at the court of the Montefeltre tyrant of Urbino — was of less help to Castiglione's position as generalissimo of the papal forces than to that of mediator between the Medici pope Clement VII and the emperor Charles V.

In stressing the concept of feudal honor, Castiglione represented some thirteen mercenary families whose intermarriages had muscled them into a feudal power structure in which honor and fighting ability were allegedly inherited. But they remained well aware that their power also depended on the regular delivery of money, weapons, and supplies to keep their companies from deserting or plundering bystanders. The Montefeltres' own reputation rested less on their heroic conduct than on their caution in risking their venture capital only on victories made certain by advance negotiation. Castiglione was to be undercut by the bad faith of the pope. He allegedly died of shame when his new employer Charles's unpaid mercenaries sacked Rome in 1527. In appealing to the Borgias to save Italy from the barbarians, Niccolo Machiavelli (1469-1527) displayed equal contempt for feudal honor and *condottieri* financial caution. But in ignoring the technical problems of supporting long-service troops over ever-longer distances with increasing quantities of nonrenewable supplies, he also ignored the forces which had already rendered the Roman system of courtly education obsolete.[7]

In 1740 Maria Theresa was midway between Charles V's abdication in 1556 and the last Habsburg's deposition, but military educators had not yet systematically faced problems which, when compounded by the further expansion of empires, trade, banking, manufacturing, transport, literacy, and the applied sciences, were to be the proximate cause of the strategic and tactical failures of the world's best-educated armies in 1914-18. Seventy-one years later, one American writer suggests that academies should not try to educate soldiers at all:[8]

> Social scientists have demonstrated that . . . personal traits and expectations are formed before college age. Those who are drawn to a "life of the mind" . . . are generally not attracted to the military profession. The few philosophically minded officers . . . were prepared to blossom long before they entered college. The vast majority . . . adapt to the military because they value a physically demanding life style, have an aptitude for dealing with technology, and value . . . the exercise of unquestioned authority. Indeed . . . they are carefully screened for these traits by . . . psychological testing instruments and interviews.

The modern officer, he continues, cannot absorb "an ever expanding body of technical knowledge" while "learning all . . . about the human condition," if only because few educators can "synthesize the practical requirements for technical understanding and the equally practical requirement to understand humanity." The contradictions of a noble country life-style, the vulgarities of engineering, and the immoralities of real politics do not go well with "duty, honor, country." Since he fights for honor and his men for money, he must know enough about the grammar and rhetoric of economic and political power to retain their confidence. But "without the technical capacity to fight, the values that we want to protect may be destroyed." The officer can be educated in, at best, two of our three cultures. "He cannot be a person for all seasons, no matter how hard he tries or how hard we try to help him."[9]

A final problem for princely selectors, tutors, educators, and trainers is the sporadic international testing of their military, as distinct from their cultural and technological, products. Soldiers, educators, and technocrats are all demand-oriented. For princes, soldiers are necessities, educators and technologists classical luxuries but modern necessities. By accepting Christianity, and implicit in it the dignity of labor, the Late Roman Empire and its barbarian rivals could still enlist civilian technicians with some knowledge of languages, arithmetic, and geometry as record keepers, paymasters, engineers, and teachers to train and discipline the more than forty technical specialists listed by Commodus's military jurist as part of each legion.[10] Their utility to a Frankish war chief is suggested by Clovis's (?466-511) use of an orphaned legion's fortress, treasury, and armory at Soissons before he decided that all this was worth a mass and founded the Merovingian dynasty.[11] But educational survival for new princes was not easy as taking over economically and technologically stagnant old empires. It was not until the Age of Reason that Europe's new monarchs had the time and resources to expand their courtly and guild academies to take advantage of the long-term economic developments opened to them in overseas trade and colonization, internal transport, gunpowder, a money economy, a power technology, and the vulgarization and nationalization of religion, sciences, art, and technology by printing and the Reformation.

Until then, the new dynasts' military educational products must be estimated in the old way, from very scattered and self-serving literary and biographical evidence based on learning-by-doing after, at most, a secondary and adolescent education. The Spanish court had trained Philip II (1527-98), William of Orange (1533-84), Alexander Farnese, duke of Parma (1542-92), Philip's son, Don Carlos (1545-68), and Charles's natural son, Don John of Austria (1547-78). Historians' judgments still rest on their performances as princes. A somewhat different view of the Spanish noble officer came from the well-educated volunteer Miguel de Cervantes (1547-1616). For their mastery of the technical problems of artillery, engineering, and logistics, comparisons of Maurice of Nassau (1567-1625), Spinola (1569-1630), Wallenstein (1583-1634), Gustavus Adolphus (1594-1632), Montecucolli (1609-80), Turenne (1611-75), Conde (1621-86), Marlborough (1650-1722), and Eugene of Savoy (1663-1736) would cover the years of professionals' mastery of swamps and forests which had repelled the Romans. Courtly education was thoroughly Machiavellian, to the displeasure of Catholic and Protestant educators, but their emphasis on modern languages and mathematics met the needs of the middle-class mercantilists who nationalized imperial expansion after the overextended Iberian empires had been defeated in northern and western Europe. Even there the devastation wrought by Turenne's disciplined mercenaries in the Rhineland was so close to the plundering described in Hans Jakob von Grimmelshausen's (1620-76) *Simplicissimus* that it besmirched Louis the Great's civilized cultural image.[12]

By 1750 Louis XV had begun the process of rationalizing and reforming France's armed forces and their training and education. Louis XIV's resource managers — Colbert (1619-83), Vauban (1633-1707), and Louvois (1641-91) — had not had the time or resources to do this, while French-language schools and academies were spreading throughout Europe. The reforms of Louis the Well-

Beloved, an astute perpetual adolescent, pleased the poor and glory-hungry nobility, the rationalizing middle class, secular critics of Louis XIV's pieties, and a national desire to reverse humiliating defeats by British and Austrian forces in the Wars of Jenkins' Ear and the Austrian Succession (1739-48). Locke's blank pages were already proving attractive to educational Utopians of a self-regulating clocklike world. The ordinary noble officer needed a disciplined secondary education away from the corruptions of the court. Specialists would go on for advanced training in artillery, engineering, and other military arts, and researchers would hold maneuvers at schools of application.[13] State and private schools would all be part of a national university from which the principles of agriculture, art, or war would trickle down to the working world. The resulting uniformity turned out to be well suited to the modernizing process of alienation, conversion, and homogenization led by classically trained rhetoricians who turned with every wind of imperial fashion. Languages, mathematics, and drawing — the most useful communications techniques for pre-photographic, preelectronic societies — were the bases of secular and national education, as the Age of Reason's educators fitted square and round pegs into square and round holes to create a Newtonian clocklike polity in which, to these Augustans, whatever was, was right. In the process, however, educators would have to hone down those ovoids of passion, dissent, nationalism, vulgarity, and technical innovation which would eventually reduce all but two people's empires to ruins.[14]

Modern business managers, teachers, and soldiers are so demand-oriented and tradition-minded that tracing changes in their procedures involves considerable problems of definition both for traditionalists and for those who had to adapt traditional methods for dealing with increasing numbers of innovators and innovations in the world beyond the parish or the company. The timing of change is imprecise because l ilitary and educational crisis testing may delay institutional reforms until quieter times. The Enlightenment simply expanded the imperial tradition of disciplined secondary education for nobles wishing to enter state service with the required social, linguistic, and arithmetical graces. Branch or professional training was on-the-job or in special schools of application. Except for certain practical professions, soldiers had few contacts with philosophers in the universities. By contrast with the medieval universities, these were now bastions of princely religions.

Marcus Aurelius saw himself as "rational and social; . . . my city and country, so far as I am Antoninus, is Rome, but so far as I am a man, it is the world. The things then which are useful to these cities are alone useful to me."[15] His successors removed Rome's ideas to the City of God; its techniques and institutions survived in the Rome of Gregory the Great (?540-604; pope 590-604). Masses of materials can still illuminate the French Revolution's liberal and conservative, revolutionary and counterrevolutionary mentalities, but, true to their traditions, many military and educational historians still treat it as a Tolstoyan epic of great captains, states, ideas, and alumni. Thomas Carlyle's (1795-1881) *French Revolution* (1837) produced his *Heroes and Hero Worship* (1840). It had let new men and ideas break through a fossilized society. But what its herods learned in their adolescent academies and adult schools of application remains clouded by what we all know about Carnot (1753-1823), Bernadotte (?1763-1844), Napoleon (1769-1821), and Wellington (1769-1851). All were soldier-statesmen. Two were nobles, two middle-class, three technicians. The longest-lived were the most successful, and each fostered a different aspect of that popularization of the military, technical, economic, and political institutions which produced such tragic results for the European peninsula and East Central Europe after 1914.[16]

When he purchased a lieutenant colonelcy in 1793, the future duke of Wellington had finished Eton and the French School of Equitation at Angers and had served in five regiments, in the Irish Parliament, and as aide-de-camp to the Lord Lieutenant. He commanded a brigade in Flanders while Napoleon was commanding the artillery in Toulon. He sailed for India in command of the 33rd Foot with a library of classics and moderns in 1796, when Bonaparte took command in Italy. Nothing in his later career suggested reform in a British system of officer selection, self-education, and regimental training which underwent little change throughout Victoria's reign (1837-1901). For a nation of exporters, the system fostered self-reliance, enough honesty for officers to need private incomes even after the abolition of purchase, and long periods of exposure to other cultures and ovoid and eccentric characters. Xenophon's Spartan and Shakespeare's Tudor mercenaries lived on in Rudyard Kipling's (1865-1936) India. Without a popular system of technical and university education, the British military guild system was more relevant for another emerging insular empire than for the modernizing nations of

Central Europe, to which — as to Colonel Blimp's inventor — this model of a modern army was one of lions led by country donkeys or an occasional mulish messmate.[17]

Bernadotte was the most successful middle-class product of the Old Regime's discriminatory system of military education and training. The son of a provincial lawyer, through his legal apprenticeship he was a master of analysis, revolutionary rhetoric, and respect for constituted authority. After his father's death, he enlisted in the Royal Marine Regiment at seventeen and rose to regimental sergeant major at twenty-five. He became a lieutenant at twenty-nine in 1792, when careers were opened to talents. In 1799, at thirty-six, he was minisser of war. In 1810, at forty-seven, he was elected crown prince of Sweden. His princely career was one of Machiavellian self-education, enlivened by military exploits which eventually won him a Marseilles banker's daughter whose elder sister had married Joseph Bonaparte. That they survived the Revolution to marry their son Oscar I (1799-1859; king of Sweden 1844-59) to Princess Josephine, the daughter of Eugene de Beauharnais and the granddaughter of the king of Bavaria, was a triumph of middle-class mobility. It was won not on the playing fields of Eton but in those drawing- and bedrooms in which Arabella and John Churchill and Sarah Jennings had attained ducal status. Wellington's rise had much to do with the Augustans' method of selecting officers for a courtly education. Bernadotte was a product of the parallel process of selecting literate legionary technicians to bridge the gap between the cream and the dregs of society.[18]

The Caesar who eventually convinced himself and his Spartans that he was a new Alexander was the son of a Corsican nobleman. After he and his brother Joseph had been tutored in French, Napoleon went to a provincial military college at Brienne, finished at the luxurious Royal Military College in Paris, and passed by examination into an artillery regiment at sixteen. Like that of the most recent great captain, Frederick II, Napoleon's education gave him everything but senses of honor and intellectual humility. In the logic and rhetoric of war and politics, both were well trained. Both saw themselves as drivers and managers of Newtonian round-and-square-peg-and-hole machines, which had only to be better disciplined than that which had carried French culture but not French arms across Europe, the mystery which Voltaire (1694-1778) had raised in the first popular history of modern civilization, *Le Siécle de Louis XIV* (175%). In the imperial arena, Napoleon's education failed him. By settling for discipline and doubling his Prussian patrimony, Frederick stayed in the Concert of Europe.[19]

Another lawyer's son, Lazare Carnot, was the elder of two brothers whose marriages to the daughters of an army contractor named Dupont helped to found a Jacobin engineering and educational dynasty. Carnot had been tutored in Paris for two years before passing the examination for the engineers' school at Meziéres. Not quite twenty when he was commissioned, he spent the next eighteen years in scientific and political self-education before both he and his engineer brother were elected to the new Legislative Assembly (1792). The precise and logical style of his defenses of Vauban's (1633-1707) obsolete fortifications system made him the Organizer of Victory for the Committee of Public Safety and the Directory. His quarrels with Napoleon ended by his returning to service as Napoleon's engineering advisor. Exiled for deserting the Bourbons for the third time, when Napoleon made him a count and minister of the interior during the Hundred Days, he was the model manager for a square-and-round-pegs-and-holes machine of educated citizens, each ready "to exercise his constitutional rights with discretion and responsibility," with a technical efficiency "appropriate to his estate."[20]

Colbert's, Vauban's, and Carnot's social-engineering ideas still informed the officer selection, education, and training systems institutionalized in an ideologically and socially divided France from the Bourbon Restoration (1815) to the end of the Second Empire (1870). Competitive admissions mixed noble and middle-class officers and raised the educational and training standards for both. Both were needed to manage their unlucky long-service peasant and working-class conscripts. Cadets now entered at eighteen for more rigorous training at St. Cyr, the Napoleonic polytechnic school, and advanced training in their branch schools or regiments. A staff officer, for example, after one year at the staff school, served two years each with the infantry and the cavalry and one with the artillery. The resulting system for producing long-service specialized guildsmen was widely imitated, not least in the United States and in an Italy united in 1860 by Piedmont-Sardinia with the help of the Second Empire. And it was to fit in with the major innovation in advanced general military education produced after Prussia's defeat in 1806-7.[21]

The military successes of the Prussian war academy and general staff from 1801, when the forty-six-year-old Hanoverian staff officer Gerhard Scharnhorst (1755-1813) joined a fossilized Prussian army, to its abolition in 1919 as a menace to the peace of Europe are well known, but it is hard to evaluate its products' role in reforming and then freezing officer education and training at a higher level. The war academy was not a cadet college or adult school of application for Prussian nobles. It was a scientific academy with permanent, student, and corresponding members and the task of trying out new ideas in seminars, exercises, and field maneuvers, communicating the results to the prince and his army, and training officers to advise field commanders who had already had staff training. The idea of a scientific staff to bridge the gap between theory and practice was not new, but it was most successful in an encircled, disunited state whose weakness in manpower forced it to substitute disciplined education and training for numbers.[22]

The technological problem which, in the end, brought about the collapse of German military science was the tactical connection between weapons and ideas. But the generational punctuation marks on that feedback process which led from a Hanoverian sergeant major's son who came of age in the year of the American Declaration of Independence to the specialized professional-education failure which gave the graduates of the new American war colleges their first experiences of an overseas industrialized war can only be approximated. In any case, both general civic and military professional education can relate each modern empire's armed forces to its "Constitution . . . Government, Customs, Climate, Religion, Commerce, etc." Carl von Clausewitz (1780-1831), the war academy's closet intellectual, modeled himself on Montesquieu (1689-1755). He heaped mainly modern observations and maxims into piles which others might erect into principles. This was not enough for such Newtonian machine-builders as the Swiss bank clerk Antoine Henri Jomini (1779-1869), who discovered Napoleon's secret in Frederick's idea of throwing his army across his enemy's line of communications. That Napoleon's system was wasteful where food supplies and roads were far less developed than in northwestern Europe was discovered later. God was on the side of Carnot's conscript battalions so long as they were activated by hunger, revolutionary fervor, their officers' thirst for status, plunder, and glory, and Napoleon's willingness to risk his capital on increasingly Alexandrian ventures.[23]

Though he was not trained as an artilleryman, Scharnhorst, like Carnot, made his name as a peacetime military educator and organizer. His forum was a new artillery school in Hanover, to which he was assigned as a twenty-eight-year-old lieutenant. His military handbooks and field manuals supported a small farm, a wife who was a sister of the first director of the University of Berlin, and his military journal. In 1793 he fought against his fellow engineer Carnot's army in the Netherlands and analyzed the French capture of Menin and success in revolutionary war. He was promoted to major and assigned to the Hanoverian staff before joining the Prussians with the rank of lieutenant colonel, more than double his former pay, and a patent of nobility. His war academy survived the military reformers' forced exile to Russia, his death as Blücher's chief of staff in 1813, and the political infighting of the postwar era, but it did so by focusing on nonpolitical, Newtonian scientific managerial problems rather than on seeking the ideal Platonic principles of politics and war.[24]

Partly because of his distrust of suspected royalist and Jacobin subordinates, Napoleon appointed Spartan lion-donkeys to independent commands outside of the two Gauls and Germany. While his imperial system of loyal commanders, long-service conscription, and machine-like training survived until 1870, it did not solve the problem of supplying and controlling mass armies. Yet it was this problem which an industrializing Prussia had to solve to unite its encircled territories to defeat Austria and co-opt liberal nationalists with the profits of a united Germany. The chief of the general staff who solved these problems from 1858 to 1888 was Helmuth von Moltke (1800-88). A scientific geographer or geopolitician, he conquered time and distance by completing local mobilization before using railroads and telegraphs to win more-than-Napoleonic victories. After 1870 his planning and training institutions and methods were adopted by every mass-conscript army, though conservatives still limited their numbers to those which could be officered by a slowly growing nobility. William the Great ([I] 1797-1888; regent to emperor 1858-88), who had fought against Napoleon, saw no reason to change Moltke's military education and training systems, but his more modern grandson William II (1859-41; emperor 1888-1918) felt the need for a more assertive foreign policy, a high-seas fleet, and an overseas empire to increase national power, prosperity, and consciousness and to outbid an increasingly literate, cohesive, and socialist proletariat.

The Frederician and Wilhelmine systems of officer selection, education, and training were not militaristic; neither modern Sparta was run for the interests of a military caste. The general staff's isolation from dynastic politics tended to isolate it from both internal and external struggles for power. Its success in solving the solvable logistic and communications problems of mass-conscript armies kept it working at even more elegant Jominian solutions for multiplying mass by mobility for decisive victory in battle. Like other general staffs it assessed only the offensive capabilities of a whole new generation of mass-produced rapid-fire infantry and artillery weapons. A war lord who knew nothing about the friction of war never questioned its plans for dishonoring treaties. It could not stop his diplomatically disastrous break with Russia, naval and colonial adventures, and overblown militaristic rhetoric. A successful system for training Spartan robots did not encourage nonconformist personalities. The similar specialization of German university life did not encourage university questions about the new science of war. There was no real dialogue between the most intellectual of general-staff chiefs, Alfred von Schlieffen (1833-1913; chief of the general staff 1891-1905) and the military historian Hans Delbrück (1848-1929). In trying to fight the last war better, staffs were looking for more Jominian examples, such as that subsumed by Delbrück from Hannibal's victory over the Romans at Cannae in 216 B.C.. In this highly specialized technical, economic, political, and military system, no special interest prevailed except that of a monarch who was a man for every fashion.[25]

As the German Empire infiltrated and then incorporated East Central Europe, each new nation Germanized its army. All were competent, and some dominated their states, but few were able to fit their Roman-German imperial ideas and institutions to their geopolitical circumstances. Again, judgments of the products of this system of officer selection, education, and training are too dependent on military biographies and autobiographies. German views of lions led by political donkeys and pied pipers to two technical, economic, and political disasters are not encouraging. Nationalist dreams of sovereignty over lands, seas, hearts, and minds on the inner European fringe of the world island, except for Albania's, were Utopian.[26]

This may be the answer to the idea that educating Spartans is a contradiction in terms made especially so by the proliferation of specialized modern military technologies. To paraphrase Clausewitz, a world in which electronic technologies have made counting resources and figuring the odds far easier has done nothing about the passions which motivate changes from friends to foes, doubters to believers, innocent civilians to combatants, and medieval to modern.[27]

The following generalizations are unprovable, and some may not be worth discussing. But in suggesting how the persistence of imperial military and educational ideas and institutions affected the pace and direction of modernization in East Central Europe, it can be contended that in 1740 monarchs were still educating their official families to honor those ties of blood and soil, ideological conformity, and technical pragmatism which had brought peace and prosperity to Augustan and Antonine Rome, technical, economic, political, and military modernization had already forced some Renaissance monarchs to hire and train more specialists. Changes, often sparked by violent generational crises, tended to be institutionalized in quarter periods of international relations under the balance-of-power system. Between 1720 and 1900, Enlightened politicians twice expanded and reformed their systems of selecting, educating, and training their service nobilities. By 1900 the Bourbon-Hohenzollern system had become so professionally specialized that its products were removed from social, economic, and political reality. Except in preaching the need for a Central European garrison state, in the sense of running that state in the interests of a military caste, it was not militaristic. This was a tragedy for the emerging nations of East Central Europe, whose expert military technicians could not save their nations from German infiltration, conquest, and the consequences of two German defeats. Only a humanistic, professional, and technical education can produce professionals who do not lose sight of their social responsibilities.[28]

NOTES

1. Marcus Aurelius Antoninus (121-80; emperor 161-80), from a family made patrician by Vespasian (emperor 69-79), was Hadrian's (emperor 117-38) choice to succeed Marcus's uncle Antoninus Pius (emperor 138-61). His thanks to his family and mentors illustrate a system of educating and adopting heirs observed by Polybius (?205-?125 B.C.) in the Hellenizing Scipionic Circle. Marcus's *Meditations*, in Greek, were written at his base camp at Carnuntum, south of the Danube near Hainburg, Austria, and Bratislava.

2. Millar, in *The Emperor in the Roman World (31 B.C.-A.D. 337)* (Ithaca, 1977), begins with Marcus Aurelius at Sirmium (Sremska Mitrovica, Yugoslavia). My quotation is from the Roman Republican Constitution of the

United States (1787). The adolescent emperors removed by their guards were Gaius ([Caligula] A.D. 12-41; emperor 37-41), Nero (37-68; emperor 54-68), and Marcus's son Commodus (161-92; emperor 180-92). On one of these failures of the Augustan system of choosing and educating princes, see Miriam T. Griffin, *Nero: The End of a Dynasty* (London, 1984).

3. For these studies on war and society in East Central Europe, Europe's great powers were agrarian and mercantile polities whose traditional soldiers and educators were still coping with the alleged imperatives of modern economic, social, technological, and political change. Both Vegetius (before A.D. 378) and Sun Tsu (after 400 B.C.) were bureaucrats in technologically stable, warring societies.

4. "Academy" in the sense of physical or gymnasium training — as a riding or royal military academy — was used first in 1734. The other definitions were earlier (*Oxford English Dictionary*, compact edition [New York, 1971]).

5. My *History and War* (Augusta, Ga., 1984) suggests that sixty-year paradigm crises and adjustments in modern great-power relations fit "epochs dominated by an expanding economy and a balance-of-power system." The "causal" factors are generational struggles for power within the sixty-year political life-span (plus five years of infancy) which was normative for classical and modern governing elites.

6. Robert R. Palmer, ed., *Atlas of European History* (New York, 1957), pp. 81-83.

7. On the mercenary princes' efforts to gain political legitimacy by playing the cultural role of the emperor, see Michael Mallett, *Mercenaries and Their Masters: Warfare in Renaissance Italy* (Totowa, N.J., 1974). The problem of domesticating the mercenaries could only be solved, Mallett thinks, by nationalization.

8. Stephen B. Sloane, reviewing *Literature in the Education of the Military Professional*, by Donald Ahern and Robert Shenk (Colorado Springs, 1982) in *Naval War College Review* 37, no. 2 (March-April 1985): 115.

9. Ibid.

10. G. R. Watson, *The Roman Soldier* (Ithaca, 1969), p. 76. Both the pay and the duties of literate soldiers with some knowledge of arithmetic and geometry were carefully outlined in the technologically self-sufficient cities known as legions. Neither Graham Webster (*The Roman Imperial Army of the First and Second Centuries A.D.* [London, 1969]) nor Edward N. Luttwak (*The Grand Strategy of the Roman Empire from the First Century A.D. to the Third* [Baltimore, 1976]) had any reason to stress the legion's technical and educational self-sufficiency.

11. Bernard S. Bachrach, *Merovingian Military Organization 481-751* (Minneapolis, 1972), pp. 4-5. The great Benedictine fortress abbeys were to

be similar refuges for Roman military technology and bastions of the Carolingian Renaissance.

12. Full titles of these great captains and princes were by this time as impressive and redundant as those of any Roman emperor. For his war against the Marcomanni, Marcus Aurelius added the title Germanicus Maximus, one which turned out to be historically correct.

13. For impressive lists of existing and projected military technical and educational institutions, see Frederick B. Artz, *The Development of Technical Education in France 1500-1850* (Cambridge, Mass., 1966). Like many histories of education and almost all histories of military education, Artz's work has a national focus, but French cultural preeminence during the Age of Reason makes this one of the best introductions to the problems of a loyal, technically competent noble imperial officer corps.

14. As Artz notes in his opening paragraphs, the origins of modern technical education "were extraordinarily diverse," because they involved educational, economic, and military theory and practice, while these, in turn, involved "the general history of education, science, technology, and government" (Ibid., p. 2).

15. *The Meditations of Marcus Aurelius*, trans. George Long (Chicago, 1952), 6. 44.

16. Leo Tolstoy's (1828-1910) *War and Peace* (1866) was an epic of free will and determinism. As a soldier, Tolstoy had strong views on the "loud cries and shining objects" of military art and training. But historians have taken only short and contemporary looks at the roles of the photographic and electronic revolutions in nationalizing and denationalizing all but two of the post-Napoleonic empires.

17. On Colonel Blimp's financial probity in a mercenary army, see Alan J. Guy, *Economy and Discipline: Officership and Administration in the British Army, 1714-63* (Manchester, 1984). That reform occurred just before the great financial scandals in the East India Company's administration, before the governor-generalships of Charles, 1st Marquess Cornwallis (1738-1805), and Wellington's elder brother.

18. A short, recent, and scholarly biography of *Bernadotte: Französischer Revolutionsgeneral und schwedisch-norwegischer König* (Göttingen, 1970). On his muscling in with the Gonzagas and the Medici, I prefer the work of an Irish lawyer, Sir Dunbar Plunket Barton, *The Amazing Career of Bernadotte 1763-1844* (London, 1929).

19. Jean Colin, *L'éducation militaire de Napoléon* (Paris, 1900), is an aptly titled classic. The best book on Frederick's political and military mentality is Gerhard Ritter, *Frederick the Great: A Historical Profile*, translated with an introduction by Peter Paret (Berkeley, 1970).

20. That the new Caesar never trusted either his middle-class marshal or his technocrat is not surprising. The quotation is from S. J. Watson, *Carnot* (London, 1934), p. 199. On the general role of the artillery and engineers in

military modernization, see Christopher Duffy, *Seige Warfare: The Fortress in the Early Modern World 1494-1660* (London, 1979).

21. Of the three systems available for East Central European modernization, the American Anglo-French system, with its Roman Republican rhetoric, was of as little use as the British system, with its Whig rhetoric. The pertinent system for landlocked agrarian states was to be that of Bourbon and Hohenzollern Jacobinism.

22. The best study of the reformers as a group is Peter Paret, *Yorck and the Era of Prussian Reform 1807-1815* (Princeton, 1966). Much of this material may be recast in his 1986 revision of Edward Mead Earle, ed., *Makers of Modern Strategy: Military Thought from Machiavelli to Hitler* (Princeton, 1943).

23. A reassessment of Jomini's and Clausewitz's roles is to be expected in Paret's revised Earle. The major works are Peter Paret, *Clausewitz and the State* (New York, 1976), and the commentaries on Clausewitz in Michael Howard and Peter Paret's translation of *On War* (Princeton, 1976).

24. The best institutional history is Walter Goerlitz, *History of the German General Staff 1657-1945*, trans. Brian Battershaw (New York, 1945).

25. On Delbrück and Schlieffen, see Arden Bucholz, *Hans Delbrück and the German Military Establishment* (Iowa City, 1985). On German militarism, see Gerhard Ritter, *The Sword and the Sceptre,* trans. Heinz Norden, 4 vols. (Coral Gables, Fla., 1969-73). Militarism as "the exaggeration and overestimation of the military, to a degree that corrupts . . . the calm considerations of statesmanship" (vol. 1, p. 5) did occur in Germany, as the result of a power vacuum at the top or "unintended militarism" rather than as an attempt to defend or enhance the class interests of soldiers.

26. Military and educational biographies, memoirs, histories, and myths have overwhelmed all but a few prosopographical studies of national and class origins rather than of mentalities.

27. The paraphrase is one of "the inquiring rather than the creative mind, the comprehensive rather than the specialized approach, the calm rather than the excitable head to which in war we would choose to entrust . . . the safety and honor of our country" (Clausewitz, *On War,* p. 112).

28. The political ineptness of the uneducated manager and technocrat is now apparent in the ancient and honorable legal, medical, and engineering professions. The first prophetic study was Jean de Bloch, *The Future of War in Its Technical, Economic, and Political Relations* (Boston, 1899). On Bloch, see the comments of his disciple, Maurice Pearton, *Diplomacy, War, and Technology since 1830* (Lawrence, Kans., 1984), chap. 5. An earlier British edition under a different title is less sharp on the American "relationships which, in the industrial age, have developed between knowledge — . . . theoretical science, industrial systems and the content of education — and action, that is, the foreign and military policies of the state,"

one of the themes of this volume (p. 9). In the United States there is a fine collection on Central European armies, compiled by Gianni Baj-Macarrie, in the U.S. Military History Institute at Carlisle Barracks. There is also a copy of an excellent survey of one army: László Mihály Alföldi, *Die Generale magyarischer Nationalität im k. u. k. Heer von 1890 bis 1914* (thesis, University of Innsbruck, 1970).

The Impact of the Military Establishment on Nationalism

Stephen Fischer-Galati

In this day and age, when wars of national liberation are regarded as the ultimate expression of peoples' historic struggles for independence, it should be difficult to question the presumed intimate connection between militarism and nationalism. In fact, even the forerunners of wars of national liberation, such as wars of national independence or armed uprisings against supranational empires, have been viewed by historians and political leaders as closely linked to both nationalism and militarism. And, in extreme cases, any confrontation within a multidenominational empire has likewise been regarded as the precursor of a war of national liberation. In truth, however, the relationship between militarism and nationalism has hardly been elucidated by historians of East Central Europe. A review of the nature of nationalism and its relationship to militarism is not likely to resolve the problems but should provide a basis for rethinking and reevaluating certain components.

What was the historic relationship between the armed forces of East Central Europe and their presumed, or actual, nationalism? Before the creation of national armies, there was, of course, no such relationship, unless one chooses to equate *natio* with nationalism. Yet, even if we were to accept the validity of that premise and believe that the leaders of the Battle of the White Mountain, for instance, were aware of their "national" interests in 1620 or that the Polish *szclachta* was aware of its national identity in its military confrontations prior to the Partitions, it would be difficult to pretend that the Serbian nobility at Kosovo, the retinues of János Hunyadi at Varna, or the Romanian armies that fought Poles, Turks, and Magyars in the fifteenth, sixteenth, and seventeenth centuries regarded their enemies as men of a different nationality. And even if we were to assume, *in extremis,* that such awareness did in fact exist in terms of differences in ethnicity, it is undeniable that the wars which antedated the eighteenth century were, in the last analysis, wars of religion, the main theater of military confrontation involving the Muslim Ottoman Empire and the theocratic Holy Roman and Russian Orthodox Empires. It is no secret that "protection of coreligionaries," which postdates the anti-Ottoman crusade as the legitimation of action against the Porte, was still in the eighteenth century the principal instrument for intervention in the internal affairs of the Ottoman Empire and, for that matter, even in Christian Poland. Nor it is possible to contest the fact that internecine confrontations involving the Ottoman power elite and the subject peoples took place between Christians and Muslims rather than between Greeks or Serbs or Bulgarians and Turks. This is not to deny the reality of a rising sense of nationality among the Christian inhabitants of Southeastern Europe in the eighteenth century but to ask whether that incipient nationalism was in any way related to military action involving Christians and Muslims.

Eighteenth-century nationalism in Southeastern Europe appears to have its origins not so much in an assumed desire to avenge, at a time propitious for "liberation from the Turkish yoke," the humiliations inflicted upon the "national states" conquered or subdued by Ottoman forces in the fourteenth and fifteenth centuries as in the deterioration of the Pax Ottomanica in the seventeenth century and the corollary increase in the financial and political power of the Phanariot Greeks. It was, in fact, the Grecization of Southeastern Europe in the eighteenth century which led to internecine conflicts within the Orthodox millet and pitted Orthodox Christian against Orthodox Christian. I think that it is fair to say that the key step toward legitimation of political — if not yet military — action within the Orthodox community in other than religious terms occurred with the alteration of identification from "Orthodox" to Serbian-Orthodox, Greek-Orthodox, Romanian-Orthodox. The Turks, however, were still identified as Muslims, and the Porte still identified the non-Muslim inhabitants of Serbian, Greek, and Romanian lands not only as external fomenters or supporters of turbulence against it but as Christians.

A case, albeit modest, has been and can be made for a connection between militarism and nationalism in the Habsburg Empire and, by extension, for convergence of these developments with developments in Southeastern Europe. It is clear, for instance, that the Serbians manning the Military Frontier knew that they were both Serbian and Orthodox and that the Romanian intellectuals of Transylvania were conscious of their being both Romanians and either Orthodox or Uniates. And it is also clear that Josephinism, in its quest for centralization of power and corollary destruction of the forces opposed to enlightened despotism and its political secularism — the Catholic church and the Magyar nation — promoted, or at least encouraged, such identifications. Nor can there be any doubt that the leaders and combatants in the bloody uprising of 1784 led by Horea, Closca, and Crisan knew that they were Romanians and that they were rebelling against Magyar landlords who, however, had to be forcibly converted to Orthodoxy. Nevertheless, the Romanians' loyalty to the supranational emperor and empire was not questioned, nor, for that matter, did the rebels consider themselves part of a Romanian military organization supportive of imperial policies directed against a "national" Magyar nobility. Thus, an organic link between militarism and nationalism prior to the first major military confrontation between the forces of secular nationalism and militarism — those of Napoleonic France — and those of the Eastern theocracies can be found only by stretching reality, and even then the link is not as firm as generally represented.

Inasmuch as modern French nationalism is intimately related to the French Revolution and the revolutionary and Napoleonic wars and wars of national liberation have also been related to those events, this inverted syllogism has equated the French Revolution and its wars with all the subsequent revolutions and wars of liberation in East Central Europe. Antirevolutionary intellectuals and political leaders, however, have a different explanation for the rise of modern nationalism in East Central Europe, namely, that it was a product of the reaction to French imperialism by the peoples who fought for God, emperor, and country against the forces of the anti-Christ Napoleon. In either case a direct connection is made between militarism and nationalism, and in both cases the connection with reference to East Central Europe is tenuous.

Taking stock of manifestations which could be described as expressions of nationalism such as the so-called Battle of the Nations, the Russian campaign against Napoleon, or the first Serbian uprising against the Porte, we may well ask whether we may, in these instances, properly speak of nationalism, whether generated by military action or not. It is doubtful that the Russian armies fought for more than God and tsar, for surely the notion of defending the Russian national state and the values of Russian civilization was alien to the enslaved peasantry. In truth, Alexander I was pursuing the war against anti-Christ not in the name of Russia's "national" interest but in the name of a conservative, legitimating divinity. The much-heralded Serbian "national and social revolution" can also be scrutinized in terms of its "national" character if not of its social one. The Serbian masses which participated in the uprising did not fight the *dahis* and the forces mustered by the Porte in the name of a specific Serbian national interest. The very acceptance by Miloš Obrenović — and the Porte — of his role of glorified Christian pasha is indicative of the fact that nationalism, whether induced by a spirit of historic vengeance or by military action against Ottoman forces, was not the overriding factor in the Serbian uprising of the early nineteenth century.

By contrast, an intimate connection can be made between militarism and nationalism in the case of the Greek War of Independence and the Polish Insurrection of 1830-31. In the case of the Greek events it is clear that the deaths and casualties incurred in combat with the Ottoman forces and, especially, with those assembled by Ibrahim Pasha were far more decisive in the development of a Greek national consciousness than the poetry of Korais and Rhigas or the messages of Western exponents of Philhellenism. However, throughout the conflict Greek nationalism retained a solid religious base: it was Greek-Orthodox directed against Muslim, rather than Turkish, oppressors. Similarly, the Polish masses which joined in the revolution of 1830-31 fought as both Poles and Catholics against the common Russian enemy even though the leaders, particularly the radicals, were secular nationalists, self-styled exponents of the French revolutionary tradition and nationalist ideology.

The advent of secular nationalism through the instrumentality of armed confrontation with "foreign" enemies was at least partially recorded in 1848. There is no need to dwell on events which have been described and analyzed ad nauseam, but it is worth noting that at least in the case of the Hungarian forces loyal to Kossuth the link between military action and modern nationalism was direct and incontestable. The masses were willing to accept the revolutionary legitimacy of Magyar nationalism and to fight for it not so much because of Kossuth's questionable identification of the *natio* and its historic interests with the "Magyar nation" and its aspirations as because the leaders could, in fact, offer the masses what the emperor did not. The substitution of historic nationalism as a legitimating force for military action directed against the traditional legitimating forces of the emperor and the church fared less well elsewhere in the empire of the Habsburgs, where the entreaties of intellectuals, students, and even military commanders ultimately failed to persuade the masses that revolutionary nationalism superseded the legitimacy of the imperial order. And even after the Russian armed intervention many of the multinational empire's inhabitants remained unprepared to support national causes directed against the emperor. On the other hand, by identifying the component units of the empire's armed forces in terms of their nationality, the emperor unwittingly facilitated the eventual forging of a close linkage between militarism and nationalism. Francis Joseph's purpose, of course, was to use the army as principal instrument for reconciliation of national differences by legitimating imperial power as representative and protective of the interests of all nationalities.

The year 1848 was, nevertheless, a turning point in the history of nationalism in East Central Europe not because of the people's commitment to revolutionary nationalism but because of factors connected with the great powers' own relations and the role assigned to national liberation movements by those powers. The Crimean War, which ended in the repudiation of foreign powers' right to protect coreligionaries in the Ottoman Empire and the corollary substitution of nationalism as the instrumentality for such intervention, the Franco-Sardinian war against Austria, the unification of the Romanian principalities, and the Seven Weeks' War and the ensuing *Ausgleich* of 1867 legitimated a direct and intimate connection between nationalism and militarism for those who thought that the promoting of wars of national independence or armed insurrections would serve the political interests of the powers and/or those of East Central European political and military leaders.

The "domino theory" which rested so heavily on internal or external fomenting of armed nationalism or "nationalizing" of revolutionary or terrorist activities became effectual, if not entirely effective, in the 1870s. The immediate and long-range consequences of these actions and of the reactions by those threatened by armed nationalism are too well known to require even recapitulation. What is deserving of comment, however, is the nature and extent of the interaction between militarism and nationalism.

It is simplistic to argue that military service, whether regular or irregular, advanced the cause of nationalism and that militarism was a prerequisite for successful action against imperialism in East Central Europe. A reasonably persuasive case for such assumptions may be made for some but not all of the successor states of the Ottoman Empire and, of course, for Romania; imagination, is, however, required to support a similar case for the Austro-Hungarian Monarchy. The illegitimacy to the Christian Balkans of the Muslim sultan and of the ruling establishment in Constantinople facilitated the military leaders' attempts to superimpose secular nationalism on religious fervor for legitimating wars or revolutions against the Porte. But this was successful only in Greece, Serbia, and Romania, whose independence either had been achieved or was not contingent on Russian political or military insemination. This was certainly not the case in Bosnia and Herzegovina, where nationalism could not be a factor in the armed uprisings of the 1870s despite the attempts of "Slavic brethren" to persuade the rebels of their common ethnic origins and national interests. And it had only limited application in Bulgaria, since that country's liberation entailed gratitude for the efforts of Russian Pan-Slavism and the Russian "liberating armies." It is true that as far as the Bulgarians were concerned these lacunae were remedied later, especially during the Second Balkan War, which pitted Christian against Christian and nationality against nationality, but it was never achieved in Bosnia, Herzegovina, or, later, Albania. In truth, Muslim nationalism was non-secular, ahistoric, and nonethnic and, as such, insusceptible to Christian or Slavic agitation and propaganda.

A corollary question is whether nationalist political indoctrination by officers in the national armies of the Balkan states and by the commanders in chief of those armies — the ruling monarchs — was more responsible for the development of secular nationalism than firsthand experience in combat against foreign enemies or historic factors related to religious differences and antagonisms. There is little reason to assume that the rank and file of the peasant armies of Southeastern Europe shared the nationalism of the officer class. In fact, it seems fair to assume that the officers were both feared and despised by individuals who had little, if any, enthusiasm for performing military service under the circumstances prevailing in the Balkan armies. They did, however, fight for God, king, and country, especially when the call to arms was directed against Muslim or other "foreign" oppressors or exploiters of the masses. Ultimately, however, the connection between militarism and the nationalism of the masses must be found in sacrifices — physical and economic — made in military confrontations.

These factors were, however, largely absent in the empire of the Habsburgs even after the *Ausgleich*. It is true that the acerbic nationalism of the Magyar military establishment was unpalatable to non-Magyar soldiers serving under its command, but it is also true that the Magyar officer class was despised and feared by all soldiers, including Magyars, for reasons not necessarily related to their nationalism. And what is true of Magyar officers is also true of officers of other nationalities who discouraged nationalism and promoted the emperor's plan of making the imperial army a "melting pot" of all nationalities. The multinational imperial army, therefore, could not be a factor in the development of nationalism except to the extent to which soldiers of various nationalities translated socioeconomic antagonism against the foreign ruling circles — represented also in the officer class — into potentially divisive and disloyal nationalist actions and activities. It is also possible to argue that at least some members of underprivileged nationalities represented in the imperial army did identify with and were supportive of the military achievements of conationals in Southeastern Europe or, alternatively, of the armed revolutionary and terrorist activities directed against the ruling establishment of the Austro-Hungarian Monarchy by conationals, whether supported by "brethren" or other would-be liberators from abroad or not, and that these associations were vital for the rise of militant nationalism within the armed forces of the empire. The plausibility of such arguments cannot be dismissed out of hand; however, it is certain that loyalty to the emperor and to the integrity of the imperial army were more characteristic of the attitudes of the soldiers and officers of that army than allegiance to divisive nationalist causes almost until the end of World War I.

All this is to say that traditional values and attitudes are hard to overcome; that secular nationalism, culminating in wars of national liberation directed against imperialism, can succeed only under unusual circumstances. In East Central Europe the success of wars of national liberation was facilitated by exploitation of the uneducated and oppressed Christian masses' hatred of the Muslim Ottoman Empire and its rulers. And even then, the substitution of nationalism for religion as a legitimating force for military action against the sovereign power had to accept convergence between secular and religious stimuli and ideologies. For these reasons successful wars of national liberation did not occur in the empire of the Habsburgs, as the legitimacy of the emperor and of the imperial order could not be challenged effectively by nationalists until military factors, largely unrelated to their efforts and activities, brought about the collapse of the empire and its resultant division into a variety of national states. It is thus hardly paradoxical that, under certain circumstances, militarism need not beget nationalism, that wars of national liberation are not inevitable, that nationalism and imperialism are not necessarily incompatible, but also that under different circumstances — especially when the legitimacy of the imperial order can be questioned by the masses — the opposite may be true.

Military Leadership and Education in Sociopolitical Responsibility

Richard Georg Plaschka

In keeping with the theme of this volume, the education and training of officers and military leaders and the impact of military education on politics and East Central European militarism, I should like to offer three remarks: one on the historical and sociopolitical image of the military and of war, another on revolutionary war and political motivation, and a final one on the sociopolitical responsibilities of military education.

The Historical and Sociopolitical Image of the Military and of War

There can be no doubt that the sociopolitical situation and functions of the military deserve more attention in our time than ever before. Military history is not merely a sequence of events such as battles and encounters but the awareness that the army is part of the developing nation and one of government's main instruments; the army is a social group differing from other groups only in its intense affiliation with the state and in its particular composition and range of action. The military historian must not only take account of this concept in domestic and international events but also consider its impact on history in general, whether political, social, economic, or legal. He will likewise have to focus his attention on the sociopolitical change to which this concept, like any personal element in history, is subject. At the same time, he will have to study the influence this concept exerts on society and the transformations effected.

Armed groups as an element of rebellion and war have repeatedly had a decisive impact on history beyond its normal evolution. Historians find such confrontations particularly important. Furthermore, national historiography opened the way for a novel, immediate approach to historical events and offered new ties with the ancestors, enabling the nation to take pride in their victories and feel grief at their defeats; it presented the nation with "hereditary enemies" and traitors in its own ranks. By holding up the ancestors' courage and abnegation as an example, history worked as an appeal to group morale. There was risk of historical oversimplification, the more so in that the public was influenced not only by historical research but also, to a much greater degree, by the contemporary mass media: poetry and songs, newspapers and periodicals, plays and historical novels. All these molded the ideas of whole generations about man in society and history by presenting dramatic historical events, whether of victory or of defeat, as determining forces for centuries to come.

The decisive events emerging from the national perspective of the nineteenth century included Valmy, Austerlitz, and Waterloo for the French; Trafalgar and the same Waterloo for the British; Lake Peipus, the Kulikovo Plain, Poltava, and Tsushima Strait for the Russians; the same Tsushima Strait for the Japanese; the Teutoburg Forest and Sedan for the Germans; Grünwald for the Poles; Bílá Hora for the Czechs; Mohács for the Hungarians; the Kosovo Plain for the Serbians; Thermopylae for the Greeks; Lepanto for the Spaniards; and the same Kosovo Plain, Mohács, and Lepanto for the Turks. Not entirely in the line of purely national patterns of interpretation, there were, moreover, the highlights of World War I — the Marne and Verdun, Tannenberg, Caporetto, and Gallipoli — and those of World War II, assuming quite different dimensions of destruction — Stalingrad and Normandy, Pearl Harbor and Midway, Dresden, Hiroshima and Nagasaki. There were also, and of no less symbolic value than these traditional images of warlike confrontations, the images of revolts, revolutions, and revolutionary wars: the Sicilian Vespers, the Hussites and the Huguenots, the Netherlands in 1568, the Thirteen Colonies in America in 1776, France in 1789, Spain, Portugal, and Latin America at the beginning of the nineteenth century, the Dekabrists in 1825, the Greeks in 1821-29, the Belgians in 1830, the Poles in 1830-31, the Hungarians in 1848-49, and confrontations with reference to the later idea of decolonization such as India in 1857-58, the Boxer Rebellion, and Adua.

Our century has brought the great revolutions in Russia and China, whose results extend into the present. The processes that come into play here are characterized by Karl Griewank in terms of three features of the phenomenon of revolution: their convulsive and, at least potentially, violent dynamics; their social basis, manifesting itself in collective and mass movements and frequently overt acts of resistance; finally, their political goal, envisioned as a renewal, a further development, a programmatic idea or ideology. More than in the past, military history must confront the phenomenon of revolutionary war.

Revolutionary War and Sociopolitical Motivation in the Twentieth Century

As early as in 1905 and 1906, Lenin, in essays such as "The Lessons of the Moscow Rebellion" and "The Partisan War," tried to integrate the development and objectives of the recent forms of revolt in Russia into the framework of his revolutionary projects, tactically as well as strategically. He had no doubt that the audacious assaults would qualify as murder and robbery according to civil law,[1] but he attributed to them a new qualitative character opposed to the old type of terror, which was individual-oriented and had become a symptom of lack of belief in the efficacy of revolt. The action of partisans, in his view, was a product of the feeling of the masses and oriented toward the party's goals.[2] This meant that terrorist combat groups with this new ideological character were to be viewed as executing a new positive order: "Partisan actions are not acts of vengeance but military operations. They are no more like adventures than the actions of riflemen in the rear of the enemy's army during a lull in the main theatre of operations are like the murders of duelists or conspirators."[3]

Lenin regarded partisan actions as necessary steps toward revolt: from strikes and demonstrations to individual barricades, from these to multiple barricades for street fighting against troops. In his mind this shift to revolt would inevitably bring the proletarian mass struggle to the point where "revolution is carried to the extreme in its use of offensive weapons," what followed being "a fierce, bloody, destructive war." The necessary consequence of this was "struggle for control of the army."[4] As for the party's position: "We have started to work on the troops ideologically and will persist in doing so." However, "we should be miserable pedants if we forgot that at the moment of revolt a physical struggle for control of the troops is needed as well. . . ."[5]

The tendency to "work on" the troops ideologically and to undertake "physical struggle" to get them under control had remarkable effects even in the Central European area during World War I, although these effects were limited to situations of matériel bottlenecks, that is, for example, to navy units at Wilhelmshaven, Kiel, and Cattaro, with certain parallels with the Black Sea navy in 1905.[6] These processes, like a number of mutinies among replacement troops of the Austro-Hungarian army in May and June 1918, were primarily socially motivated.[7]

The resistance activities in the Habsburg Monarchy during World War I involved social and national factors complementing each other. Both factors can be found a few years later in Mao's concept of guerrilla war, which integrates Lenin's ideas and transcends them. In the hardening process of war, the guerrilla units must "gradually become regular forces" if revolutionary warfare is to be successful. They have to reach the level — also demanded by Lenin — "that is expected of regular troops," especially as far as discipline is concerned: "We must see to it that every order is carried out without hesitation and any laxity rooted out."[8] Mao emphasizes the importance of a base for action for those who at the outset are the weaker ones, the oppressed, as in China, where the social goal of the Communists was at the same time a national one. He argues that guerrilla zones must gradually be transformed into stabilized "base areas" in which the revolutionary forces, both armed and political-organizational, have been successful and mobilization of the masses can be achieved.[9]

Guerrilla warfare is supposed to affect the adversary not only by expansion in space but also by maximal mobilization and internal organization: "In the course of military action we must arm the population." Those who choose to remain aloof from the struggle or even to oppose the revolution will have to reckon with the consequences: "We shall have to exterminate overt and covert traitors." No doubt is left about the severity of the actions of elimination, no doubt about the intensity of the measures for achieving integration: immersion of the masses in political propaganda, their political mobilization by a "permanent and dynamic process," and influence through "the spoken word, leaflets and bulletins, newspapers, books and pamphlets, plays and films, schools, mass organizations, and our cadres." Mao's aim: comprehensive mobilization of militant energies — total guerrilla warfare turning into total war — to the end that "the mobilization of ordinary people all over the country will create an enormous ocean in which the enemy must drown."[10]

Clausewitz had stressed the importance of political motivation in the achievement of such dynamics; war for him was "a true political instrument," "a continuation of political dealings" — "the political intention is the target, war is the means."[11] For him this political intention, the motivation for the combatants, was closely linked with the efficiency of military actions. Where political motivation was absent, where it was unclear and unconvincing, there was a risk that politics would come to be overemphasized, become independent, questionable, disconcerting. "The weaker. . . the motives and tensions are, the less the natural direction of the military element, that is, force, will fall into line with the goals indicated by politics" and "the greater the divergence will be between the political goal and the objective of an ideal war and the more war will appear political."[12]

To this situation Clausewitz opposed the fully engaging political motivation that conferred on military action impulses toward maximum intensification — war as an expression of politics which, while encompassing it totally, was absorbed in it: "The more magnificent and stronger the motives of war are, the more they encompass the whole existence of nations, and the more violent the tension which precedes war — the more the war will approach its abstract form, the more its goal will be to force the enemy down, the more the military target and the political intention will coincide, and the more purely warlike and less political the war will appear to be."[13]

These theses of Lenin, Mao, and Clausewitz seem to raise a number of questions with regard to motivation in wars in recent years.[14] The military schools and academies, although doubtless facing an imperative challenge in the technological education of their pupils, will also have to attend to those sociopolitical perspectives on the actions of armed groups, the actions of troops, and the development of their ideological attitudes.

The Sociopolitical Responsibilities of Military Education

Education was a powerful factor in the nineteenth-century rise and development of nations — starting with primary school and ending with the universities, those flagships of national instruction. The military academies, too, were elements in those networks. Their students used to be considered an elite representative of the state and its system.

The situation of students and alumni of military schools was often one of tension and contrasts. Students in officers' schools and young officers were frequently highly sensitive to authoritarian oppression and ready to risk their lives in struggles for a national cause (for example, the Dekabrists of 1825 and the students of the Warsaw military school in 1830, but also the young officers who took part in the revolt of July 20, 1944). There was also tension between national development and allegiance to the sovereign. In the case of the Austro-Hungarian Monarchy this contrast can be seen in the army's role as the defender of centralism. Military education was a support of the supranational system, counteracting centrifugal tendencies until the Monarchy's disintegration in 1918.[15] Again, there was tension for the military leader in his simultaneous responsibility for human lives and for military success, which demanded the optimal use of the forces at his disposal, sometimes in an ultimate effort. A lost battle such as Benedek's Königgrätz or a surrender like Nebogatov's was more likely than failure in civil professions to lead to prosecution.

Clausewitz once warned against the gap between theory and practice. For military schools the practice of future warfare is an even more agonizing problem than it was a few decades ago. First, there are arsenals of highly sophisticated weapons that are capable of destroying our world several times over. Second, ours is an age of the masses. It would take scarcely more than the pressing of a few buttons to exterminate the populations of whole areas, and this threat of mass destruction has meant a fundamental change in the relationship of politics and warfare. Resort to war has become a more doubtful expedient than ever. Bearing all this in mind, military schools find themselves challenged to prepare their students not only for their military tasks but also for their vocation as responsible partners in society.

What is a responsible partner in human society? In the words of a Chinese philosopher, a person who is strong of mind, sincere, and wise. Some of the traditions that inspired the military schools of the past — though not all traditions, and certainly not those which lead toward authoritarian development — justify the hope of a military education capable of meeting the demands of the future.

NOTES

1. V. I. Lenin, *Werke* (Berlin, 1958), 11:162-63, 205 ff.; cf. Claus D. Kernig, *Sowjetsystem und Demokratische Gesellschaft: Guerilladoktrin*, vol. 2 (Freiburg/Br., 1968), pp. 1127 ff; Karl Griewank, *Der neuzeitliche Revolutionsbegriff* (Frankfurt/M., 1969), 21 ff, 214-23.
2. Lenin, *Werke*, 10:106-7; 11:211-12.
3. Ibid., 10:107.
4. Ibid., 11:159 ff.
5. Ibid., 11:160-61.
6. Cf. P. M. Bogačev, ed., *Revoljucionnoe dviženie v černomorskom flote v 1905-1907 gg.* (Moscow, 1956); Richard Georg Plaschka, *Matrosen, Offiziere, Rebellen*, vol. 2 (Vienna, Köln, Graz, 1984); S. F. Najda, ed., *Voennye morjaki v period pervoj russkoj revoljucii 1905-1907 gg.* (Moscow, 1955); Ferdo Čulinovic, *1918 na Jadranu* (Zagreb, 1951).
7. Cf. Richard Georg Plaschka, Horst Haselsteiner, and Arnold Suppan, *Innere Front*, vol. 1 (Vienna, Munich, 1974); Karel Pichlík, *Bojovali proti válce* (Prágue, 1953).
8. Mao Tse-tung, *Vom Kriege* (Gütersloh, 1969), pp. 70-76, 171-74; cf. Lenin, *Werke*, 29:280, 399, 438, 545; 30:399.
9. Mao, *Vom Kriege*, pp. 158-59.
10. Ibid., pp. 161, 232 ff.
11. Carl von Clausewitz, *Vom Kriege*, vol. 1 (Berlin, 1867), p. 22.
12. Ibid., p. 23.
13. Ibid., pp. 22-23.
14. Cf. Marc E. Geneste, "Guerillakriegsführung"; in Franklin Mark Osanka, *Der Krieg aus dem Dunkel* (Köln, 1963), pp. 356-60.
15. Cf. Kurt Peball, ed., *Conrad von Hötzendorf: Private Aufzeichnungen* (Vienna, Munich, 1977); Plaschka, Haselsteiner, and Suppan, *Innere Front*, vols. 1 and 2.

II. EXTRATERRITORIAL PATTERNS

The Selection, Education, and Training of British Officers, 1740-1920

Robin Higham

A single chapter on the evolution of the officer corps of the three services which guarded Britain during the days of the Habsburg Empire requires considerable compression of the subject!

Essentially eight governing influences were at work in the process of selection, education, and training of British officers. First, the natural insularity bred a supreme confidence in the officer class as well as an independent sturdiness in the men they commanded. Second, imperial necessities governed how they would be used while the close relationship of the merchants to the parliamentary purse strings and to the aristocracy ensured funding in wartime and parsimony in peace. Third, the necessities of continental allies, the pressures from such rivals, and the entanglements of royal connections all played their part. Fourth, officers had to have the right connections socially and a sufficient outside income. Fifth, what they needed to know depended upon the technological state of the services — the navy being the most advanced and involved, the army tending to be conservative, and the air force being too young by 1920 to have yet established a pattern different than its mixed navy-army parentage. Sixth, there was an increasing need to learn management techniques as first the king, then Parliament, and finally the Industrial Revolution all made money dear. Seventh, there was the relationship of selection, education, and training to those general concepts within society which limited progress until the mid-nineteenth century. And eighth, and certainly not to be overlooked, is the fact that the noncommissioned officers to a very large extent ran the British services on a day-to-day basis.

These patterns were, then, common to the three services (though, of course, the flying ones do not appear until 1911), and their presence in the background helps explain why progress was often very slow and at other times much more rapid. It was only around 1900, for instance, that the Industrial Revolution really began to be felt at the battlefield end of the army, though its social impact had been visible in both the army and the navy from the end of the 1840s, almost eighty years after its commonly accepted starting date. Well into the second half of the nineteenth century the emphasis was more upon the second part of the rubric "an officer and a gentleman" than it was upon professionalism, except in those predominantly middle-class specialties relating to mathematics and machinery.

Throughout this long period from 1740 to 1920 Britain spent an increasing amount of time engaged in war. In fact, of all the years of the nineteenth century, only in 1868 were its armed forces not engaged in conflict in some part of the globe. At the same time, it was the leading industrial power until at least 1870. But it was not until about that date that its armed forces began to make significant strides away from the eighteenth century in terms of weapons, selection, training, education, and management of the armed forces.[1]

The Royal Navy

The professionalization of the English armed forces had really begun under Oliver Cromwell and the Commonwealth, when Parliament had ruled supreme. Then the navy had been commanded by generals-at-sea, who were exactly that.[2] Upon the Restoration in 1660, the senior service enjoyed the patronage of Charles II and of his Catholic brother, the duke of York, later briefly James II. James actually commanded the fleet at sea until beached, when the office of Lord High Admiral was put in commission. The road to the top command at sea still remained essentially a career open only to those who were able to have their feet placed upon the bottom rung of the ladder of promotion by family connections. Thus normally the son of a respectable family who wished to go to sea or who was too far down the sibling line to inherit the estates was found a berth at the age of eleven to thirteen, usually in the patronage of the captain of a ship. To these "captain's servants" the diarist Samuel Pepys, clerk to the Board of Admiralty, had added in 1676 by royal order another class, "king's letter boys," but for long they never amounted to more than about 15 percent of those in training. Not till the end of the Napoleonic Wars did the Admiralty begin to get control over nominations, not till 1838 was entrance by competitive examination, and not till 1843 did this intake become known as naval cadets. Nor was it until 1913 that the right of individual officers to nominate candidates was withdrawn.

Nevertheless, studies of 1800 officers in the mid-nineteenth century showed that 50 percent came from professional families.

In the meantime, the authorities had established a naval academy at Portsmouth, where college volunteers began their training before going to sea. Though the Admiralty was opposed in this by the clique which ruled the navy, it was itself part of the clique and recognized its concepts of privilege and patronage to such an extent that it can be argued that it generally took a forward view that the navy should be commanded by men of influence who would naturally rise to the top and that these persons should, therefore, be as well trained as possible. Perhaps the problem lay in that the school started with youngsters who would far rather have been at sea, while what they really needed to be taught had to do with high command, which was some twenty years in their futures. Ironically, all the great admirals of the eighteenth century, including Nelson, entered the navy as captain's servants. In 1773 the school's title became the *Royal* Naval Academy and in 1806 the Royal Naval *College*, but after 1837 it died. In 1857 the Admiralty decided that the policy of training all cadets at sea had not worked very well, and so the ships *Illustrious* and later *Britannia* were commissioned as schools. These hulks were, however, cold and damp, and the cadets remained "snotties" with runny noses for sixteen to twenty-four months, and so the colleges at Osborne and Dartmouth were established ashore once again in 1903 and merged in 1921. In the meantime, in 1913 there had become available a new method of entry known as the special or public schools, which because its members were older led to a commission as a sub-lieutenant in four years instead of the eight usual for the twelve-year-old who went to Dartmouth and entered as a midshipman. The advantage was that this semitrained outside supply could be regulated according to demand. Pepys had also been responsible for promulgating regulations concerning the creation of the post of midshipman, an under-officer aspiring to become a commissioned officer. Pepys laid down that he must have two years' sea service as well as coming from gentlemanly stock.

It took a considerable while in the days of sail to shift from the concept of having a captain who could fight the ship but did not know how to sail it (and so had to have a sailing master under him) to producing an officer who could command fully. This gradually evolved into the master-commander and then petered out in the nineteenth century when connections beat out competence.

Among the very few studies that we have so far of the distribution of British officers in ranks is Michael Lewis's analysis of 3,467 naval officers who served in the Napoleonic Wars and were still alive in 1845. These show very clearly that by far the best road to the top was through *interest*, starting as a captain's servant. (He also gives the distribution by highest rank attained as flag 7.3 percent, post-captain 17.25, commander 17.75, and lieutenant 57.6.) But that same distinction between gentlemanly accomplishments and technical competence reappeared in the Royal Navy when in the 1830s steam propulsion was introduced, followed by the revolutionary shift from wooden-hulled sailing ships with muzzle-loading cannon to steam-driven, steel-hulled vessels with breech-loading rifled guns firing explosive ammunition. Not until 1880 was a college for engineers founded (at Keyham), though in 1868 the body of engineers had been divided into professionals, composed of commissioned officers, and artificers, comprising warrant officers. From 1868 to 1903 engineer officers wore a distinctive purple band on their sleeves commingled with their rank braid. But in 1903 the Fisher-Selborne reforms required that all naval executive officers be drawn from the same pool of cadets. Thus the Admiralty hoped to snuff out the long-standing quarrel between the advocates of sail and of steam. However, the idea failed because it was too late. Modern technology demanded specialization, but, given a choice, few graduating cadets opted for engineering. And so in 1925 the engineering branch with its distinctive purple band was reactivated. However, in the meantime, the engineer had been admitted to the officers' mess, and a better understanding had been achieved between this below-decks specialist, often at least in fiction if not in fact a Scot, and his brother officers on the bridge.[3]

Several other trends also affected the overall education of British naval officers in the 180 years under review. In the eighteenth century there was periodic action either in major wars or in antipiracy and other patrols. Thus officers such as Horatio Nelson became captains at twenty-one and then spent long periods in that rank. If excellent, well-connected leaders, they were able to pass a great deal of that time in command, if not at sea. They were professional ship-handlers and commanders of men, but studies of the battles fought by the Royal Navy shows that its leaders were not well trained, had virtually no staff, and lacked a suitable system of communications. The "Nelson touch" is significant largely because the victor of an unusual series of battles drilled his captains in anticipating situations professionally.⁴ But from 1805 to 1914 the Royal Navy fought only one major action, and that accidentally, at Navarino in 1827. Many of its captains spent years unemployed on half-pay. It went through the midcentury revolution in equipment followed by the equally revolutionary impact of the internal-combustion engine and electricity without any proper training and sailed majestically into World War I full of untested technological innovations and without a trained staff or commanders.

The original technological revolution epitomized by H.M.S. *Warrior* had admittedly started with some smaller vessels but had largely moved forward for the first twenty years in the battleships. This had meant that command and experiment had been in the hands of senior personnel and training and education in the broadest sense had been restricted. As the Whitehead torpedo had begun to make it necessary to consider protecting the battleline with smaller vessels both to deliver and to counter these deadly underwater weapons, innovative command had devolved once more upon the youngest officers, selected for their dash and bravery. Yet in truth the road to the top in the nineteenth-century navy was more through varnish, polish, good manners, and social connections than it was through ability. And to this later in the century and early in the twentieth could be added a winning touch in competition as the emphasis upon sports and scientific proof coalesced to demonstrate superiority.⁵ In the decade or so before World War I, the two most important new arms for young officers were the submarine service and aeronautics. Not only were there opportunities for individual distinction and the mastering of complexities not understood by senior officers, but especially in the Royal Naval Air Service casualties increased the vacancies.

Losses in the naval air service in World War I exceeded those of the anti-slave-trade patrols off the West African coast in the 1830s and 1840s, when disease struck down as many as one-third of officers and men.⁶ As a consequence, the demand for sublieutenants was high and training brief. Officer candidates received a few weeks' ground school and some dozen hours' flying training and then were posted to a front-line squadron.⁷ After the war and the compulsory merger of British air services, most of the former navy pilots in the Royal Air Force were weeded out. A small core was sent to train the Japanese navy's air service.⁸

Where the Grand Fleet and the Battlecruiser Force, the main British fleet in the North Sea, were concerned, the long century of neglect of the fundamentals was brought home at Jutland in 1916. Admiral Sir John Jellicoe and Vice-Admiral Sir David Beatty failed to smash the German High-Seas Fleet because they did not command what was by the standards of the day a fully professional force. The units of the fleet had not yet learned when and how to communicate. The Admiralty had not refined the handling of intelligence. And Jellicoe had never had a chance to practice handling a unit as large as that he then commanded except under wartime conditions. The navy had lost the Nelson touch because it had not yet assimilated the new revolutions.

World War I taught it a great deal, but it was still in 1920 both fighting against recognizing some of the evidence, such as U-boat successes, and in the throes of postwar unrealism. Not really until 1924, after the "Geddes axe" economies, the Washington naval treaties, and the reestablishment of the naval air arm, could the navy be said to have returned to a staff-conscious, peacetime basis.

The Army

The history of the British army in the years 1740-1920 divides almost equally into two parts. In the first it was dominated by iss domestic role as an internal police force with colonial garrisons, which occasionally sallied into Europe. In the second it became a victorious imperial force gradually forced to look once again to playing a role in Europe.[9]

In those two periods there was a remarkable continuity of weapons. The 150-yard-range Brown Bess musket was introduced into the infantry in 1717, tested definitively in 1843, and withdrawn in 1846. Thereafter the foot soldiers were armed with 800-yard-or-more-range rifles, and by the end of the nineteenth century these were also being issued to the cavalry. Artillery was similarly pretty much standardized, except for the siege and coast-defense guns. Thus the technical burden on officers came from the Maxim machine gun, the balloon, the telegraph (and later the field telephone), the railway, and river steamers. Only when the British came up against the Boers at the end of the century did they face a foe that was mentally and physically their equal as no one had been since the days of Napoleon.

Just as the navy had not for years after Trafalgar had to face a major opponent, so neither had the army. Those remarkable maps of the jingoistic late nineteenth century with British possessions in red showed that all were garrisoned by a remarkable small force in 1830 of 51,000 at home and and about an equal number in India with penny packets spread all over the world and assisted where needed by trained native levies. By 1899 the total had risen to 250,000 plus 90,000 reserves. The officers from the best families with the largest incomes stayed in garrison at home, while their progressively less fortunate colleagues officered either the less prestigious cavalry and infantry regiments first at home, then abroad, or, if really quite impecunious, the regiments of the British East India Company until its disbandment in 1858, after which they served in the Indian army. How they got there was not, in some ways, very unlike the system in the navy. It, too, worked on patronage at first.

When George I came to the throne, he inherited an army run by colonels with funds disbursed by captains. He and his successor wished to control the army as they did that of Hanover, and so by royal warrants they gradually abolished various privileges. At the same time the army gradually increased in size from 15,851 officers and men in 1715 to 111,553 by 1762, not including at least 12,000 on the Irish establishment. Of these, 90 percent served twelve months of the year, and of the officers some 2,000 were regulars who when they reached the rank of major or lieutenant colonel (the real commanders of regiments) were handpicked for command by the monarch. The man in charge of regimental accounts was the captain, and it was he who taught the subalterns, the newly commissioned, untrained officers, all about discipline, horses, and weapons to safeguard his own investment in the regiment, especially when he was on leave. Privilege and property were the passwords of the British officer system until the abolition of purchase of commissions in 1870, even though many did not in fact enter the army by this means. Perhaps as many as 25 percent of the officers were either Scots or middle-class rather than men of birth and fortune. On the other hand, of the 374 colonels of regiments, that is, the owners of these military organizations, between 1714 and 1763, 57 were peers of the realm, 17 baronets, 25 the sons of these two groups, and 70 members of the untitled gentry. An average of half of them sat in Parliament, and most of them held a higher military rank such as major general while at the same time being an inspecting officer.[10] The road into the army and on to the top is reminiscent of Parkinson's "short list"[11] — connections were all-important.

If it was true that entry and training in the army was a matter of patronage in spite of royal attempts to control it, it is also true that the appearance of the Franco-Spanish fleet in the Channel in 1780 put the paymaster general back in control of reform again. Ironically, this caused the shrinkage of officers' pay just when both inflation and the conception of how an officer should live were on the rise. And that in turn caused the regiments to separate even more socially, so that the household cavalry and infantry became elites, while the more able sought service under the British East India Company, where seniority rather than bank account determined success. By 1797 the British were once again embroiled in a European war after having lost the American colonies, and once more in a wartime expansion the army lacked trained officers. In spite of a plethora of manuals of instruction, there were no schools (except Woolwich for engineers and artillery from 1741)[12] for either officers or NCOs. Rapid expansion diluted the forces at home too fast for assimilation and steadiness in the field. Experienced troops often could not be spared from India, and their officers could not afford to be in home regiments, especially when faced with the costs of active duty (which amounted to as much as five or six times the annual pay). In addition, a purchase system with no pension did not encourage bravery.[13]

It was against this background that in 1797 Colonel John LeMarchant presented to his friend the duke of York, the new commander in chief, the idea for an officers' school that would become the Royal Military College, Sandhurst. Four years were to elapse before it came into being, but in the meantime in 1798 the staff college was opened under General Francis Jarry.[14] Eventually a good many officers from this establishment went to aid Wellington in the Peninsular campaign and then remained in service until the 1860s as something of a mixed blessing of consinuity and deadweight.

LeMarchant's college finally opened in 1801 for cadets who were nineteen years of age, had served two years, knew how to run a company, had mastered the first four rules of arithmetic, and were fluent in French. The next year the Junior Department was set up for those thirteen to fifteen who knew math and Latin. They were to pass out to regiments at the age of seventeen. Sons of officers killed in action were to be educated free. Except for the need to know battlefield commands, what was taught was very similar to the instruction in other

English public schools of the day. (The U.S. Military Academy at West Point, founded in 1802, was modeled upon LeMarchant's conception.) By 1811, when LeMarchant was ordered to command a brigade of cavalry and was killed in Portugal, two hundred officers had passed through the Senior Department, and fifteen hundred cadets from the Junior were also in the Peninsula. Twenty graduates were eventually killed in Portugal and Spain and twelve at Waterloo.

From 1813 on, cadets who sought a commission without purchase had to pass rigorous examinations before their eighteenth birthdays in both normal academic subjects and fortifications á la Vauban and be proficient in military drawing. But until the death of the duke of Wellington in 1852 the myth persisted that the British had beaten Napoleon by birth and not musketry. In fact, the establishment of a school of musketry in the British army and the requirement that one officer and one NCO from every regiment had to be trained there was not realized until 1853. The requirement that every Sandhurst cadet know how to use a rifle was delayed until forty years after the Iron Duke died. Meanwhile the Whigs had abolished scholarships for orphans in 1838 on the grounds that it was unwise to have officers without means. But the fact that there were no library, no books, and no recreation, only studies and a little bad food, merely reflected the state of other public schools. The cadets were beginning to resent this as the country and, therefore, the nature of the cadets themselves changed. But it was not until 1862 that matters were brought to a head when the entire cadet body mutinied after carefully preparing a fort on the grounds and stocking it with dry loaves of bread as ammunition. These they successfully used to shell all emissaries up to the new commander in chief, the royal duke of Cambridge, who sensibly agreed to their demands. Three meals a day, a privilege which had already been granted troops in 1844, to curb drunkenness, were instituted, sofas supplied, billiards and anterooms set up, and a reading room established. By the time that Governor Sir Harry Jones, the last Peninsular veteran but one at the college, died in 1866, a quiet revolution had taken place.[15]

In 1856 Wellington College had been founded nearby to supply boys to the military college. In 1857 a parliamentary committee proposed merging Woolwich and Sandhurst, but this was not done until 1947. Nevertheless, the Senior Department was spun off as a proper staff college. At the same time, the Indian Mutiny caused profound changes on top of the necessity for reforms made evident by the poor performance of the army in the Crimean War. The Indian army was placed under the War Office and its own training college at Addiscombe closed in favor of sending its cadets to Sandhurst. The age of entrance to the military college itself was raised to sixteen to eighteen, with cadets already expected to have acquired the gentlemanly traits at a public school; poor officers' sons became queen's cadets, and the college, instead of being self-supporting, was carried on the army estimates. By 1870 reform was driving the British army because events on the continent were showing the country that it could no longer afford the luxury of an inefficient, unprofessional army. Concurrently, imperial successes buoyed its popularity.

Thus came the reforms of Secretary of War Sir Edward Cardwell, which among others limited army appointments, with the exception of that of the royal commander in chief, five years, required civil-service examinations for a commission on the same basis as the Northcliffe-Trevelyan reforms required for civil appointments, limited promotion to merit and seniority (thus abolishing purchase), and provided funds to pay for all commissions then extant. The reforms were to have included the closing of Sandhurst, but while the cadets were dispersed to their homes following an outbreak of scarlet fever, the War Office miscalculated the exams and passed too many candidates. The solution was to offer seniority to those who passed at Sandhurst, and this became the accepted solution, so that from 1874 on customarily all infantry and cavalry officers in the British army did so. Thus in the late 1870s and early 1880s most of the leaders of World War I were cadets there; the cadets of the next decade became the field commanders of that war, those of 1895-1905 the captains of 1914 and lieutenant colonels of 1918, and those after 1906 members members of the high command in World War II.

The last quarter of the nineteenth century was the scene of change in a number of ways. The first commandant who had himself been a cadet took his place. The tone was set by cadets from Eton and Harrow, the leading English public schools, meaning that future generals came from the same political and social milieu as many of their civilian masters, just as by World War II they also shared the experience of the trenches on the western front in 1914-18. Cricket was well established as a sport. A study of the cadets who attended between 1878 and 1899, including the later prime minister Sir Winston Churchill, showed that of an average intake of 330, 23 came

The Selection

from Wellington, 11 from Bedford Grammar School, 18 from Clifton, 17 each from Eton and Harrow, 12 from the United Services School, Westward Ho, 11 from Cheltenham, and 10 from Winchester. All these schools had preparatory classes for Sandhurst. In the same period an average of 161 were sons of army officers, 15 sons of naval officers, and 87 the offspring of private gentlememof no other known profession or affiliation. Of the average entry, no fewer than 222 had studied at crammers before being admitted.[16] In other words, by the late nineteenth century the army was an attractive career and one that many families could afford or that those in the army felt offered good prospects of success and ample rewards. Perhaps one reason for this was that the pay was not only stable but worth more in the nineties than it had been in the forties when the scales were set. More than this, even at Sandhurst changes were being made to help level costs and keep cadets out of debt. Polo was abolished in 1894, the year after a modern accounting system was installed to control mess bills.

On the whole, Peninsular tactics had stood the British army in good stead in its colonial actions, so the parade-ground maneuver of forming a square to repel cavalry still had value as long as fighting dervishes and others were still in vogue, but the Boer War was a shock. It demanded new tactics. These hit Sandhurst over the Easter recess in 1902. From them on, the army developed effective tactical drill formations, and in the fall khaki made its appearance in place of blue working clothing, wine and beer were allowed, and other changes followed fast. Suddenly the military college seemed in the lead instead of a backwater. Rugby versus Woolwich, an annual cross-country run, and compulsory physical training (though the latter had been available since 1860) were introduced. In 1911 the barracks were enlarged to hold 424 more cadets, and during the 1914-18 years some 5,000-odd were pushed through in short courses. In all, 3,200 former cadets died in World War I, compared with 246 killed in action between 1855 and 1898. The western front ate up young front-line officers partly because of the lack of training and education of senior officers and their staffs.

This was a matter which had periodically been tackled more in a practical than in a theoretical manner. Neither the War Office, wherein resided the Secretary at War (amalgamated in 1855 with the Secretary of War), nor the House Guards, the home of the commander in chief, had a staff of more than a half-dozen before the bureaucratic explosion of the mid-nineteenth century. Generals in the field operated in much the same manner, with their commissariat services in civilian hands through the Crimean War. As long as the army's wants were simple and could in part be supplied by the countryside, the system sufficed. Similarly, a general's staff was made up of officers assembled for the campaign. However, the demands of even the limited Crimean campaign after a long period of peace, the presence of newspaper correspondents, and the evident incompetence of the staff forced change.

In 1856 the newly appointed duke of Cambridge obtained the appointment of a Council of Military Education and ordered it first to consider the proper task of the Senior Department at Sandhurst. At the same time, in consultation with Albert, the prince consort, the duke issued General Order No. 685, laying down the qualifications for staff officer from January 1, 1858. These included, upon the insistence of the prime minister, legible handwriting. Shortly after this the committee reported, the prince consort amended, and the queen approved the conversion of the Senior Department into the staff college. It moved to nearby Camberley in 1862.

The problem with the new staff college was that its instructional staff still thought of it in much of the old way. In a confusion of staff with technical duties, the emphasis was upon mathematics. In fact, not until the late 1890s did the course begin to provide real training in staff duties. Perhaps it did not matter much, for of the first 144 officers trained only 81 got staff appointments, while in most cases regimental prejudice against those who "deserted the family" discouraged many officers from seeking advancement in this manner. Moreover, most colonial campaigns simply did not require people with the designation "p.s.c." (passed staff college) after their names. By 1869 the number of candidates for the fifteen annual vacancies had dropped to twenty-one. This brought on a royal commission of inquiry and a new mandate. Henceforth the college was to seek to obtain the best officers, train them practically, and give them reasonable assurance of the appointments for which they were trained and best-fitted. This new order at once attracted candidates, and in 1871 there were forty-nine. In 1877 six officers were assigned from the Indian Staff Corps, and in the following year the new commandant was himself a p.s.c. In 1881 "Staff Duties" was added to the syllabus in place of "Photography," and the first battlefield tour was undertaken, to Metz. In 1885 mathematics was abolished, being required

The Selection

on the entrance examination instead, and the age for sitting was reduced to thirty-seven. The next year the number of places, which had risen to forty-eight, was increased to sixty.[17]

At about the same time, Field Marshal Lord Wolseley, the leading soldier of the day, was becoming very influential, and for the next decade his oversight over the college led to the gradual eradication of the inessential and of flagrant cheating and the implementation of practical training. Having commanded a number of large expeditionary forces, Wolseley was fully aware of the necessities for staff work and was not out simply to "Prussianize" the army. Though the staff college was closed briefly in 1900, during the Boer War, it was opened again before the end of the year with the work much more closely tied to field realities. Reflecting the changes taking place in the army itself as a result of the embarrassments of the South African war, in 1906 the six professors were replaced by a directing staff of deputy-assistant adjutant generals. Two naval officers were added to the students, followed, in 1909, by two Australians and one Canadian. Yet in spite of the lessons of the Boer War, on the outbreak of the 1914 conflict the college was closed. It was not opened again until 1919, when a large number of the students proved to be officers of considerable experience, the first two classes containing twenty brigadier generals, three brevet colonels, and seventy-seven brevet lieutenant colonels.

The army had great need for replacements. In spite of the fact that a staff college had also been founded at Quetta, India, officially in 1907, it and Camberley produced only enough staff officers for the peacetime needs of the small British army. From 1914 to 1918, 219 (49.2 percent) of the p.s.c.'s on the army list of 1914 were killed or died of wounds. More than this, the concept of a staff officer had for too long been too narrow, and when, starting in 1906, the staff college became "the brains of the army," involved in the switch of British strategy from a colonial to a continental one allied with France and opposed to Germany (a complete reversal of the position in the eighteenth century), there simply were not enough officers trained to understand and advise properly on the problems. But, in spite of the report of the Esher Committee after the Boer War, neither the gentlemen who ruled the country nor their close relatives who ran the army were prepared to treat defense as a business and manage it on that basis.[18]

The Royal Air Force

Military aviation began only very shortly before the 1914 war. In Britain officers were required to obtain their Royal Aero Club pilot's certificate before they could get military instruction, and they were then only seconded from their regiments for four years so as not to ruin their careers. Flying was treated as an adventure, just like detachment to some frontier force.[19]

When World War I broke out, losses mounted and replacements had to be found at a far more rapid rate. Selection processes placed the emphasis upon officers and gentlemen. At a time when there was increasingly a shortage of junior officers due to trench warfare, the cream of the crop was being given flying training. But trainees only got fifteen hours of flight instruction, and casualties were at about the same level as for infantry subalterns — 8,000 dead out of 14,166.[20] Command tended to go to survivors, and in day fighter squadrons these were the more experienced officers — providing their machines held up and did not catch fire, for they had no parachutes. In late 1917 the training was increased to fifty hours, with a marked decline in the casualty rates in the Royal Flying Corps, the army's air arm until April 1, 1918. A great deal was owed to the new hands-on training system of Major R. Smith-Barry. Bomber crews sent on unescorted sorties suffered as heavily, except at night. As in the regimental army from which the whole system evolved, much of the training was expected to be done on the squadrons, when they had the time. The weakness of this was that when they were heavily engaged and taking casualties, they did not have the time and so took even greater losses as neophytes had to be committed raw to battle. Only after the end of the war in 1919, when the reversion of the air force to its two parent services was in contemplation, did Chief of the Air Staff Sir Hugh Trenchard publish a plan to create a college at Cranwell, a dream realized in 1919,[21] with a staff college founded at Andover some time later.

By 1920 the Royal Air Force was only emerging from the ancillary stage. It had learned a good deal in World War I, when it reached a strength of 290,000. It would still be much influenced by that conflict in its approach to the selection, training, and education of the officers who served in World War II. More a middle-class service than its seniors, it was less concerned in 1920 with the image of an

The Selection

officer and a gentleman and more with survival as it was reduced to 10 percent of its wartime size.

Conclusions

During the 180 years of Habsburg predominance in East Central Europe, the British services made the transition from the eighteenth to the twentieth century, from a comfortable compatibility of weapons in both services to an increasingly bewildering array of weapons and ancillary equipment. This revolution both reflected the Industrial Revolution and directly impinged upon the officers and gentlemen who ran the services, since they were in theory required to have sufficient knowledge to make intelligent decisions about the procurement and employment of these new implements and engines of war. Very little was done, however, to train those outside the engineers and artillery and later the signals in these mysteries.

Naval officers kept themselves on deck except to inspect living quarters. Engines were the domain of those below decks, generally regarded, until the Selborne Scheme, as a breed apart. Thus neither from a strategic, a staff, nor even a social point of view were the essentials of naval warfare integrated in selection, training, or education. Much the same can be said of Sandhurst, which was for years a public school, and of the army staff college. And the nascent air force began life essentially as a species of cavalry with an unwanted naval arm.

The reason was not difficult to discover: until the beginning of the twentieth century even naval officers were promoted largely by interest. When there were examinations, they were such as could be passed by public-school boys or reasonably competent technically qualified officers. Concepts of cadet training and education mirrored the slow pace of public-school and grammar-school education; it is scarcely surprising that something as advanced in management concepts as general-staff training should not be some way behind on an island where neither an ill-fated fleet nor an embarrassingly defeated army existed. The overconfidence of "splendid isolation" inhibited the modernization of the fighting forces, especially since the ruling classes controlled both.

NOTES

1. The basic introduction to the subject is Robin Higham, ed. *A Guide to the Sources of British Military History* (Berkeley, 1971). A revised edition under the guidance of Gerald Jordan of York University is in preparation and will be published by Garland in New York in 1987.

2. This section relies heavily on three books by Michael Lewis, a former professor at the Royal Naval College at Greenwich: *The Navy of Britain* (London, 1948), *A Social History of the Navy, 1793-1815* (London, 1960), and *The Navy in Transition: A Social History, 1814-1864* (London, 1965). Additional short explanations are to be found in C. Northcote Parkinson, *Portsmouth Point* (Cambridge, Mass., 1949). For a discussion of the 1,800 naval officers of the mid-nineteenth century mentioned below see Lewis, *1793-1815*, pp. 27 ff. and 201. Common as one would expect statistics on the size of the navy to be, they are not easily found. In peacetime in the eighteenth century it stood at about 13,000 seamen and at the same in 1817 with a peak in between of over 100,000 during the Napoleonic Wars. By 1914 there were 151,000 officers and men and in 1918 347,000.

3. The transition to steam is covered in a number of works including the massive series of volumes by Arthur Marder which starts with *The Anatomy of British Sea Power* (New York, 1940) and ends with the five-volume *From the Dreadnought to Scapa Flow* (New York, 1961-70); Oscar Parkes's detailed *British Battleships, 1860-1950* (Hamden, Conn., 1972) deals with the heavyweights (Anthony Carew, *The Lower Deck of the Royal Navy, 1900-39: Invergordon in Perspective* [(Manchester, 1981)]. Much that has been written, however, is either on high policy or lowly hardware, with not much in between on the interrelationships of technology, tactics, and training. N. A. M. Rodgers, *The Wooden World: The Anatomy of the Georgian Navy* (Annapolis, 1986) fills a gap and presents a fresh picture.

4. On the Nelson touch, see Ludovic Kennedy, *Nelson's Captains* (London, 1951), and Dudley Pope, *The Great Gamble: Nelson at Copenhagen* (New York, 1972).

5. On this see the biography of the leading gunnery expert Sir Percy Scott by Peter Padfield, *Aim Straight* (London, 1966), and of the founder of the *Naval Review* by Barry D. Hunt, *Sailor-Scholar: Admiral Sir Herbert Richmond, 1871-1946* (Waterloo, 1982).

6. Christopher Lloyd, *The Navy and the Slave Trade* (London, 1949), p. 288.

7. Neither P. K. Kemp, *Fleet Air Arm* (London, 1954), nor the Navy Records Society, *The Naval Air Service*, vol. 1, *1908-1918*, ed. S. W. Roskill, gives any exact figures for instruction. Roskill has a 1914 report which shows seven and three-quarters hours after receiving a Royal Aero Club certificate. This probably meant about fifteen hours, or the same as in the Royal Flying Corps at this time.

8. See H. G. Brackley, *"Brackles": Memoirs of a Pioneer of Civil Aviation* (Blakeney, Norfolk, 1952), pp. 93-225.

9. A modern overview of the army is Correlli Barnett's *Britain and Her Army* (London, 1970). Other recent works which provide further guidance beyond that mentioned in n. 1 are H. C. B. Rogers, *The British Army of the Eighteenth Century* (London, 1977); Alan J. Guy, *Oeconomy and Discipline: Officership and Administration in the British Army, 1714-63* (Manchester, 1985); J. A. Houlding, *Fit for Service: The Training of the British Army, 1715-1795* (Oxford, 1981); Hugh Thomas, *The Story of Sandhurst* (London, 1961), to which should be coupled John Chandos, *Boys Together: English Public Schools, 1800-1864* (New Haven, 1984); Hew Strachan, *Wellington's Legacy: The Reform of the British Army, 1830-1854* (Manchester, 1984); Frederick Myatt, *The Soldier's Trade: British Military Developments, 1660-1914* (London, 1974); Byron Farwell, *Eminent Victorian Soldiers: Seekers of Glory* (New York, 1985) and *Mr. Kipling's Army: All the Queen's Men* (New York, 1981); Edward M. Spiers, *The Army and Society, 1815-1914* (London, 1980); Gwyn Harries-Jenkins, *The Army in Victorian Society* (London, 1977); and John Sweetman, *War and Administration: The Significance of the Crimean War for the British Army* (Edinburgh, 1984).

10. Guy, *Oeconomy and Discipline*, p. 137.

11. C. Northcote Parkinson, *Parkinson's Law* (Boston, 1958).

12. The Story of the Royal Military Academy, Woolwich, has been told in two parts, the first by Sir Frederick (Gordon) Guggisberg, *The Story of the Royal Military Academy* (London, 1900), and the followup by Colonel K. W. Maurice-Jones, *The Shop Story, 1900-1939* (Woolwich, 1954). Instruction at The Shop was always much more technical, and there was a much shorter lead time between the appearance of an item in the civilian marketplace and the inclusion of it in the instructional curriculum. Very shortly after 1900, for instance, X-rays and motorcycles were included, while until shortage of money stopped it, the cadets regularly had summer camps where they did live firing with field guns and engaged in other practical work.

13. On purchase see Anthony Bruce, *The Purchase System in the British Army, 1660-1871* (London, 1980).

14. To the small centennial volume by F. W. Young, *The Story of the Staff College, 1858-1958* (Camberley, 1958), should be added Brian Bond, *The Victorian Army and the Staff College, 1854-1914* (London, 1972).

15. The last Peninsular veteran on the staff was Sir George Wetherall, governor from 1866 to 1868, when he died at the age of eighty.

16. Thomas, *Sandhurst*, p. 151.

17. The history of the staff college is summed up briefly in Young and amplified in Bond (see n. 14).

18. See John Gooch, *The Plans of War: The General Staff and British Military Strategy, c. 1900-1916* (London, 1974).

19. The best coverage of the early history of the war in the air is now in the first volume of the new official history of the Royal Canadian Air Force, S. F. Wise, *Canadian Airmen and the First World War* (Toronto, 1980); Denis Winter, in *The First of the Few* (Athens, Ga., 1983), describes the fighter pilots of the RNAS and of the RFC, which were merged on April 1, 1918, to form the Royal Air Force. The immediate postwar years are described in Robin Higham, *Armed Forces in Peacetime: Britain, 1918-1940* (London, 1963).

20. Smith-Barry's Gosport system was so good that it lasted through the two World Wars, but typically he was an outspoken Etonian who was dropped from the postwar air force as quickly as possible. His practical methods cut the death rate in training in half (Winter, *First of the Few*, pp. 36-37).

21. E. B. Haslam, *The History of Royal Air Force Cranwell* (London, 1982).

The Royal Prussian Cadet Corps, 1871-1918:
A Prosopographical Approach

John Moncure

The Great Elector Frederick William of Brandenburg had established three schools to train young nobles as officers in an army that was rapidly growing and becoming more technologically advanced. In 1717 Frederick William I, the soldier king, brought the 130 cadets of these schools to Berlin and founded the cadet corps, with the intention of educating the sons of officers — almost all of whom were noble — who could not otherwise afford to school their children. This entrance requirement not only provided social welfare to those who had dutifully served the state and ensured a loyal officer class and co-opted nobility; it also served as the fatal legacy which, in 1918, led the Allies to abolish the cadet school, the Hauptkadettenanstalt, in Article 176 of the Treaty of Versailles. To the framers of the peace, the cadet corps perpetuated Prussian militarism and a class bias incompatible with the newly forged Weimar Republic.

The legacy did not die there, becoming a historiographical argument that flared periodically on the fringes of the historical community. Critics of the institution fall into three categories: those who object to the brutal discipline, those who condemn the low academic standards, and those who consider the entire school system a prop for an otherwise uncompetitive nobility. The last two types of critics are cousins. If the Military Education Commission had intended to prevent the erosion of aristocratic monopoly by training below-average nobles to be officers, either the academic standards of the schools would have been lower than those of a *Realschule* (to which the cadet school was considered equivalent) or the faculty would have produced one set of exams for commoners and another for Junkers. Certainly the German military leadership was capable of such thinking. War ministers objected to any increase in the size of the army, and therefore the officer corps, because it would mean "taking on more democratic and other elements that were not fit for this career" and inevitably "reaching down into circles unsuitable for the expansion of the officer corps, which . . . would expose it to the danger of democratization."[1]

The authors of the attacks on the cadet school are often alumni and occasionally respected scholars, but they always see the institution as a sinister reflection of the brutality of monarchistic, militaristic Germany. In his memoirs Ludendorff grumbled about his lost youth, although, in view of his standing, these remarks were overlooked by his fellow members of the National League of Former Cadets.[2] The novelist and former cadet Fritz von Unruh delivered a withering attack on the cadet corps in a speech at the Paulskirche in Frankfurt on May 18, 1948, in which he described the institution as the prototype of the concentration camp.[3] One old cadet, a well-known sociologist and son of an old noble-military family, condemned the academic standards in his memoirs.[4] A letter in the *Frankfurt Allgemeine Zeitung* by a Professor emeritus Georg Madelung charged that the cadets were "bulwarks of the crown against liberalism and socialism and of the nobility against the bourgeoisie."[5] Remarks by Hans-Ulrich Wehler, Walter Goerlitz, and Roger Parkinson emphasize the atavistic aspects of Prussian military education.[6] The only monograph on the subject by a professional historian, *Das preussische Kadettenkorps* (1978), agrees with this last assessment.[7]

The principal counter to this impressive array of authorities is *Kadetten*, a simple chronicle written by a former director of the Bundeswehr Museum. He presents the discipline as hard but fair, the academics appropriate to the cadets' ages and professional needs, and the product thoroughly superior.[8] While one ought not dismiss his view outright, it is nonetheless naive and alone in the historical community.

However, not even the most articulate condemnations by modern social historians can disguise or reconcile the disturbing evidence that confronts us: How, if applicants were accepted on the basis of social and political desirability, to prevent the bourgeoisification of the officer corps, did the cadet school at Lichterfelde produce the Ludendorffs and Mansteins and the host of brilliant tactical commanders who twice in this century terrorized a continent? After all, being socially acceptable does not make one tactically or technically proficient.

The answer is not complex. In fact, it is a blend of the divergent opinions mentioned above, and more. During the period of empire,

1871 to 1918, the Prussian cadet corps evolved into a school system with three distinct functions. It continued to provide education for the sons of officers, whatever their social class. It blended the outlook of its nobles and an ever-growing bourgeoisie into a single officer-class perspective. Most important, it provided talented young men an avenue to the most prestigious positions in the army regardless of social class.

The Prussian cadet corps must be considered in the context of the Prussian military education system as a whole. Unlike most major armies of the period, which produced all their officers in state-run schools, the Prussian army had two principal sources of commission (fig. 1). The officer-candidate system accounted for 65-70 percent of Prussia's regular officers and the cadet corps for the rest.[9] The cadet schools were merely the foundation for an officer's education. After several years of preparatory school (*Voranstalt*) and two years of cadet school, most cadets were posted to a regiment for six months as *characterizierte Portepée-Fähnriche* (provisional ensign). Military academy followed promotion to *Fähnrich* (ensign). After successful completion of an examination and a vote of the officers of his regiment, the cadet would be promoted to *Leutnant* (second lieutenant). Formal education continued for most line officers in the various infantry or cavalry schools. A select few were chosen in about their tenth year of service to attend the three-year staff-college course followed by duty in the general staff and accelerated promotions.

Because of the federal nature of the German Empire, the kingdoms of Bavaria and Saxony retained control of their armed forces and maintained their own academies throughout the period of empire.

The good press of the academies still in existence ensures that their alumni are remembered and the institutions themselves are sufficiently hallowed in the public eye, but those that fell to the victor's sword or the revolutionary's torch are fast receding into an obscurity they may not deserve. This is especially true of the Royal Prussian Cadet Corps. No biographer of a major Western military figure spares his reader a discussion of his cadet education: at best brief mention, more often a detailed analysis of the school's influence on his outlook and a report on his academic standing and cadet responsibilities. Anyone familiar with the genre knows, for example, that General Omar Bradley and his wartime superior General Dwight D. Eisenhower were classmates or that Douglas MacArthur was first in his class and

FIG. 1

THE PRUSSIAN ARMY COMMISSIONING PROCESS.

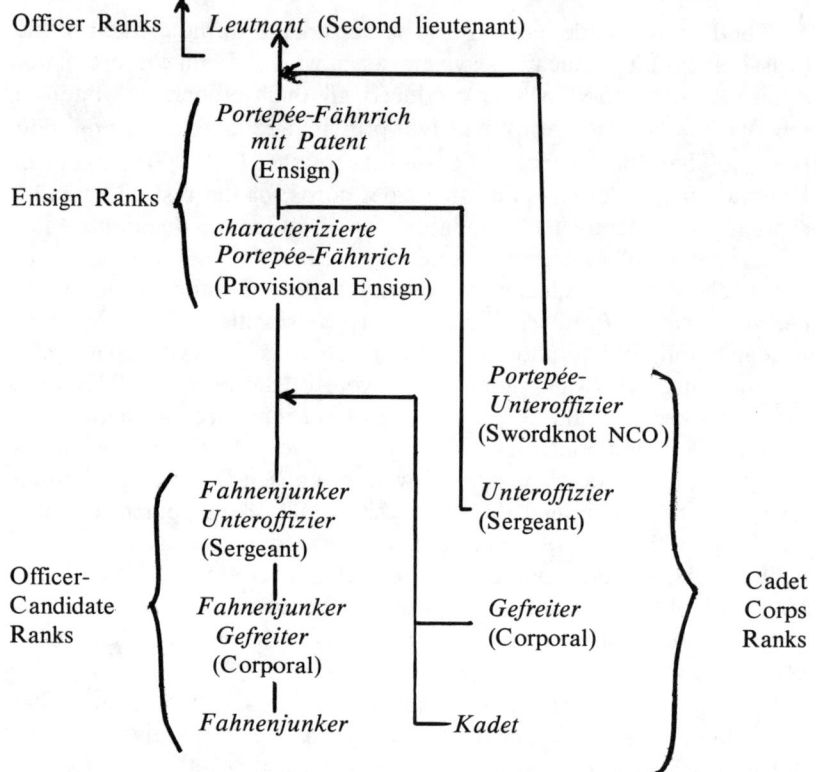

the highest-ranking cadet in his last year, as was Field Marshal the Earl Haig from Sandhurst. Anglo-Saxon biographers of German generals, however, are far less likely even to mention their subjects' academic training, and if they do they mistranslate and misrepresent the organization and function of the school. Kenneth Macksey, author of the most recent biography of Guderian, devotes almost a page to the cadet schools but fails to point out that his subject had passed through a special academic course which led to the coveted *Abitur* (qualifying for admission to a university) and accelerated promotion.[10] Although six of the seven men treated in biographical sketches of Germans in Carver's *War Lords* were graduates of the Hauptkadettenastalt, in two cases this is not mentioned and even in those in which reference is made to schooling only a phrase is devoted to the subject.[11] It is as if the nomenclature and organization of the Prussian cadet school intimidated biographers so much as to make them avoid the topic entirely.

Yet there can be no doubt that the institution, for good or for evil, produced a disproportionate share of Germany's civil and military leaders. Prior to World War I numerous former cadets served in the highest positions. Of thirteen war ministers under the Empire, at least eight were graduates of the cadet school, including von Roon, von Waldersee, Bronsart von Schellendorff, von Heeringen, and von Einem. The prolific military writer General von Verdy du Vernois was also a product of the cadet school. Cadet-school graduates figured prominently in World War I as well. Paul von Hindenburg, Erich Ludendorff, Hermann von Francois, Colmar von der Goltz, Georg von der Marwitz, and Oskar von Hutier all graduated from the cadet school between 1866 and 1884. Even in the Weimar Republic former cadets appeared in prominent positions, including Chancellors von Papen and von Schleicher, Field Marshal von Blomberg, and Generals Heye, von Hammerstein-Equord, and Reinhardt. Their names appear prominently as leaders of the anticommunist paramilitary (Freikorps) units as well. Not surprisingly, former cadets led the Wehrmacht in World War II. Hermann Göring graduated in 1914. Half of Germany's Prussian-born field marshals, including von Rundstedt, von Brauchitsch, von Kluge, von Witzleben, and von Manstein, were educated by the king, as were Generals Guderian, von Falkenhorst, Blaskowitz, and Student.

The complexity of organization of the cadet corps is partially responsible for the summary treatment it has received at the hands of historians and biographers of its celebrated alumni. The school system consisted of nine institutions on two different levels spread throughout Prussia. Eight preparatory schools, situated so as to keep their cadets as close to home as possible,[12] fed the cadet school, which moved from downtown Berlin to the suburb of Gross Lichterfelde in 1878. The education they provided was equivalent to that of a *Realschule*, or modern secondary school. It differed from the classical *Gymnasium*, which prepared the intellectual elite for the university, in that it taught modern instead of classical languages.[13] Because the schools were financed by the crown instead of the students' parents, their academic standards came under frequent scrutiny. Low standards would indicate that the General-Inspektion des Militär-Erziehungs- und Bildungswesen, which approved applications, was more interested in "character" — a Prussian euphemism for aristocratic background — than intellectual promise. The commandant of cadets of West Point, Emory Upton, visited European military schools in 1878 and reported that the Prussian cadet school was not only inferior to his institution but a very ordinary secondary school as well.[14] In evaluating this opinion, it is important to remember, first, that the cadet school hardly performed the same function as West Point and therefore makes a poor comparison and, second, that Upton is a virtually unimpeachable source. In any event, his opinion was seconded and contradicted by numerous observers and alumni to the extent that the issue comes down to a matter of whom one chooses to believe.

The preparatory schools (fig. 2) taught the lower grades, Sexta to Obertertia. Each school had two companies of a hundred boys. Each year-group in the company sat as a class. Thus, assuming roughly equal class sizes, one teacher addressed about twenty boys. This compares favorably with contemporary Prussian civilian schooling, which averaged more than fifty pupils per teacher.[15] The course of study included languages, mathematics, history, and military instruction — equivalent to the curriculum of a *Realschule*. Certainly the potential for an excellent education existed.

The cadet school consisted of two main classes, the Untersekunda and the Obersekunda. At the conclusion of the second of these, most cadets entered the army. The curriculum was mathematics-intensive and included tactics and fortifications. Two special courses, the one-year Selekta and the two-year Prima, were also offered. These courses conferred several benefits, including the notoriety that

The Royal Prussian Cadet Corps

FIG. 2.

ORGANIZATION OF THE CADET CORPS IN 1914

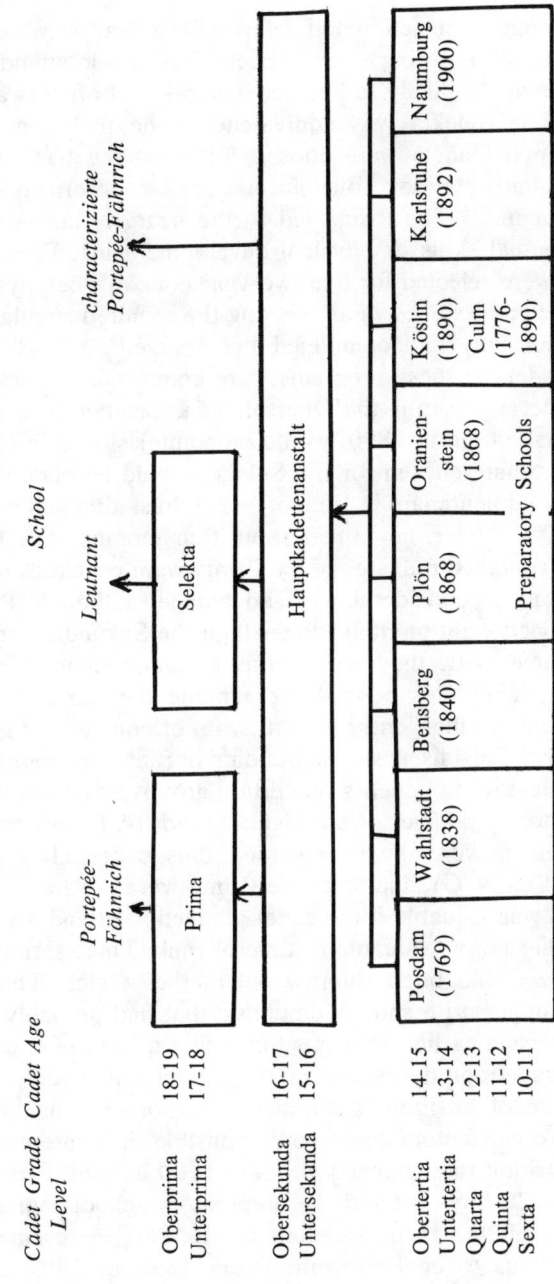

accompanied selection and deferral for a year or two of the substantial expense of outfitting a new officer. Cadets who attended these courses were twice as likely to become general-staff officers as those who did not. The Selekta was equivalent to the first year at the military academy. Cadets were chosen for it on the basis of demonstrated leadership abilities; one former cadet described them as "All-American."[16] The Prima led to the *Abitur.* Cadets with noteworthy intellectual skills or physical development insufficient for regimental duty were selected for this two-year course. The physically immature were commissioned upon meeting the required standard, regardless of whether they had completed the course.[17]

Cadets in these programs were commissioned at different grades. A cadet completing the Obersekunda, gazetted to a regiment as provisional ensign in 1890, would be commissioned in October of 1891. A classmate chosen for the Selekta would be commissioned directly to second lieutenant in June of 1891; thus, although he finished school a full year later, he gained about four months' date of rank over his entry cohort. Graduates of the Prima were posted as ensigns. This put them at a considerable disadvantage; although they were commissioned eight months sooner than the Sekunda graduates posted in the same year, they were months behind their entry cohort. After 1900, their dates of rank were made the same as for the Selekta graduates of their entry cohort, who, of course, had graduated a year earlier.[18] This discussion about date of rank is neither trivial nor pointless. Bestowing benefits on certain groups as opposed to others gives clues to the policies of the higher authority. In this case, graduates of the Selekta were always rewarded; thus, cadets always coveted places in that class. Graduates of the Prima were rewarded with the *Abitur,* which was valuable if the cadet planned to attend a university but for a soldier not as valuable as date of rank. Thus, serious students were penalized and often shunted out of the service. The royal order of 1900 indicated a shift of emphasis that had probably begun as much as a decade earlier. It seems likely that quality of education improved as competition for spots in the Prima stiffened.

Rate of attrition is another indicator of education level. While many other factors could be responsible, it is interesting to note that the attrition rate changed at about 1900 as well. From 1871 to 1890 about 220 boys entered the preparatory schools annually, while 217 cadets left the Hauptkadettenanstalt. This represents a net attrition rate of just over 1 percent. From 1890 to 1899 about 280 boys replaced 272 graduating cadets, or almost 3 percent attrition. But from 1900 to 1909 about 320 boys replaced 234 cadets,[19] the rate soaring from almost nothing to 26 percent! There are several possible explanations for this phenomenon. Disenchantment with the military would explain the change, but in Wilhelmine Germany this hardly seems likely. Dramatic changes in the physical requirements or levels of hazing could also account for increased attrition, but there is no evidence in memoir or official literature to support such a theory. If the cadet corps stopped replacing cadets who had resigned, the attrition rate would appear to rise. However, cadets at the preparatory school at Culm (Köslin), for whom considerable information exists through 1907, consistently remained an average of about three and one-half years prior to entering the Hauptkadettenanstalt. The rate of transfers to and from various preparatory schools and the rate of dropouts fluctuated but manifests no trend in any direction.[20] It is most reasonable to assume, then, that while the quality of education at Lichterfelde varied from year to year, around the turn of the century Prussian military leaders realized that they needed sharp minds as well as "character" to lead their army.

That the Hauptkadettenanstalt continued to provide education to the sons of officers is clear. Of a sample of 556 cadets (5 percent of the total) two-thirds were sons of army officers.[21] Even allowing for a bias toward this occupation on the part of cadets who reported their fathers' occupations, the statistic is revealing. An additional 12 percent (67) were the sons of owners of East Prussian estates, many of whom held reserve commissions as well; these are not classed as officers' sons because their fathers were probably well-off enough to have financed their educations in any case. Clearly, then, the king was looking out for his officers and their children.

The cadet education leavened the Prussian officer corps with a strong loyalty to the person of the king, a concept of duty to the state, and a sense of self-discipline. The family background of cadets was likely to form a sound basis for a *königstreue* education. Fully 77 percent earned their livelihood in the king's service. Royal Prussian cadets did not come from socialist or anarchist households. Almost nine out of ten boys were sons of officers, landowners, or civil servants.[22]

The king reinforced this socialization process by taking a personal interest in each cadet; he met each senior cadet just prior to graduation. The ritual interview played itself out almost without variation.

The class about to graduate assembled in the Feldmarschalsaale, on the walls of which were described in bas-relief the deeds of the Prussian warriors of the past. The cadets stood at attention in a single line. The king entered the room with his entourage, resplendent in full-dress uniform, and stepped in front of each cadet. The cadet took two steps forward, announced his name, his father's occupation, and the regiment to which he hoped to be assigned. The king spoke to each man, recalling the good services his ancestors had performed for former Prussian kings: "Ah, yes, your grandfather was a young hero at Jena and Leipzig, and your father served in the Reserve Guard Regiment." In 1888, William I spoke to the assembled cadets, saying, "I am glad to have met you, even if only *en passant*. You were educated at the expense of the state; be thankful for it when you are in the army. Do your duty, hold high the honor of the army; only then will you be the standard-bearers of honor [*Träger der Ehre*]." With this, the interview ended and the cadets returned to their barracks.[23] This story is impressive not only in that the king — even William I in his dotage — was able to recall the families of so many cadets but in that, through this single ceremony, he bound to his person almost a third of his new officers. In account after account of this meeting, the writers describe themselves as having been awestruck by the attention the king had shown them.[24] Officers considered themselves the king's (not the emperor's) knightly retainers and referred to military service as being *im Königs Rock*.

Another important mechanism of this socialization process was the tutor (*Erzieher*), an officer responsible for the cadet's morale and development.[25] He was not the company commander; that was a separate post. He served, as it were, as guidance counselor to about twenty cadets. As one former cadet recalled, he looked after one's character: "Once in a while [he] would call a couple of cadets to his rooms and give them coffee or cocoa"; his duty was "to shape you" and "to keep your monarchist ideals alive."[26] Obviously, the assignment of a hundred or so officers to this task demonstrates the emphasis that the army placed not only on "character" but on political reliability.

The regimen was spartan.[27] This observation may appear obvious, but it is an important consideration on two counts. Dilettante noblemen did not fit in the cadet corps. Noble cadets were probably not from the cream of court society. In fact, in the forty-eight years of the Empire, only seven cadets, to be sure all noble, joined the dandiest of Prussian units, the Regiment des Garde de Corps. By comparison, over a hundred cadets joined the First Foot Guards during the same period, and the average for an ordinary infantry regiment was about forty.[28] The life-style cadets experienced at Lichterfelde — parades, inspections, punishment — made them well suited to the army.

Despite all this evidence that the Hauptkadettenanstalt supported the nobility and suppressed any notions of democracy or socialism, it nonetheless provided an opportunity for advancement of talent, without regard to comparatively humble origins. Cadets remember it that way. Countless memoirs and interviews suggest that within the school no favoritism was bestowed on noblemen.[29] Statistical evidence supports their opinion. Corporal is a cadet rank awarded to cadets who would eventually complete the Selekta or Prima and would be the only rank the remainder would ever see. In the last forty-eight years of the institution, over five hundred cadets graduated from the Sekunda as corporals.[30] If social-class bias existed, nobles would appear in disproportionate numbers at this grade, but this is not the case. From 1871 to 1879, while only 42 percent of cadets were bourgeois, they occupied 45 percent of the corporal positions. In the first decade of this century, 59 percent of the cadet corps were commoners, and they held 61 percent of the corporal positions.[31] While noblemen may have gained entrance to the institution more easily, once inside it, their advantage evaporated.

The size of the bourgeoisie in Prussia and the number of bourgeois cadets increased throughout the period of empire. From 1871 to 1874, only 40 percent of cadets were not nobles. Their representation increased steadily until the war years, when they occupied 78 percent of the spaces.[32] As Eckert Kehr has demonstrated, the social status of an army officer was enviable indeed.[33] Since the school was a "ticket" to social position, the middle class came more and more to represent the upper tier of German society. This story repeats itself in the Selekta, the most prestigious group in the school. The class of 1886, the first for which all members of this group are identifiable, was 42 percent bourgeois, while they were 44 percent of the class as a whole. The Selekta of 1910 was 66 percent bourgeois, while the class of 1910 was 64 percent bourgeois. In 1914, the bourgeois were 75 percent of the Selekta and 73 percent of the class as a whole.[34] The data for the Prima reflect the same trends.

There can be no doubt that the accusers of the Prussian cadet corps and the crown can say with justification that the institution buttressed the social class that most closely supported the monarchy. But this argument is incidental to the purpose of the cadet corps in the nineteenth century. Germany needed intelligent, dedicated, professional officers to lead its increasingly technical, rapidly growing army. Such men as had always filled those positions — the nobility — were unable to meet the requirements in quality and quantity demanded by the state. Yet the military class could not be discarded. The high command sought a compromise that would maintain the traditional relationship between the nobility and the state, yet ensure that the army was well led. The model for its solution was the three-track German education system. Just as children were divided at an early age into schools that would perpetuate their social-class membership and decide their life work, the cadet corps provided multiple programs, but according to ability rather than class.

Within this almost feudal political institution and society, the leaders of Prussia created a modern military school that rewarded excellence and served as a means of upward mobility for men of talent. The Prussian cadet was younger than his British, French, or American counterpart. He was probably less well-grounded academically, but he was surely more accustomed to the rigors and rituals of active service. He was as likely to be competent on the battlefield as he was unlikely to turn on his royal master.

NOTES

1. The war ministers in question were von Einem, writing in 1904, and von Heeringen, writing in 1913, as cited in Eckert Kehr, *Economic Interest, Militarism, and Foreign Policy*, trans. Grete Heinz, ed. Gordon Graig (Berkeley, 1977), p. 65.

2. Erich Ludendorff, *Meine militärischer Werdegang* (Munich, 1933), p. 6.

3. Jürgen-Konrad Zabel, *Das preussische Kadettenkorps* (Frankfurt am Main, 1978), p. 1.

4. Leopold von Wiese und Kaiserswaldau, *Kindheit* (Hanover, 1924), pp. 46, 47, 80.

5. Georg Madelung, "Ein Lanze für Kadetten Anstalten," *Frankfurter Allgemeine Zeitung*, no. 111, May 14, 1963.

6. Hans-Ulrich Wehler, *Das Deutsche Kaiserreich 1870-1918* (Göttingen, 1983), pp. 126, 127; Walter Görlitz, "Die Offiziere harte Schule," *Welt*, January 28, 1967; Roger Parkinson, *Tormented Warrior* (London, 1978).
7. Zabel, *Das preussische Kadettenkorps.*
8. Freiherr von Brand, *Kadetten* (Munich, 1981).
9. Statistical compilations of biographical sketches of 11,155 graduates of the cadet school from 1871 to 1918 are presented in the unpublished draft of John Moncure, "The Royal Prussian Cadet Corps 1871-1918: A Prosopographical Approach" (Ph.D. diss., Cornell University) (hereafter Moncure, Database).
10. Kenneth Macksey, *Guderian: Creator of the Blitzkrieg* (New York, 1976), pp. 4, 5.
11. Michael Carver, ed., *The War Lords* (Boston, 1976).
12. Cadets whose fathers were officers tended to change schools when their fathers were transferred (Moncure, Database).
13. The complete course of instruction included Latin, German, French, geometry, trigonometry, geography, history, physical science, and military drawing (Henry Barnard, *Military Schools and Courses of Instruction and the Art of War in France, Prussia, Austria, Russia, Sweden, Switzerland, Sardinia, England, and the United States* [New York, 1872], p. 316; Military Education Commission, ed., *Accounts of the Systems of Military Education in France, Prussia, Austria, Bavaria, and the United States* [London, 1870], p. 216; Emory Upton, *The Armies of Europe and Asia* [New York, 1878], p. 211).
14. Upton, *Armies*, pp. 212, 360.
15. Thomas Alexander, *The Prussian Elementary School* (New York, 1918), p. 97.
16. Horace Wetzell, interview, August 11, 1983.
17. *Aufnahme-Bestimmungen und Lehrplan des Königlichen Kadettenkorps* (Berlin, 1899), p. 4.
18. [Kurt] von Rabenau, *Die deutsche Land- und Seemacht und die Berufspflichten des Offiziers* (Berlin, 1906), pp. 174, 175.
19. Moncure, Database.
20. Neuschäfer, *Stammliste des Königlichen Kadettenhauses Culm-Cöslin (1. Juni 1776-1. November 1907)* (Berlin, 1907).
21. Moncure, Database.
22. Ibid.
23. Emil Ilgner, *Kadetten-Erinnerungen* (Berlin, 1932?), p. 105. For the address of William I and the text of the conversation, see Magnus von Eberhardt in Richard Feiber, *Leben und Treiben in Königlich Preussischen Kadettenhaus Bensberg*, self-published manuscript dated 1942, Bundesarchiv-Militärarchiv document KORPS 54; Walther Schulze, *Damals, als ich Kadett war* (Leipzig, n.d.), p. 101.

24. [Constantin] von Altrock, "Aus dem Kadettenzeit," *Reichskadettenblatt*, no. 5 (September 1925), pp. 51-53.
25. Wetzell, interview.
26. Ibid.
27. This is not the universal opinion (see Upton, *Armies,* p. 8), but sufficient evidence exists to be certain that the schools seemed rigorous to the cadets (Zabel, *Das preussische Kadettenkorps*, p.1; Ludendorff, *Meine militärischer Werdegang*, p. 6; Wetzel, interview; Manfred von Richthoven, *The Red Battle Flyer*, trans. Ellis Barker [New York, 1918], pp. 22, 23; H. M. Morgan, *Assize of Arms* [New York], p. 138; von Wiese und Kaiserswaldau, *Kindheit*, pp. 75-76; Schulze, pp. 32-33; Hans Eberhard von Besser, *Wahlstaetter* [n.p., 1934], pp. 10-11).
28. Moncure, Database.
29. Ilgner, *Kadetten Errinerungen*, p. 76; Wetzell, interview, p. 15.
30. Moncure, Database.
31. Moncure, Database.
32. Moncure, Database.
33. Kehr, *Economic Interest*, pp. 98, 99. Morgan (*Assize of Arms*, p. 112) observed this as well.
34. Moncure, Database.

III. THE HABSBURG IMPERIAL SYSTEM

The Education of Habsburg Army Officers, 1848-1918

István Deák

The origins of Austrian military education reach back to Wallenstein, the great captain of the Thirty Years' War, who founded a military academy in 1624. This school did not, however, survive its creator. A Baron Richthausen von Chaos established a school for military engineers in Vienna in 1666, and in 1693 this school moved to a place outside the walls of the city that would later be called Stiftskaserne and that now houses the Austrian War Archives and other military institutions. It was Eugene of Savoy, an innovator in many things, who turned that school into a regular academy for military engineers (*k.k. Ingenieurakademie*) in 1717. This was still a private institution that charged tuition.[1] The first state-supported military schools were set up by Maria Theresa in the 1750s, but not even this great imperial reformer was primarily interested in the training of officers. Her real concern was to provide for military orphans, the sons of deserving officers, and the younger sons of the minor landed nobility — a preoccupation which remained with the Habsburg rulers to the end. Her best schools were actually not schools at all: the Hungarian and Italian Noble Bodyguards, established in Vienna and Milan respectively. These units offered a general education to a few dozen sons of penniless Hungarian and Italian nobles. Some of the young Guards used the opportunity to acquire Jacobin revolutionary ideas; the majority became well-trained officers. This rudimentary system of military education was subsequently expanded by Joseph II and his successors, so that by the mid-nineteenth century there were a number of military schools with well-established traditions. Foremost among them was the Military Academy at Wiener Neustadt, near Vienna, founded by Maria Theresa in 1752, which supplied the army with its best-educated infantry, ranger (*Jäger*), and cavalry officers.[2] Even today, the Military Academy trains future Austrian officers.

Until the mid-nineteenth century, the Military Academy took in an annual contingent of a hundred boys eleven to twelve years of age and kept them for seven or eight years before commissioning them as junior lieutenants (*Fähnrich*, later termed Lieutenant Second Class). Less deserving students were supposed to become noncommissioned officers, but in reality graduates were almost invariably commissioned. From 1852 on, boys between the ages of eleven and fifteen were directed into other schools and the Military Academy became a high school only. Later it became a genuine academy, for young men between eighteen and twenty. The cadets were primarily the sons of soldiers: the lower the rank of the father, the more likely his son was to be admitted to a "free place," which meant room and board as well as a little pocket money. This, at least, was the theory; in practice, as one bitter critic of the Austrian army wrote in his memoirs, he, the son of a two-star general, had been admitted automatically to a free place.[3] Some students had "half-free" places, and a few paid the full fee, which amounted to eight hundred gulden annually. This sum, the equivalent of a captain's yearly basic salary, was one that only foreign princes, landowning aristocrats, and the very rich bourgeois could afford to pay.

The academy was under the command of a general, and the majority of its teachers were officers, but before 1852, especially in the lower classes, much of the teaching was also done by Piarist (Calasanctian) fathers. In fact, the academy was a curious cross between a monastery and a barracks. At first only Catholics were admitted, but later Protestants and then, toward the end of the nineteenth century, Jews and Muslims were admitted as well. Mass was celebrated every day (replaced later by a brief prayer rattled off at great speed), but religion seems to have played only a very minor role in the life of the cadets, just as it would later in their lives as commissioned officers. Religious instruction was treated as a necessary bore, typically offered by a Czech padre whose Bohemian accent was a frequent source of amusement to memoirists.[4] Religious services were a formality, as much a part of the pomp and circumstance of an officer's life as grand parades, guard duty at the imperial palace, and solemn military funerals.

The curriculum emphasized theoretical knowledge; mathematics and geometry counted for four points, German and French for two, and history, geography, and natural history for only one. Fencing, gymnastics, and music counted for nothing — at least until the 1850s. Inevitably, the students treated the professors of important subjects, all military men, with great respect and the teachers of unimportant subjects, often priests or civilians, with a good deal of contempt. The cadets suffered under an enormous burden of thirty-five to thirty-eight hours of classes weekly. About sixty subjects were taught, all under strict supervision and iron discipline.

The cadets slept in the same meticulous order which regulated their working hours: always in their own platoon and arranged by height. Reveille was at five or six in the morning, and from that moment on every movement of the cadets was scrupulously controlled. They marched in close order to the washroom under the supervision of a "class sergeant" (*Klassenfeldwebel* or *Inspectionsorgan*, an elderly NCO) to wash in cold water with a few soap crumbs kept in a small bag (a hot bath was provided only once a month).[5] Then came mass, a breakfast of black bread and water (in winter, warm milk), and, finally, work in the classroom. Lunch and dinner were quite sumptuous; in general, the cadets ate better and lived more comfortably, despite everything, than they had at home or would again as junior officers.

Study consisted mostly of memorization, followed, late in the afternoon, by a walk in the academy park. There was the "Grand Tour," undertaken on Sundays, and the "Little Tour" on weekdays, in close order, with one class marching fifty to a hundred feet behind the other, always on the same path, every day of the year. One ex-cadet calculated that he had walked the Grand Tour five hundred times and the Little Tour three thousand.[6] The cadets, called *Zöglinge*, never saw the rest of the enormous park, where hunting and forestry were practiced on a broad scale.

Classes were strictly separated; even the members of parallel sections were forbidden to meet. Brothers at the same school were allowed to get together once a month, and then for only an hour.[7] When classes did meet, it was only to fight one of those famous battles — recounted in so many memoirs — in which furniture was destroyed or set afire and a few participants ended up in the hospital. Curfew was strictly enforced, and leaves were granted with great reluctance. Honor students were occasionally allowed to eat out, but only on Sunday afternoons and only if invited and accompanied. Vacation was in September, but if the family was far away (as it often was) or if it lacked the money for travel (as it often did) or if the cadet was under interdict (as most were), then there was no vacation. The official *Reglement* emphasized the basic principle of the school: "the young people are to be prevented from following their natural inclination toward laziness."⁸ Thus, some cadets were never allowed to leave the academy. Even Sunday mornings were devoted to work, but, this being a Catholic country, there were several religious holidays. When finally commissioned after seven or eight years of virtual imprisonment, the ex-cadets often felt utterly lost in the great world. There were legendary stories of a young lieutenant who, upon arriving in Vienna, which he had never seen, was afraid to step off the sidewalk and could not find his hotel because he was unable to conceive of more than one hotel in a town.⁹ And such people were expected to take over platoons of raw recruits in some remote corner of the Monarchy!

Entertainment at the academy consisted of mild games and the far more brutal illegal rumbles. Smoking was prohibited but practiced in secret. There were occasional trips to the local theater to see specially expurgated plays. Reading material was scarce and censored. Before 1867, the discovery of a copy of Goethe's *Goetz von Berlichingen* in one's trunk could be cause for an appearance before the company commander; a copy of *Werther* could lead to incarceration and one of the poems of Heine to incarceration reinforced by fasting. Surprisingly, the reader of Schiller, a far more irreverent poet than Goethe, was encouraged, perhaps because so many of Schiller's heroes were soldiers.¹⁰ James Fenimore Cooper's Leatherstocking tales seems to have been the favorite reading of the young cadets. Correspondence was supervised, as were the rarely authorized visits of family members. Punishment was varied and imaginative; it ranged from no dinner to imprisonment up to eight days in a dark cell with a wooden bunk, bread-and-water rations, and "light irons," the latter to be removed every third night. Even more feared was lashing, called *Schilling*, carried out under medical supervision and often resulting in hospitalization. Quitting school was extremely difficult; nor were expulsions very frequent.

The students' unwritten code of behavior was in direct conflict with the official code, foreshadowing the two conflicting codes of behavior that officers had to live by. Much divided among themselves, the students presented a united front to the authorities. Complaining to a supervisor or informing on one's comrades was seen as the worst of crimes, and one was expected to suffer bullying without a murmur. The freshmen, called "Benjamins," were routinely mistreated by the seniors, called *Burgherren* (lords of the castle), who were assigned to each dormitory room. The bullying of former "civilians" (called

Philister) was particularly odious, whereas the *Fisolen* (Austrian for "green beans"), who came from the lower-level military schools, knew how to defend themselves.

A sense of camaraderie must have helped, as did homoeroticism. The memoirists are very shy on the subject, but at least two of them mention that there were many "romantic friendships" which had "the character of love affairs." Older boys tried to choose their beloved ones, called *Schmalzel*, from the younger classes and risked severe punishment to spend a few minutes with them. At the very least, they could cast longing eyes at each other. The weaker or more effeminate partner in such a relationship was commonly referred to as *die Dame*. Permission to hold hands or walk arm in arm at one of the rare excursions counted as a supreme favor. The cadets spent every free moment in the morning pomading their hair (pork fat would do if nothing else was available) and sprinkling themselves with strictly forbidden perfume. These friendships should not necessarily be interpreted in a physical sense, for which in any case there was little opportunity. Rather, the passion felt for one's *Schmalzel* represented the only affectionate relationship many boys had enjoyed since they had turned six or seven. However, Oscar Teuber, a writer of very popular military reminiscences, mentions rather casually that at the Military Academy it was possible to bribe the warden for permission to join a friend in the punishment cell, "for the pleasures of sweet intimacy." That the authorities closed their eyes to such special friendships is shown by the fact that the class sergeant sometimes admonished the cadets to choose their *Schmalzel* from among their own classmates.[11]

The memoirists are unanimous not only in their description of the discipline and the terror but also in their emphasis on the enthusiasm, youthful idealism, and ethical purity of the cadets. For them, the emperor was a demigod, and so were the supervising officers, with whom they had, incidentally, little contact. The cadets had more mixed feelings toward their teachers, the military ones of whom could send a student to jail, and they professed boundless contempt for the class sergeants, whom they called *Fetzen* (the rags that served as a foot soldier's substitute for socks). The sergeants, mostly highly decorated war heroes of lower-class origin, shared their quarters with the students; they nagged — but were not allowed to punish — the cadets and were terrorized by them in return. Beating up the sergeant in the dark of night seems to have been a favorite pastime. The sergeants endured because of the prospect of an officer's commission at the end of their long stay, but it is an apt comment on the vast class difference between future officers and enlisted men that the cadets' brutalization of the *Fetzen*, the only nongentlemen with whom they were in contact, was so casually tolerated.[12]

Ideological training in mid-nineteenth-century Austria was incredibly primitive, at least from the point of view of modern notions, and perhaps because of this very effective. The teaching of history consisted mainly of a listing of the great deeds of former Habsburg rulers; military history consisted more or less of the same thing.[13] One of the most important subjects was military writing style, in which (fortunately for the historian) calligraphy was considered equally as important as the memorization of the complex formulae by which the higher-ups were to be addressed. It was perfectly good form to conclude a petition to His All-Highest Majesty with the fervent wish "to expire in deepest reverence at the feet of His Most August Presence."[14] God, Emperor, and Fatherland were mentioned in the same breath (the earlier formula was Throne and Altar), but the meaning of "Fatherland" was never defined. Nor could it be, considering that Austria, even at its most unified, consisted of a vast number of theoretically sovereign kingdoms, principalities, margravates, counties, baronies, and seigniories.

The cadets hailed from all parts of the Monarchy. The majority of them had German-speaking parents, but this did not necessarily mean that they were German. In fact, the cadets sometimes distinguished between those who used "Army German" (*Armeedeutsch*) at home, regardless of their family's ethnic origin, and genuine German nationals. During the Franco-Prussian War, in 1870-71, when the Austrian military was aching to avenge the humiliation suffered at Königgrätz, the cadets ostracized and often mistreated the ethnic Germans in their midst. There were many conflicts between these so-called *Einfach-Österreicher* (plain Austrians) or *Armeedeutschen* (Army Germans) and the ethnic Germans, whom their opponents referred to as "Prussians." Croats were called *Krowaten* or *Krowatowitsche*, and their protection was often sought, because these boys from Border Guard families were reputedly stronger and more mature than the others. Ethnic Hungarians were also much sought after because of the sumptuous food packages they received from home. Poles had the reputation of being wealthy aristocrats and poor students; Czechs, Italians (*Katzelmacher*), and Romanians were all seen in the light of their national stereotypes. In the first year, a cadet was forbidden to speak his mother tongue, and some cadets were forced to relearn their mother tongues later in language courses offered by the school.[15]

Officers, noncommissioned officers, officials, and teachers tended to use German in everyday speech whatever their mother tongue, and the imperial census takers wanted to know only what language was used in everyday affairs. The army itself was uninterested in such matters. The detailed personal records (*Conduite-Listen* or, later, *Qualificationslisten*) of the officers mentioned neither nationality nor mother tongue (although, beginning in the 1890s, the students' records began to indicate the latter). Consequently, the researcher must arrive at his shaky conclusions concerning ethnicity from a combination of name, birthplace, legal residence, religion, and language abilities. The trouble is that soldiers and their sons were seldom born in the province of their ethnic origin and were often raised in a foreign environment. As for names, one need only glance at the rank lists of the period to appreciate the many amazing interethnic name combinations. My own study of the careers of a thousand Austrian officers selected at random from two separate generations (1870 and 1900) suggests that about 55 percent of Military Academy graduates were likely to be German — more than double the proportion of Germans in the Monarchy. There is nothing to show that the Germans among the graduates made better careers for themselves than the non-Germans. On the other hand, Military Academy graduates considerably outpaced graduates of other schools and officers without a formal education. Admission policy definitely favored the well-connected, but at the academy itself there seems to have been no favoritism or discrimination. This is easily understandable if we consider that, from the emperor's point of view, race, religion, and even social class were of little consequence; what mattered was whether one was a loyal and useful subject.

The language of education and communication at the academy, as at all the other military schools, was German. The students were spared the burden of Latin and Greek but had to learn French, "Bohemian" (i.e., Czech), and either Hungarian or Italian — apparently all badly taught. This was a serious matter considering that, once transferred to his regiment, a young lieutenant was expected to instruct his recruits in their language, not in his own. Yet even if all of the ten major languages spoken by the Monarchy's inhabitants had been taught to the cadets, they would still have been at a loss when confronted with the soldiers of, say, an Italian regiment in the Austrian army that spoke the widely different dialect of Milan, Venice, or Bergamo.[16]

In the 1850s, exercise and sports counted for little in the life of the cadets — they would become important later. Gymnastics were considered lower-class in any case. Fencing, riding, and dance instruction, on the other hand, were required and very popular.

The day of liberation came on August 18, the emperor's birthday, when the young lieutenants were commissioned. For the occasion, the army proved as generous to the graduates as it would be stingy with them later as commissioned officers, providing them with uniforms, silver, elegant linen, and luxurious underwear. At mid-century, the average worth of these gifts was calculated at nine hundred gulden, but the parade uniform of some cavalry regiments alone cost a thousand.[17] Later there would be fewer and fewer such benefits. Before commissioning, the cadets usually visited a tailor to have the collars on their uniforms heightened: this was a source of dandy pride for them and an irregularity much disliked by the military authorities.

The ceremony of "passing out" or commissioning (*Ausmusterung*) is invariably described by the ex-cadets as the "greatest day of my life," and there can be little doubt that they were sincere when they swore to give their lives for the emperor. The school had probably not treated them much worse than they would have been treated in civilian establishments. Nor was strict discipline unknown to youngsters who, for the most part, came from military families, in which authoritarianism was even more pronounced than in civilian ones. The cadets had been taught more science at the academy than they would have elsewhere. They had learned to be gentlemen, which would count for more than anything else in the regiment. Of politics they knew nothing; they took their absolute devotion to the ruler for granted. There was now one more walk in the park, in freely formed groups at last; from there, the road led directly to the troops and, for many, to acute disappointment.

The Military Academy could not, of course, fulfill all the needs of the army. The other elite institution, the engineering academy founded by Eugene of Savoy (actually two academies, one for gunners and the other for engineers), changed its name and location a number of times but consistently trained highly qualified artillerymen, builders, and sappers. Its graduates demonstrated superior knowledge, formed exclusive castes, and were well respected. Socially, they were more middle-class than the Military Academy graduates, and they provided Central Europe with some of its foremost scientists and technical innovators.

All of this was still insufficient to supply the bulk of the armed forces with officers. There were also a number of middle-level schools, known as *Schul-Compagnien*, for the training of noncommissioned officers (the best of whom would make it to the level of officer).[18] A few of these, for instance, the Pionier-Schule at Tulln in Lower Austria, were considered elite institutions. The average troop officer, however, attained his commission not by going through school but by entering a regiment. Thus, he was first a soldier (usually at age fourteen or fifteen), then a regimental cadet, and finally an officer.

There were many ways in mid-nineteenth-century Austria for a youngster to become an officer without having completed a middle- or upper-level military school. He could enlist as an ordinary soldier and earn an officer's golden sword tassel (*portepée*) by moving up through the ranks, usually as a result of extraordinary valor on the battlefield. There were many such cases, especially among the Croat, Serb, Romanian, Swabian German, and Székler Hungarian soldiers of the eighteen Border Guard regiments. He could complete an elementary military school (*Unter-* and *Obererziehungshaus*) and enter the army as a cadet, with a fair chance of becoming an officer. He could also enter a regiment directly as a cadet (provided that he could pay for his uniform and equipment) and then hope for a commission. But even among such cadets there was a bewildering variety. The so-called imperial cadets received monthly pay and had the right to every third lieutenant's position in the regiment. The others were mere "regimental cadets," and their only hope was the goodwill of their colonel or, even more, of the "Proprietor of the Regiment" (*Regimentsinhaber*), a most unreliable source of favors.[19]

The monarchy attempted to care not only for the sons but also for the daughters of its soldiers. It was again Maria Theresa who created an officers' daughters' educational institution in 1775, at St. Pölten in Lower Austria. There the daughters of impecunious or dead officers were trained to become governesses for aristocratic families. This way, the empress argued, the great families would be less interested in importing governesses from abroad. It was expected that these girls would eventually marry officers and thus perpetuate the military establishment. Graduates were provided with a gift of 250 gulden, and if they stayed on as governesses for at least six years, they were permitted to marry an officer without depositing the customary security (*Heiratskaution*). If they found no husband and grew too old to work as governesses, they received a life-time pension of 150 gulden yearly.[20]

In 1786, the officers' daughters' institution moved to Hernals, near Vienna. It was complemented in the first half of the nineteenth century by two smaller schools for the orphan daughters of enlisted men and noncommissioned officers; girls there were trained to become "maids for middle-class families." Finally, in the mid-nineteenth century, a second officers' daughters' institution was set up at Sopron (Ödenburg), in western Hungary. Founded by a local women's organization, the Sopron school was taken over by the Joint War Ministry in 1877 and thereafter was similar to the Hernals preparatory school. After a while, Hernals came to train not only governesses but teachers as well, and by the end of the nineteenth century its more talented students were being encouraged to acquire a *Gymnasium* certificate (*Matura*). In 1907, the educational subsidy for all officers' orphans was extended to the age of twenty-four, which enabled some Hernals graduates to study at the university. All in all, the daughters of officers had better educational opportunities than women in civilian life. At first, the girls at Hernals and Sopron were subjected to strict discipline; later, the system became more liberal, and girls were taught not only sewing, French, and piano but also the arts and sciences. The overall aim was to turn them into "respectable ladies." In 1905, Hernals had thirty-one regular and nineteen "outside" teachers, a good number in relation to the fewer than two hundred pupils.[21]

The young officer in 1850 was a loyal subject of his ruler, but in general he was either unprepared for army life as a result of his having been isolated at school or well versed in practical matters but lacking in education. All this was shortly to change. The war of 1848-49, in which a hastily organized Hungarian national army nearly defeated the imperial forces, was a bitter lesson. It resulted in a growing demand for reform, especially in military education, and some attempts were made in the following decades to introduce changes. The schools were reorganized in successive waves, but not until the

Compromise of 1867 and the concurrent triumph of liberalism were substantial reforms introduced.

The first changes were in fact quite superficial. For instance, in the 1850s, the three academies — the Military Academy at Wiener Neustadt, the Engineering Academy at Klosterbruck bei Znaim, and the Artillery Academy at Olmütz — gave up their first four classes to four new cadet institutes in which boys between the ages of eleven and fifteen prepared for entry into the academies. The new system increased to 800 the number of well-educated cadets available for admission to the academies. The latter now functioned as secondary schools and trained a total of 720 students — 450 at Wiener Neustadt and 135 at each of the two technical academies, among them many entrants from nonelite preparatory schools.[22] However, most officer candidates were still trained in the *Schul-Compagnien*, which also served the needs of the army for noncommissioned officers. Others came up from the regimental cadet companies, where education was uneven if not totally lacking. Discipline became even more extreme in all the schools. Students were locked up in the institutions; they were spied on constantly and were expected to spy on others. The aim was to turn them into obedient and hardy warriors. For example, an imperial regulation of 1859 stipulated that the cadets' sleeping quarters be kept at $8X$ Réaumur ($10X$ C.) at night and that the mess halls be left practically heatless. Only the infirmary and the classroom were to be heated to a blissful $19X$ C.[23]

The terrible military defeats of 1859 and 1866 increased the pressure for fundamental political change in the Monarchy and, with it, a reform of the military schools. The Battle of Königgrätz in 1866 was widely interpreted as a victory of the Prussian school system over the Austrian system. (The French were to analyze their own situation in a similar light following their defeat at Sedan in 1870.) Austrian military observers as well as the civilian press admiringly compared the self-reliant Prussian junior officer with the heedlessly heroic, over-disciplined, and militarily ignorant Austrian officer, and urgent calls went out for a new type of officer to lead a new army.

Amazingly, in at least one memorable case the cadets took reform into their own hands. When, in January 1867, the commander of the cadet institute at Marburg (today Maribor in Slovenia) ordered the lashing of lazy students and not only, as heretofore, those guilty of serious infractions, the older cadets (boys of fourteen and fifteen) conspired to make a revolution. On February 1, 1867, when the cadets were armed with rifles (without bullets) and bayonets for field exercises, they took over a building, set up barricades, and chanted revolutionary slogans. When they nearly stabbed the commanding colonel who had tried to negotiate, a *Jäger* battalion was ordered to surround the building. Unfortunately for the cadets, while their accumulated food supply was adequate for a long siege, the question of water supply had been overlooked in the excitement. They surrendered by midnight of the same day in exchange for the promise of a partial amnesty and the abolition of lashing for insufficient diligence. Although there had been an orgy of destruction in the building, practically no one was punished or expelled from the institution. Almost as if in response to the revolt, corporal punishment was abolished in all military schools in October of 1868, and as a further major concession the cadets were now permitted to keep a significant part of the pocket money sent by their parents.[24]

The 1867 Compromise resulted in the creation of four separate armies in the Monarchy: the joint army, the Austrian national army, the Hungarian national army, and, as an annex of the latter, the Croatian national forces. All four military establishments had their own schools, and while the Hungarians (and Croats) insisted that Hungarian (or Croatian) be spoken in their national forces and national military schools, the joint army and the Austrian national army or *Landwehr* continued the old anational or supranational tradition. What concerns us here is the military schools of the joint army.

The fundamental provision of the reorganization of military education that followed was that all officers receive military school training. By requiring a certain measure of education of everyone, the new system closed the door to ambitious enlisted men and noncommissioned officers, but their sons were still perfectly welcome in the military schools and thus also in the officer corps. In fact, because the sons of the nobility now increasingly shunned an officer's career, while the well-to-do bourgeoisie never developed an interest in the profession, the army took more and more sons of the petty bourgeoisie into the military schools. This caused the generals no end of worry, as is shown by numerous memoranda on the lowering of class and educational standards in the officer corps. There is no reason to believe that the generals were right, at least with respect to education; in fact, the education and training of officer candidates improved significantly after 1867.

After the last great reform of military education, devised by Colonel Adolph von Wurmb, in 1874, there were three types of schools for training career officers: academies, cadet schools, and schools for the professional retraining of reserve officers. Still at the top of the system were the military academies, which drew their students primarily from specially established military preparatory high schools (*Militär-Unterreal-* and *Militär-Oberrealschulen*). Civilian high-school students could also be admitted to the academies at the age of seventeen, that is, before they had earned the *Matura*. The academies offered a three-year curriculum which led to commissioning as a full lieutenant. (The rank of lieutenant second-class no longer existed.)

The Military Academy supplied the army with only one out of every eight infantry officers, while the ratio in the cavalry was one out of every two; most of the other officers came from the newly established cadet schools, four-year institutions whose graduates entered the army not as officers but as noncommissioned ensigns (*Kadet-Offiziers-Stellvertreter*, known after 1908 as *Fähnriche*). Commissioning as a lieutenant usually followed after one year of army service.

There were, in 1900, only two joint army military academies, the Military Academy at Wiener Neustadt and the Technical Military Academy at Vienna. There were eighteen cadet schools, one each for the cavalry, the artillery, and the engineers and fifteen for the less prestigious infantry. Whereas the academies took in an annual contingent of about 250 freshmen, the eighteen cadet schools were ready to admit over 2,000 youngsters — in practice, there were never enough students. Tuition at the cadet schools was exactly half that at the academies, but in both types of institutions the majority of students paid nothing. The academies admitted the talented and the well-connected, which more or less amounts to saying that they admitted the sons of the military and civil-service elites. The Military Academy class of 1874 included, among its ninety-five graduates, seventy-one sons of officers, the son of a military official (*Militärbeamter*), and thirteen sons of civil servants, a total of eighty-five young men whose fathers were in state service. With 90 percent of the graduates coming from a military or civil-service background, the occupations of the fathers of the remaining 10 percent seem almost immaterial. In any case, they included four estate owners, a rentier, a Protestant minister, three professionals, and one peasant. Of the ninety-five graduates twenty-eight (30 percent) had a noble predicate (five barons, two *Ritters*, and twenty-one from the lower nobility), but except for the two Polish *Ritters* and a few Austrian, Hungarian, and Polish untitled nobles, these boys were not from the old nobility. Rather, they were the sons of ennobled officers and officials.[25] In brief, in the 1870s the primary function of the Military Academy at Wiener Neustadt was to train the sons of upper-echelon officers and civil servants. To cite another example, out of eighty students selected at random at the military preparatory high school at Mährisch-Weisskirchen, there were, in 1899, nine boys whose fathers were generals or admirals.[26]

Yet, by the turn of the century, new elements had appeared at the elite military schools, and by the eve of World War I, the social composition of the Military Academy had changed significantly. Of the 133 graduates of the class of 1913, only 50 (37.6 percent) were sons of officers; another 6 were the sons of noncommissioned officers (in 1874 none had been), and 11 were the sons of military officials (in 1874 one had been). Thus sons of military men constituted only half (67) of the class. Even if we add to this the surprisingly large number (32) of students whose fathers were civil servants, the entire state service made up only 74.4 percent (99 students) of the class (in 1874 it had been 90 percent). The occupations of the other fathers are not without interest: there were among them 5 estate owners, a rentier, a factory director, a hotel owner, and a wholesale merchant as well as 9 professionals (including an artist), 4 merchants, 4 business employees, 4 artisans, 2 farmers, and a doorman. Clearly, the class of 1913 was less representative of the officer corps and of state service in general than the class of 1874 had been. Furthermore, it included a goodly number of boys of lower-middle-class background. Characteristically, it had only one titled nobleman, a *Freiherr* whose father was a two-star general and whose title represented a mark of personal distinction. There were also two *Ritters* and 29 lower nobles, almost all from the new or service nobility.[27]

The graduates of the military academies had a good chance of making it into the general staff and thus ending up as generals. The students at the cadet school were trained to serve with the troops, but crossing over from one type of school and career into another was quite common, and many a poor cadet-school student went on to the general staff and from there to a general's rank.[28]

The third road to a professional career led through the reserve-officer's commission. The Austrian and the Hungarian military laws of 1868 enabled conscripts with a high-school education or its equivalent to serve one year instead of three. By creating this institution, the liberal Austrian and Hungarian governments hoped to fill the officer corps with educated civilians in uniform as well as to attract the bourgeoisie to the military profession. The "one-year-volunteers" (*Einjährig Freiwillige*) were conscripts just like the ordinary recruits, but they enjoyed many privileges, and they alone qualified for reserve-officer's school. Once they had completed their brief training, the "volunteers" were usually made warrant officers, and three years later a substantial minority became lieutenants in the reserve. Then, if they wished and qualified, reserve lieutenants could attend a special course to transform themselves into career officers.[29] There were hundreds of such cases, but the liberals' dream of making the army officer corps more liberal remained only a dream. By 1900 there were 12,744 reserve officers, as opposed to 16,714 career officers, but politically and ideologically the reservists and the former reservists who had become career officers made no difference. The officer's vocation appealed even less to the educated and career-minded middle class than to the old nobility, and the few reserve officers who chose a professional army career were mostly unemployed "diploma-holders."

Students at the military preparatory schools and at the academies were overburdened with knowledge. They were expected to acquire a combined humanistic and scientific erudition (minus Latin and Greek) and to complement it with such subjects as public law, economics, astronomy, geodesics, the building of fortifications, terrain drawing, the major tongues spoken by the peoples of the Monarchy, the handling of complex weapons, field exercises, drill, tactics, strategy, horseback riding, fencing, swimming, dance, and athletics. History continued to be taught in accordance with the official dictum that "thought-provoking [*reflektierende*] or critical presentations are to be avoided; on the other hand, every opportunity must be used to strengthen the patriotic and military consciousness [*Gesinnung*] of the pupils."[30] The military schools had no special textbooks in the humanities and social sciences. History books continued to list the Roman and German rulers and to present euphoric accounts of the great deeds of Habsburg princes. The quality of teaching left much to be desired: the best specialists came from the general staff and the higher military technical institutions; the humanities, social sciences, and languages were often taught by officers who were frustrated poets or writers and should not have been in the military in the first place. The army had set up schools for the training of military teachers; still, pedagogical ability seems to have been rare among them.

In the race for good grades, crucial for admission to a desirable regiment or to the elite *Jäger*, Military Academy students lost or scarcely developed any interest in ethical or religious problems, civic duties, and social or political culture. But at least now there was more freedom. Long gone were the stern Calasanctian fathers, the daily mass, and the compulsory confession. The class sergeant had vanished in 1868, along with fasting, corporal punishment, and imprisonment in a darkened cell. Students at the academy were now free to smoke, to keep their pocket money, to stay out on Sundays, to go to the theater, to write uncensored letters, to read nearly anything they liked, to cultivate the arts, and to walk anywhere in the park. Hazing by upperclassmen remained, however, as did the dual moral standard. Instead of the airs of a bully, students now tended to display an air of cultural superiority that made them obnoxious not only to their liberal and socialist critics but often also to their comrades in the cadet schools. Only one thing remained common to all military students, no matter where they were trained: their unconditional devotion to Francis Joseph, the only supreme commander they, their fathers, and sometimes even their grandfathers had known.

The cadet schools came much closer to being democratic establishments, if not in spirit then at least in the cultural and social background of their pupils. Because there were never enough applicants, a junior-high-school average of *genügend* (satisfactory), the lowest passing grade, sufficed for admission to an infantry cadet school. Failure in Latin and Greek was discounted, and the compulsory entrance examination was treated as a farce.[31] Thus the cadets were often those who had not made it into the *Gymnasium* or whose parents were too poor to pay the costs of a civilian senior highschool. Yet even the lowly infantry cadet schools seemed to demand the impossible of their inmates. In February 1893, Anton Lehár, brother of the composer Franz Lęhár, received generally excellent grades in the following subjects for the first semester of his fourth year at the Vienna infantry cadet school: comportment, industry, ability, character, behavior, accoutrement, German, Hungarian, French, geography, history, arithmetic and algebra, geometry, geometric design, practical geometry, physics, chemistry, calligraphy, freehand drawing, service regulations, drill regulations, army organization, weaponry, terrain study and terrain drawing, tactics, military engineering, fortifications and fortress warfare, military administration and business style, field exercises and the training of troops, gymnastics, fencing, service rules and proper conduct (*Anstandslehre*), singing, music, and social dance.[32] Interestingly, Lehár was given no religious instruction in his senior year.

The military schools of the joint army remained stubbornly indifferent to the social background (except in the case of archdukes), ethnicity, and religion of their students, and I have not come across a single complaint about intramural discrimination.

The language of education and communication at the joint army schools was still German, but the first cracks began to appear in the system when Hungarian students insisted on the use of their language in public and when, in 1904, the Hungarian government succeeded in introducing Hungarian as a compulsory language at Wiener Neustadt. Joint army schools in Hungary were now obliged to teach a number of subjects in Hungarian, even to students who did not come from that country. Moreover, pupils born in Hungary had to learn Hungarian no matter where they studied.[33] This, together with the fact that joint army regiments originating in Hungary were expected to be stationed in that country and that the Hungarian government did its best to replace non-Hungarian officers in these regiments with Hungarian citizens, meant that now even the joint army was beginning to split up.

The army high command feared Hungarian separatism; the Hungarian government worried about the anti-Dualism of the army and the underrepresentation of Hungarians in the officer corps and the military schools. In reality, between 1867 and 1914, Hungarians made considerable advances at the military schools and thus ultimately in the officer corps as well. In the academic year 1880-81, the joint army had a total of 2,033 military students; of these, only 395 had been born in Hungary (not including Croatia-Slavonia and the port city of Fiume): this represented only 19.4 percent of military students at a time when Hungarian citizens constituted 36.2 percent of the Monarchy's total population.[34] Worse still, a large part of these Hungarian-born students were in reality Saxons, Zipsers, and Swabians — that is, members of the German minority in Hungary. Other so-called Hungarians were ethnic Serbs or Romanians. By the beginning of the twentieth century, however, this situation had changed dramatically. Not only did the Hungarian national army now have its own military academy, the Ludovika Akadémia, a military preparatory high school, and two infantry cadet schools, where the overwhelming majority of students were native speakers of Hungarian,[35] but the proportion of ethnic Hungarians in the joint army schools now surpassed, for the first time, the proportion of ethnic Hungarians in the Monarchy's total population. In 1911-12, the joint army had 4,380 military students; 960 of them, or 21.9 percent, were native speakers of Hungarian,[36] and this at a time when the Hungarian ethnic group constituted about 18 percent of the Monarchy's total population.[37] Hungarian ethnic representation in the joint army military schools was greater, in 1911-12, than the proportion of all Hungarian-born students, whether ethnic Hungarians, Germans, Serbs, or Romanians, had been in 1881.

Two obstacles to establishing complete parity with Austria even in military affairs remained. One was the chronic underrepresentation of ethnic Hungarian teachers in the joint army military schools: the introduction of compulsory Hungarian in many schools offered a partial remedy for this shortcoming. The other was the uneven distribution of ethnic Hungarian students in the different military schools. The Military Academy at Wiener Neustadt always had an inordinate number of Hungarian students preparing for the cavalry branch; on the other hand, there were almost no ethnic Hungarians in the artillery and the other technical schools. As late as 1897, the Artillery Cadet School at Vienna did not have a single Hungarian-born student. In 1899, there was one such student, apparently quite unqualified.[38] But by 1912, the Hungarian *honvéd* had finally obtained an artillery branch and had set up an artillery section at its academy. This made the *honvéd* a full-fledged army. Simultaneously, ethnic Hungarians were becoming more conspicuous in the artillery and technical schools of the joint army. There would have been nothing wrong with Hungarians' developing an interest in all aspects of military service had not the Hungarian leadership aimed at splitting up the joint army. In Hungarian eyes, every Hungarian-born officer of the joint army was a future commander in His Apostolic Majesty's Royal Hungarian forces. Clearly, the joint army was fighting a losing battle, even in terms of military education.

Not only Hungary but all the kingdoms and provinces of the Dual Monarchy were unevenly represented in the joint army military schools. In 1880-81, for instance, the greatest number of students came, proportionally (in descending order), from Lower Austria (Vienna included), with an almost purely German population, Silesia, with a mixed German, Polish, and Czech population, and Moravia, with a majority of Czechs and a respectable minority (29 percent) of Germans. The lowest number of students came, proportionally (in ascending order) from Galicia, with a mixed Polish and Ruthene (Ukrainian) population, Hungary, with an ethnic admixture of Hungarians, Romanians, Germans, Slovaks, Serbs, and Ruthenes, and, surprisingly, traditionally loyal and warlike Tyrol and Voralberg, with a majority of Germans and a large minority (38 percent) of Italians. In 1880-81, the Lower Austrian representation in the military schools was proportionally almost six times that of the Galician and five times that of the Hungarian.[39] By the turn of the twentieth century, however, the balance had begun to change in favor of the primarily Slavic and Hungarian provinces and kingdoms.

World War I brought inevitable changes in the life of the military students as well as a huge number of reform projects. Students were commissioned early to replace the subalterns killed at the front. In fact, casualties among the junior officers were catastrophic. The Military Academy graduated 133 lieutenants in 1913; of these, 40 (30 percent) died in the war, the majority of them during its first weeks. Another 27 graduates (20.3 percent) were badly wounded: thus 69 graduates (51.9 percent) were lost.[40]

The planned school reforms aimed at further liberalization and at establishing equality between the academies and the cadet schools,[41] but there was no time to institute these changes. During the first two years of the war, the students were well provided for, but then hunger gradually set in. Nor was there much heating. News from the front was kept from the students, one reason, perhaps, that there was still no national conflict at any of the schools. When the Monarchy collapsed, some students did not know where to go; the soldiers' sons, in particular, had no idea of their nationality. In November of 1918, after Emperor-King Charles had been abandoned even by his noble bodyguards, student companies from the Military Academy and the Traiskirchen artillery school mounted guard at the Schönbrunn Palace to protect their former ruler from the revolutionaries. Then Charles was interned by the new Austrian government, and, on December 2, 1918, the last Habsburg army military students handed over their equipment and horses to the Vienna city police. From there, they dispersed to their new fatherlands.[42]

Military education in the Habsburg Monarchy changed with the changing times. Under Maria Theresa, students were separated into noblemen and commoners, but even the latter enjoyed six-course dinners, wine, and the service of lackeys. In the post-Napoleonic restoration period, they were locked up, spied upon, and treated as potential troublemakers; all the subjects they were taught were treated as corollaries of religion and ethics. In the absolutist era after 1849, the students were trained to be brave, rough, practical soldiers. In the post-1867 period, they were brought up to be educated men and leaders. At all times, the students' devotion to the emperor was taken for granted, and there is no evidence that more than an insignificant minority wavered in their near-religious attachment to the ruling house. Especially after 1867, the students were offered an enormous amount of scientific and practical knowledge. What they were never taught was the folklore, customs, problems, and aspirations of the Monarchy's many peoples. They were taught to lead men, not to treat them as individuals. The officers may have been able to speak the language of the recruits, but they did not know, and in their vast majority did not care to know, how to win them over. Thus, they could only delay the breakup of the Monarchy; they never learned to fight nationalism with a new and revolutionary supranational ideology.

Appendix

THE THERESIAN MILITARY ACADEMY AT WIENER NEUSTADT IN 1912-13

Excerpts from the *Jahresbericht der k. und k. Militärakademie in Wiener Neustadt, 1912/13* (Wiener Neustadt, 1913), pp. 75-78:

Teachers, supervisors, and administrators, 55; of these, teaching personnel, 42 (teacher: student ratio 1:10).
Students, first year, 150; second year, 150; third year, 138; total, 438. Of these, commissioned on August 18, 1913, 134: 82 (including one Chinese) to the joint infantry and *Jaeger*, 34 to the joint cavalry, 15 to the *Landwehr* infantry branches, 3 to the *Landwehr* cavalry branches.

Religious distribution of students

	Number	Percentage
Roman Catholic	381	87.0
Greek Catholic [Uniate]	4	0.9
Greek Oriental [Orthodox]	20	4.6
Evangelical, Augsburg Confession [Lutheran]	23	5.3
Evangelical, Helvetic Confession [Reformed]	5	1.1
Mosaic [Jewish]	3	0.7
Confucian	2	0.5

Distribution of students by domicile

	Number	Percentage
Alpine provinces [more or less today's Austria]	115	26.3
Carniola [a large part of today's Slovenia] and the Adriatic Littoral	16	3.7
Bohemia, Moravia, and Austrian Silesia	136	31.0
Galicia and Bukovina	33	7.5
Lands of the Hungarian Holy Crown	136	31.0
Foreigners	2	0.5

Note that (1) even though Bohemia, Moravia, and Silesia (today mostly in the Czechoslovak Republic) provided 136 students, only 28 students spoke Czech as their mother tongue and (2) of the 136 students from Hungary and Croatia-Slavonia, only 71 spoke Hungarian as their mother tongue.]

Distribution of students by mother tongue

	Number	Percentage
Germans	277	63.2
"Czechoslavs" [*Tschechoslawen*]	28	6.4
Poles	16	3.7
Ruthenes	1	0.2
South Slavs [Serbs, Croats, and Slovenes]	35	8.0
Italians	5	1.1
Romanians	3	0.7
Hungarians [*Magyaren*]	71	16.2
Chinese	2	0.5

Distribution of students by previous academic preparation

	Number	Percentage
Civilian high schools [*Realschulen, Gymnasien, Realgymnasien*]	144	32.9
Military high schools [*Militär-Oberrealschulen*]	229	52.3
Cadet schools [*Kadettenschulen*]	65	14.9

On these, acquired a high-school graduation certificate [*Matural*], 162.

Distribution of students by payment categories [Platzkategorien]

	Number	Percentage
Paid nothing	411	93.8
Paid partial or full fees	27	6.2

Citizenship of students admitted in 1912-13

	Number	Percentage
Austrian	97	64.7
Hungarian	53	35.3

Grades for 1912-13

Excellent [*Vorzugsschüler*]	63
Very good	165
Good	185
Satisfactory	4
Unsatisfactory	1
Other	20

NOTES

1. On the Austrian technical military academies, see Moriz Ritter von Brunner and Hugo Kerchnawe, *225 Jahre Technische Militärakademie 1717 bis 1942* (Vienna, 1942); F. Gatti and A. Obermayr, *Geschichte der k.u.k. Technischen Militärakademie 1717 bis 1942* (Vienna, 1942); Heinrich Schalk, *250 Jahre militärtechnische Ausbildung in Österreich* (Vienna, n.d. [1967]); and Ernst Freiherr von Palombini, "Erinnerungen," Kriegsarchiv, Vienna, B/1959, pp. 83-104. A concise source on the history of Austrian military education is Otto Kainz, "Die Offiziersheranbildung in Österreich," *Militärwissenschaftliche Mitteilungen* 66 (1935):161-87; 67 (1936):776-88, 868-84. A more substantial account is G. Poten, *Geschichte des Militär-Erziehungs- und Bildungswesens in Österreich-Ungarn*, Monumenta Germaniae Pedagogica 15 (Berlin, 1893).

2. The most important source on the history of the Military Academy is J. Svoboda, *Die Theresianische Militär-Akademie zur Wiener Neustadt und ihre Zöglinge von der Gründung der Anstalt bis auf unsere Tage*, 3 vols. (Vienna, 1894-97), with three manuscript supplements of later date. Also recommended are Peter Broucek, ed., *Ein General im Zwielicht: Die Erinnerungen Edmund Glaises von Horstenau*, 2 vols. (Vienna, Köln, Graz, 1980), 1:110-11 et passim: Johann Jobst, *Die Neustädter Burg und die k.u.k. Theresianische Militärakademie* (Vienna, Leipzig, n.d. [1909]); Joseph Ritter Rechberger von Rechkron, *Das Bildungswesen im Österreichischen Heere vom Dreissigjährigen Kriege bis zur Gegenwart* (Vienna, 1878); and Carl Baron von Torresani, *Von der Wasser- bis zur Feuertaufe: Werde- und Lehrjahre eines österreichischen Offiziers*, 2 vols. (Dresden, Leipzig, 1900), 2:40-42.

3. Fenner von Fenneberg, *Österreich und seine Armee* (Leipzig, 1842), p.30.

4. See Broucek, *Ein General im Zwielicht*, 1:96, 131, and Torresani, *Von der Wasser- bis zur Feuertaufe*, 2:79, 138.

5. There are dozens of eyewitness accounts of life at the Military Academy. Of particular interest are Fenner, *Österreich und seine Armee*, pp. 28-43 et passim; Moriz Edler von Angeli, *Wien nach 1848* (Vienna, 1905), pp. 114 ff.; Heinrich Ritter von Födransperg, *Vierzig Jahre in der österreichischen Armee . . . 1854-1894*, 2 vols. (Dresden, n.d. [1895]), 1:3-4; Wilhelm Hirsch, Edler von Stronstorff, "Erinnerungen," Kriegsarchiv, Vienna, B/1003, pp. 10-21; Anton Ritter von Pitreich, "Mein militärischer und politischer Werdegang," Kriegsarchiv, Vienna, B/589, no. 3, pp. 8 ff., and Torresani, *Von der Wasser- bis zur Feuertaufe*, 2:3-172.

6. Hirsch, "Erinnerungen," p. 15.

7. Födransperg, *Vierzig Jahre*, 1, pp 3, and Hirsch, "Erinnerungen," p. 11.

8. *Reglement für die kaiserlich-königlichen Militär-Bildungs-Anstalten* (Vienna, 1859), p. 12.
9. Angeli, *Wien nach 1848*, pp. 114-15.
10. Oscar Teuber, *Im Cadeteninstitut: Lose Skizzen aus dem miltärischen Jugendleben*, 3d ed. (Jena, 1881), pp. 52-53.
11. Torresani, *Von der Wasser- bis zur Feuertaufe*, 2:91n; Teuber, *Im Cadeteninstitut*, pp. 22-26, 93-94; and Teuber, *Tschau! Lose Skizzen aus dem Militär-Akademie*, 2d ed. (Prague, 1881), p. 139.
12. Broucek, *Ein General im Zwielicht*, 1:103; Hirsch, "Erinnerungen," p. 12; Torresani, *Von der Wasser- bis zur Feuertaufe*, 2:75-79, 107-8; Teuber, *Im Cadeteninstitut*, pp. 16-19 et passim; idem, *Tschau!*, p. 33.
13. Broucek, *Ein General im Zwielicht*, 1:13.
14. Fenner, *Österreich und seine Armee*, p. 51.
15. Teuber, *Im Cadeteninstitut*, pp. 7-13.
16. Fenner, *Österreich und seine Armee*, p. 104.
17. Ibid., p. 42n. Also Pitreich, "Werdegang," p. 15, and Torresani, *Von der Wasser- bis zur Feuertaufe*, 2:172-89.
18. On the *Schul-Compagnien*, see Angeli, *Wien nach 1848*, pp. 115-17, and Anton Freiherr Mollinary von Monte-Pastello, *Sechsundvierzig Jahre im österreichisch-ungarischen Heere, 1833-1879*, 2 vols. (Zurich, 1905), 1:30. Also *Reglement für die kaiserlich-königlichen Militär-Bildungs-Anstalten*.
19. On the institution of regimental cadets, see Angeli, *Wien nach 1848*, pp. 117-20; Fenner, *Österreich und seine Armee*, pp. 50, 114-20; Födransperg, *Vierzig Jahre*, 1:5-93; Mollinary, *Sechsundvierzig Jahre*, 1:31-35; Franz Xaver Schubert, "Nachlass," Kriegsarchiv, Vienna, B/833, no. 2, pp. 1-13, and *Sechzig Jahre Wehrmacht, 1848-1908* (Vienna, 1908), pp. 13-15.
20. See Erzsébet Gangel, *A soproni m.kir. "Zrínyi Ilona" honvédtiszti leánynevelőintézet története, 1850-1936* (Budapest, n.d.), p. 18; and Adele von Arbter, *Aus der Geschichte der k.u.k. Offizierstöchtet-Erziehungs-Institut* (Vienna, 1892).
21. See *Militär-Schematismus, 1905* (Vienna, 1905), p. 1064.
22. *Reglement für die kaiserlich-königlichen Militär-Bildungs-Anstellen*, pp. 6-7.
23. Ibid., p. 81.
24. Teuber, *Im Cadeteninstitut*, pp. 118-32. See also k.k. General-Commando in Graz to the Imperial War Ministry, February 7, 1867, Kriegsarchiv, Vienna. Unfortunately, the report of Feldmarschalleutnant Heinrich Rupprecht von Virtsolog, head of the investigating commission on the events (*Exzesse*) of February 1, 1867, at Marburg, had been discarded.

25. Statistical data on the Military Academy class of 1874 have been computed from the résumés contained in Svoboda, *Die Theresianische Militär-Akadémie*, 1:263 ff.
26. Statistical data on the Militär-Oberrealschule at Mährisch Weisskirchen have been computed from the *Classifikations-Listen* of that school for 1899, in the Kriegsarchiv, Vienna.
27. Statistical data on the Military Academy class of 1913 have been computed from the résumés contained in the 1909-19 (unpublished) supplement to Svoboda, *Die Theresianische Militär-Akademie*.
28. On the post-1874 military academies and cadet schools, see Poten, *Geschichte*, pp. 335 ff.; Broucek, *Ein General im Zwielicht*, 1:94-137; Alfons Danczer, et al., eds., *Unter den Fahnen: Die Völker Österreich-Ungarns in Waffen* (Prague, Vienna, Leipzig, 1889), pp. 550-65; Ludwig Hesshaimr, ". . . lass eine goldne Spur . . . mein Lebensweg vom Soldaten bis zum Künstler, 1872-1954" (Rio de Janeiro, 1954), Kriegsarchiv, Vienna, B/765, no. 1,; Otto von Kiesewetter, "Der Offizier der alten österr. ung. Armee," 4 pts., Donation Kiesewetter, Kriegsarchiv, Vienna, B/1861; Anton Freiherr von Lehar, "Lehar Geschichten" (Vienna, 1942), Kriegsarchiv, Vienna, B/600, nos. 1 and 2, part 2, pp. 10-15; Adolf Stillfried von Rathenitz, "Erinnerungen aus meinem Leben," Kriegsarchiv, Vienna, pp. 58-69; *Schwartz-gelbe Armee-Sociale Fragen*, 2d ed. (Dresden, Leipzig, 1899),, pp. 15-60; Ulf Sereinigg, "Das altösterreichische Offizierskorps, 1868-1914: Bildung, Advancement, Sozialstruktur, wirtschaftliche Verhältnisse" (Ph.D. diss., University of Vienna, 1983), pp. 51-55; August von Urbanski, "Das Tornisterkind: Lebenserinnerungen," Kriegsarchiv, Vienna, 5/58, no. 4, pp. 9-13; and Theodor Ritter von Zeynek, "Das Leben eines österreichisch-ungarischen Generalstabsoffiziers," Kriegsarchiv, Vienna, B/151, no. 2, pp. 9-13. For a sampling of school histories, see *Historische Schilderung der k.u.k. Militär-Unterrealschule in Kismarton [Eisenstadt]* (Kismarton, 1909); Gotthold Krebs, *Die k.u.k. Militär-Oberrealschule zu Mährisch-Weisskirchen* (Vienna, Leipzig, 1906); *Lehrplan der k.u.k. Militärrealschulen* (Vienna, 1912); *Lehrplan der k.u.k. Militärakademien* (Vienna, 1918); and Adolf Proksch, *Geschichte der k.u.k. Artillerie-Kadettenschule in Wien* (Vienna, 1907).
29. On the reserve officer system, see Danczer et al., *Unter den Fahnen*, pp. 16-18, 112, 260-63; Kiesewetter, "Offizier," pt. 4; Sereinigg, "Offizierskorps," pp. 46-48; Anton Kainz, "70 Jahre Reserveoffiziere in Österreich," *Militärwissenschaftliche Mitteilungen* 68 (1937): 353; Lorenz Seutter [Laurentius Rettues], "In goldenen Schnüren," Kriegsarchiv, Vienna, B/139, pp. 220-32; *Dienstverkehr des Reserveoffiziers* (Vienna, 1915); *Der Weg zum Einjährigen-Freiwilligen-Begünstigung nach dem Wehrgesetze vom Jahre 1912* (Vienna, 1917), and H[ugo] Schmid, *Heerwesen*, vol. 2, *Österreich-Ungarn: Lehr- und Lernbehelf für Militärerziehungs- und

Bildungsanstalten, sowie Reserveoffiziersschulen, dann für das Selbststudium (Vienna, 1914), pp. 13-14.

30. See Poten, *Geschichte,* p. 372. Also *Lehrplan der k.u.k. Militär-Akademien* (Vienna, 1898), and *Lehrplan der k.u.k. Militärrealschulen.*

31. Interview with the Hungarian colonel Kálmán Kéri, who had been a pupil at the artillery cadet school at Traiskirchen. Lower Austria, between 1915 and 1918 (Budapest, December 4, 1984). Kéri's father was an engineer with the Hungarian State Railways.

32. "Mittheilung über die Studien-Erfolge," k.u.k. Infanterie-Schule in Wien, 1892-1893, Lehár Nachlass, Kriegsarchiv, Vienna.

33. *Historische Schilderung,* p. 63, and *Lehrplan der k.u.k. Militärrealschulen,* pp. 14, 42.

34. Percentages calculated from data in Mór Pásztory, *Az osztrák-magyar monarchia statisztikája* (Pozsony, Budapest, 1884), pp. 164-65, and Ungarische-Delegation, *A közös ügyek tárgyalására kiküldött magyar országos bizottság hadügyi albizottságának jelentése, 1881,* no. 17 (Budapest, 1881), pp. 128-29.

35. See *Utasítás a pályázók felvételére nézve a m.kir. honvéd nevelő és képző intézetekbe* (Budapest, 1898); *Aufnahmebedingungen der Militär-Bildungs-Anstalten* (Budapest, 1912), pp. 50-90; Tibor Papp, "Die Königlich ungarische Landwehr, 1868-1914," manuscript (Budapest, 1978), pp. 60-72.

36. Percentages calculated from "A Hadügyi Albizottság jelentése," in *A közös ügyek tárgyalására a magyar országgyűlés által kiküldött s Ő Felsége által 1912. évi szeptember 23-ra Bécsbe összehívott Bizottság irományai,* no. 20 (Budapest, 1912), p. 138.

37. One of the more controversial achievements of the Hungarian government was to have the Joint War Ministry, after 1893, inquire into the ethnic background of officers and military students. The statistics were at first based on "language," later on "nationality." How these data were compiled (whether, for instance, cadets or their parents were asked about their mother tongue) remains unclear; the Kriegsarchiv in Vienna seems to contain no information on the methods used.

38. Proksch, *Geschichte,* p. 17.

39. Pásztory, *Statisztikája,* pp. 164-65, and Ungarische Delegation, pp. 128-29.

40. Statistics based on the biographies contained in the 1909-19 (unpublished) supplement to Svoboda, *Die Theresianische Militär-Akademie.* Note that the sources disagree on the number of graduates.

41. See Rainer Egger, "Der Stand des österreichisch-ungarischen Militär-Erziehungs- und Bildungswesens 1918," *Österreichische Militärische Zeitschrift* 6 (1968):424-30.

42. Interview with Kéri, Budapest, December 11, 1984.

The Theresian Military Academy in Wiener Neustadt

Gertrud Buttlar-Elberberg

The Theresian Military Academy in Wiener Neustadt is the oldest military school in Europe, closely linked with Maria Theresa, archduchess of Austria, queen of Hungary and Bohemia, and, as the wife of Francis I, Empress of the Holy Roman Empire. The beginning of her forty-year reign (1740-80) over the Habsburg Empire was marked by wars against Bavaria and Prussia, desperate efforts to protect her inheritance. The performance of the army in the War of the Austrian Succession gave the first impetus to a comprehensive reform of the Austrian military, including the founding of the Military Academy.[1]

From the beginning of the eighteenth century it had been evident that bravery and physical fitness alone no longer made an efficient officer. To meet the requirements of modern warfare, officers needed a great deal of technical knowledge. The counts Friedrich Wilhelm Haugwitz and Leopold Daun, military advisors to the empress, explained to her the importance of the education of young officers. It is thought to have been Haugwitz who suggested the creation in Austria of a corps of aristocratic cadets on the Prussian model. For the housing of the cadets, the imperial castle of Wiener Neustadt, then little used, was considered. In order to prepare young men for the cadet school, a special school in Vienna, or "nursery" (*Pflanzschule*), was planned.

Maria Theresa gave her consent and support to all these proposals. On December 14, 1751, she decreed the establishment of a corps of aristocratic cadets in Wiener Neustadt, to be housed in the old castle, and a military preparatory school in Vienna.[2] In November 1752 cadet education began in earnest.[3] The commanding officer of both the cadet school and the preparatory school was Count Leopold Daun; Major General Count Franz Ludwig Thurheim was made responsible for the everyday life of the school. Sons of impoverished aristocratic families and occasionally of brave nonaristocratic officers were admitted as cadets. The young officers who graduated from cadet school soon distinguished themselves by their military and scientific education, becoming a model that has endured to the present.[4]

An earthquake destroyed much of the castle at Wiener Neustadt in 1768, nearly putting an end to the school. The imperial architect Nicolo Paccassi, commissioned to rebuild it, advised Maria Theresa to move the school to Vienna instead, but she insisted on the restoration. One tower was rebuilt, and in the process the rooms for the cadets were modernized and made more comfortable.[5]

Very important reforms in the education of officers took place during the reign of Emperor Joseph II. After his father's death in 1765, Joseph II became co-ruler with his mother and took charge of military affairs. He appointed General Count Franz Kinsky, a member of his circle, to command the Military Academy. (The cadet school became an "academy" in 1769.) Kinsky fundamentally reformed the academy's curriculum at his emperor's behest. He was interested in pedagogy and maintained close contact with the noted Swiss educator, Johann Heinrich Pestalozzi.[6] The educational program he designed was characterized as "a combination of enlightened rationalism and military monastic rule," and it was quite successful,[7] realizing his aim to "educate justice-loving men who are true servants to their country, to themselves as well as to others."[8] The museum of the Military Academy contains eleven interesting pictures by Bernhard Albrecht, the drawing master of the academy, painted during the Kinsky tenure (1779-1805), that give a very good impression of the kind of education cadets there received at the time.[9] Kinsky's educational program was probably a strong barrier against the influence of French revolutionary ideas. Although a cadet was a defendant in the Vienna Jacobin trials, this was the only such case[10] and the man later became a teacher.

From 1805 until 1849, Archduke Johann, brother of the emperor Francis I, was commanding officer of the Military Academy. He had no influence on the educational program.[11] While more and more young men from bourgeois families were being accepted into the academy and the number of young aristocrats was declining, the program set up by Kinsky remained virtually unchanged until the middle of the nineteenth century. Gradually, however, satisfaction with it declined, and after 1848 critics became more vocal, claiming that the system offered "too much theory and too little practice." They also objected to the fact that cadets spent all their time inside the academy, as if they were in a monastery, and consequently found it difficult to adjust to practical life.

These criticisms led to fundamental reform. In 1849, the academy's directorship was abolished, and it was directly subordinated to the War Ministry in Vienna. Basic courses were transferred from the academy to the newly founded cadet schools, junior high schools in fact. From that time on, the academy provided higher and academic education only. Further, it was no longer a school of theoretical education. Cadets received military equipment, and on parade and in military maneuvers they formed a battalion. The program became more spartan, as was considered appropriate for the preparation of officers. The officers who graduated from the Wiener Neustadt academy changed the Austrian army for the better.

After the defeat at Königgrätz in 1866, new reforms were introduced into the army and the academy. In 1879 the length of the course of instruction was fixed at three years and only young men with high-school diplomas were admitted.[12] In 1894, Emperor Francis Joseph I granted the academy its prsent name, the Theresian Military Academy.[13] The graduation parade (*Ausmusterung*) of cadets, marking the solemn completion of their education and their entry into the army, was celebrated, during the reign of Francis Joseph I, on August 18, the emperor's birthday, and called for the presence of the emperor or a member of the imperial family.[14] After the death of Francis Joseph I in 1916, the graduation parade was held one day later, on Emperor Karl's birthday, August 19. The site of this military festival was Maria Theresa Square, behind the old castle. The most important part of the ceremony was the oath taken by the young officers: "True unto death."

The end of World War I and the dissolution of the Austro-Hungarian Monarchy in 1918 brought an end to the Theresian Military Academy. On November 2, 1918, Major General Guido Baron Novak von Arienti, then its commanding officer, announced to the cadets assembled in Maria Theresa Square that it had ceased to exist.[15] The education of officers during the First Republic (1922-34) took place in the Forces School (*Heeresschule*) in Enns, a small town in Upper Austria. The army officers who had been educated at Wiener Neustadt pressed for a reestablishment of the traditional academy, however, and in 1934 they managed to have the education of officers transferred from Enns to Wiener Neustadt with the help of the war minister, Carl Vaugoin, a former officer.[16] On August 29,

1934, the battalion of cadets reentered the castle of Wiener Neustadt. On September 1, 1934, the school resumed its old name. After an interval of sixteen years, on September 2, 1934, Maria Theresa Square again saw a graduation parade; fifty-five lieutenants educated in Enns were graduated from Wiener Neustadt.

A reform of the education of officers seemed necessary once again because of modern technical developments. Education had to be broadened in matters such as arms technology and motorization. Separate education for infantry, cavalry, armored troops, artillery, engineering, signal sciences, and the air force was introduced. Tactics had to undergo special reforms to reflect changes in technology and warfare. The commanding officer of the Military Academy between the World Wars was Major General Rudolf Towarek. The first officers to receive the full three-year education at Wiener Neustadt since 1918 graduated in March of 1937, some months earlier than originally planned because the army urgently needed officers.[17]

The *Anschluss* of 1938 meant the end of the Theresian Military Academy once again. Towarek was pensioned off and was succeeded by Colonel Karl Moyses. The cadets were ordered to enter the German *Wehrmacht*.[18] In 1938 there were three graduations. The castle at Wiener Neustadt became the home of one of the five German military schools. For a year (1938-39) the commanding officer of the military school at Wiener Neustadt was Colonel Erwin Rommel, later well-known as a field commander in Africa.[19] Because Wiener Neustadt was one of the most important centers of war industry, producing fighters and V-1 and V-2 missiles, from August of 1943 through April of 1945 the town was very heavily bombed by the Allied air forces, and in March of 1944 a great part of the castle was destroyed by Allied bombs.

After the end of the war, the reconstruction of the castle of Wiener Neustadt — for ten years situated in the Soviet zone — took a long time, but in 1958 it was completed and the officers' training school for the second Austrian Federal Army could be transferred from Enns to its new-old home.[20]

NOTES

1. Adam Wandruszka, "Maria Theresia," in *Ausstellungskatalog "Maria Theresia und ihre Zeit," Wien, SchloY Schönbrunn* (Vienna, 1980),

pp. 7 ff., 269 ff.; Johann Christoph Allmayer Beck, "Das Heer der Kaiserin," in *Maria Theresia und ihre Zeit* (Vienna, 1979), pp. 83 ff.
  2. Johann Christoph Allmayer Beck, "Die Theresianische Militärakademie von ihrer Gründung bis 1918," in *Alma mater Theresiana, Jahrbuch 1977* (Wiener Neustadt, 1977), pp. 7 ff.
  3. Johann Jobst, *Die Neustädter Burg und die k.u.k. Theresianische Militärakademie* (Vienna, 1908), pp. 12 ff.
  4. Allmayer-Beck, "Theresianische Militärakademie," p. 12.
  5. Jobst, *Neustädter Burg*, p. 77.
  6. Ibid., p. 29.
  7. Allmayer-Beck, "Theresianische Militärakademie," p. 13.
  8. Ibid.
  9. Dorothee Horn, *Wiener Neustadt: Festung, Residenz, Garnison Wiener Neustadt* (Wiener Neustadt, 1972), pp. 163 ff., nos. 96-106.
  10. Allmayer-Beck, "Theresianische Militärakademie," p. 13.
  11. Jobst, *Neustädter Burg*, pp. 36 ff.
  12. Allmayer-Beck, "Theresianische Militärakademie," pp. 15 ff.
  13. Ibid., p. 17.
  14. Ibid.
  15. Anton Wagner, "Die Theresianische Militärakademie in der Ersten Republik (1918-1938)," in *Alma mater Theresiana, Jahrbuch 1977* (Wiener Neustadt, 1977), p. 19.
  16. Ibid., pp. 20 ff.; Paul Wittas, "Verlust und Wiedergewinnung der Wiener Neustädter Burg zwischen den beiden Weltkriegen," in *Alma mater Theresiana, Jahrbuch 1964*, pp. 44 ff.
  17. Wagner, "Theresianische Militärakademie," pp. 24 ff.
  18. Rudolf Marwan-Schloser, *Die Neustädter Burg-Theresianische Militärakademie: Ein historischer Überblick 1194-1984* (Wiener Neustadt, 1985), pp. 82 ff.
  19. Ibid., pp. 85-86.
  20. Gertrud Gerhartl, *Wiener Neustadt: Geschichte, Kunst, Kultur, Wirtschaft* (Wiener Neustadt, 1978), pp. 497-98, 512 ff.

IV. NATIONAL PATTERNS

The Training of Bulgarian Officers, 1878-1918

Ljudmil Petrov

The Russo-Turkish War of 1877-78 was national-liberating and antifeudal in character, and it ended in the Treaty of San Stefano of March 3, 1878, which established a Bulgarian state in the ethnic territories of the Bulgarian nation. Impelled by their imperialist interests, the Western European countries, especially Britain and Austria-Hungary, called the Congress of Berlin to consider and revise the terms of the treaty, replacing it with the Treaty of Berlin of July 13, 1878. The Berlin treaty liquidated a considerable portion of the progressive results of the war, and in relation to Bulgaria it was particularly unjust in that it destroyed the national unity of the Bulgarian people.[1] The Bulgarian territories between the Balkans and the Danube were declared the Principality of Bulgaria and subordinated to the Ottoman Empire while those to the south of the Balkans were designated the autonomous region of Eastern Rumelia, with a governor general appointed by the sultan; the remaining territories of Macedonia and Thrace were returned to the Empire, and northern Dobruja and Bulgarian Pomoravie were given to Romania and Serbia respectively. The treaty not only did not settle but even deepened the national and international contradictions on the Balkan Peninsula, turning it into the powder keg of Europe for decades to come.

The results of the war, however partial and incomplete because of the Berlin treaty, could only be preserved and guaranteed by an independent Bulgarian army. Therefore, as early as the first half of 1878, the Provisional Russian Government, under the direction of Prince Dondukov-Korsakov, was active in the creation of such an army, and on July 15, 1878, the Bulgarian Zemska Army was established.[2] In the following year it was designated the Bulgarian Army. It served during the initial period as "a primary factor in the political system of the Third Bulgarian State,"[3] its main purpose in the field of foreign policy being to ensure the sovereignty and independent development of the Principality of Bulgaria (after 1908 the Kingdom of Bulgaria) and to seek a just solution to the national problem by liberating from Ottoman feudal oppression the Bulgarian population beyond its borders. Consequently the activities of Bulgarian governments were directed at the consolidation, refinement, and modernization of the army, matters of paramount importance to the military policy of the state,[4] while military policy in turn periodically proved of paramount importance to the overall policy of the country. It was only natural that the army served as well the "internal" goal of preserving bourgeois domination and capitalist socioeconomic relations. The personnel of the army increased from 25,349 in 1888 to 60,898 in 1912; its organization was improved, and modern material and technical means, arms, and military technology were gradually provided.

One of the most significant problems in the development of the Bulgarian army was the recruitment and training of officers. The success of the army in wartime operations very largely depended on the resolution of this problem. The importance of the officer corps was the greater in that it was the officers who largely determined the political character of the army. Therefore the Bulgarian political and military leadership paid the utmost attention to the creation and training of the officer corps. This is a subject that has not hitherto been explored.

An analysis of the historical development of the army and in particular of the officer corps calls for the distinction of three stages. The first stage lasted from the establishment of the army to the Serbo-Bulgarian War in 1885; the second stage was the development of the army in peacetime from 1886 to 1912; the third stage ran from 1912 to 1918, when the growth and development of the army took place in the context of the Balkan Wars (1912-13) and World War I (1915-18).

An important feature of the first stage was the existence of two Bulgarian states with separate armed forces. The first contingent of 135 officers for the army of the Principality and for the police of Eastern Rumelia was recruited by the Russian army and included the few Bulgarian officers in Russian service.[5] On September 11, 1878, the first four Bulgarians were promoted to the rank of officer by Prince Dondukov himself.[6] During the succeeding years of the period the demand for officers was filled by graduates of the Military School in Sofia or a military school abroad; foreigners could be enlisted in the army of the Principality only by special permission of the Sobranie.[7] An analysis of documents reveals an effort to make the army conspicuously national in character and to avoid admitting unqualified persons on the basis of their social positions, and these two facts predetermined its militancy and efficiency.

Regulations governed the organization of the officer corps and established the rules for promotion to higher ranks. The length of service at a given rank could be reduced only in wartime and if "special insignia of honor" had been earned; the skipping of ranks was prohibited. The strict order observed in promotion contributed to the maintenance of discipline and ethics in official relations among officers. At the same time, the role of the monarch was beginning to be felt more strongly, promotion to the rank of general depending on his support.[8]

In accordance with the idea of the creation of a mass Bulgarian army as a bulwark of the state, as early as the middle of 1878 the Provisional Russian Government began preparations for the establishment of a Bulgarian military school.[9] The Military School in Sofia was opened on November 26, 1878.[10] The initial period of training was two years; after 1881 it became three years in the preparatory grades and two years in the special (Junker) grades. The preparatory grades covered general subjects and the special grades military ones. The preparatory grades accepted candidates who had not graduated from high school, while high-school graduates entered the first (junior) special grade. Upon completion of the course Junkers were accorded the rank of first officer.[11] Up to the Serbo-Bulgarian War the commanders of the school and most of the lecturers were Russian officers. The course of study was based upon Russian regulations[12] and was similar to the programs of the Russian Junker schools. It was General Parensov, the first minister of war of the Principality of Bulgaria, who was largely responsible for the efficiency and high quality of the Junkers' education. Under his influence Suvorov-Dragomirov's principle —training the army in peacetime in what would be required of it in wartime — became the rule. Thus, showiness was subordinated to practical military knowledge and skills. The respect accorded Parensov as the founder of the Bulgarian army was clearly expressed by Tsar Ferdinand and the Ministry of War in 1914.[13]

During the period 1878-85 the Military School provided the army six batches of graduates, about 450 officers.[14] Progressive educational principles and the lack of a class-political criterion for enrollment resulted in the attraction of youths from a broad social spectrum into the school and justifies the assertion that the Bulgarian army was democratic during the first years after the Liberation even in its commanding personnel.[15] In 1885, just 17 percent of officers came from wealthy families, while 30.1 percent were from middle-income families and 52.9 percent from poor ones.[16] For all these reasons, officers had great prestige in Bulgarian society, and this helped them to fulfill their functions efficiently in both war and peace.

In 1879 the foundations were laid for a systematic increase in officers' qualifications during practical service with military units. Studies were made obligatory for commanders, and the Ministry of War issued instructions for their proper execution.[17] As a result of the training at the Military School and the in-service training of commanding officers, the basic strategic and tactical concepts of the Russian army were acquired and adapted to the particular circumstances of Bulgaria and the Balkans and recent innovations in warfare. In the field of strategy the basic concepts were the enemy army as the main strategic object, the necessity for full mobilization from the very beginning, the importance of the element of surprise, careful selection of the direction of the main assault, and rapid advance. Strategic defense was disregarded, defense being considered a transitory phenomenon in war, and special attention was paid to the necessity of determining the right moment to shift from defense to decisive counterattack until the enemy forces were totally destroyed.[18] The basic tactical concepts on which training was based were that the offensive is essential and defense transitory; that the most powerful means of destroying the enemy is accurate firepower and headlong assault; that forces and means must be concentrated in the direction of the main assault; that quick pursuit is necessary for success; and that in defense it is necessary to strengthen the outposts and the main position and to establish general and local reserves. The tasks of tactical utilization of the various branches during different kinds of combat had been appropriately set.[19] It is reasonable to say that by as early as the very first years after the Liberation, Bulgaria had adopted a modern set of theoretical views on waging war.

The status and training of officers in Eastern Rumelia reflected the complexity of the political situation. In the period 1879-85 a large number of officers of the Principality of Bulgaria enlisted in the Eastern Rumelian militia, thus frustrating the attempts of Western European officers to acquire positions of command in it.[20] As a result, the Eastern Rumelian militia was trained according to Russian regulations and instructions by officers dedicated to the Bulgarian national cause.

As part of the Bulgarian national army, it played an important role at the time of the unification of the Principality of Bulgaria and Eastern Rumelia and in the military defense during the Serbo-Bulgarian War.

During the initial years after the Liberation, the demand for officers was acute, and the Military School was not in position to meet it. Therefore, training of young Bulgarian officers abroad was widely resorted to. Such training was possible only in Russia, which opened wide the doors of its military schools. Bulgaria, for its part, preferred Russia to the other countries because of its cultural and linguistic affinity and because of the role Russia had played in the Liberation, as well as for its generous assistance in the creation of the Bulgarian army. There were also purely military reasons, for the Russian army and its commanders were famous at the time for their training. Another predisposing factor was the exceptionally warm attitude of the Russian authorities and society toward the Bulgarian graduates and the facilities the latter were offered in achieving admission to the military schools.[21] Thus, of the 595 Bulgarian officers in the Serbo-Bulgarian War, 132 had graduated from Russian military schools.[22]

That war was the first historic test of the Bulgarian army and its officer corps. On the eve of it, the Russian government recalled its officers from Bulgaria, leaving the mobilized Bulgarian army with an officer shortage of about 35 percent.[23] The young Bulgarian officers acted responsibly and with initiative; they skillfully applied the strategic and tactical concepts they had learned and coped brilliantly with command. The basic reason for the Bulgarian victory was the mass enthusiasm and heroism shown in the defense of the nation's sovereignty, but an essential military precondition was the high level of training of officers and troops in the spirit of the efficient Russian science and art of warfare. The German military literature on the war stressed that an important reason for the victory was the ability of the Bulgarian officers to make decisions independently both before and during combat and their good qualities as commanders.[24] It was because of the legitimacy of the war, the high moral and political spirit of the warriors, and the excellent training of the officers that the well-trained and well-supplied Serbian army was destroyed within two weeks.

After the Serbo-Bulgarian War, the development of the Bulgarian army and its officer corps entered its second stage. The training and education of the army continued to be under the strong, although no longer exclusive, influence of Russian military thought. In 1886 Russian regulations, instructions, and directions began to be introduced. Officers were required to surpass their inferiors "in knowledge, experience, and character";[25] initiative was encouraged, and senior commanders were expected to intervene only when their juniors were wrong.[26] Thus, the ideas adopted from the Russian army about the role of the officer were developed in a positive direction.

The Military School in Sofia remained the only center of officer training for the peacetime army. After 1887 the duration of the course of training was three years. In 1900 a military high school with four cadet grades was established, but it was closed in 1908 because the cadet system did not meet the need for military specialization. The Junker system was restored, with a three-year course of training consisting of one preparatory and two specialized Junkers' grades. The program of specialized military education consisted of tactics, topography, fortifications, artillery, military administration, jurisprudence, military methods and ethics, military geography, military hygiene, and other topics.[27] An important indicator of the refinement of the program was the establishment at the school in 1909 of infantry, cavalry, and artillery specialties, which allowed education to be differentiated according to branch in the second year.[28] This further contributed to the specialization of troops. Thus the Military School went beyond general military training to provide the Bulgarian army with well-trained specialized junior officers.

It is not unreasonable to assert, on the basis of this analysis of the program, that the Military School provided the peacetime army with a well-trained annual complement of active officers. The participation of Bulgarian officers in the Balkan Wars and World War I is further support for this conclusion.

Analysis of the experience of the Serbo-Bulgarian War and a correct appreciation of the role of reserve officers for the successful conduct of military operations caused special attention to be paid to the training of the reserves for the needs of the wartime army. In 1889 the Military School opened an additional grade of nine months' duration for reserve officers.[29] After 1892 each of the six divisions operated a so-called divisional school command in which reserve officers were trained for nine months.[30] After 1901 the reserves were trained at the School for Reserve Second Lieutenants, the School for Fortress Reserve Second Lieutenants, and the School for Artillery Reserve

Second Lieutenants, which ensured good conditions for training with an intensive eleven-month program.[31] Thus, the training of reserve officers produced excellent results, and the schools became a model for a number of foreign armies.[32] The officer corps of the army was completed by retired active officers and sergeant majors who had enlisted in the reserves as officers after their discharge. The promotion of reserve officers was regulated; they were allowed to rise no higher than captain.[33] The training programs and the requirement for periodic retraining show that the military command was aware of the importance of the reserve officers as command personnel in the mobilized army during wartime and therefore took care in peacetime to see that sufficient well-trained personnel were prepared.

An important aspect of the improvement of officers' qualifications was higher military education for some. During that period such education could only be obtained abroad, as there was no staff college in Bulgaria. During the Serbo-Bulgarian War there were just thirteen officers who had graduated from Russian military academies. Because of the break in political relations between Russia and Bulgaria in the period 1886-97, officers were no longer dispatched to be educated there. It was only after 1897 that the four Russian military academies once more opened their doors to Bulgarian officers, each of them annually admitting four Bulgarians. After 1889 officers were sent to Austria-Hungary,[34] and in the subsequent years they went to Italy, France, Belgium, and Germany as well. An analysis of the data of that time shows that Russia maintained its role as the main educational center outside Bulgaria: between the years 1900 and 1908, of 193 officers who had some higher training, 102 had been educated in Russia.[35] For the whole period from 1878 to 1915 the number of Russian-educated officers was 263, about 75 percent of the foreign graduates, and another 250 officers had been probationers for various periods in units of the Russian army.[36] During World War I, of 524 officers with academic education, 392 (75 percent) had graduated from Russian military academies, while the remaining 132 had studied in Western Europe.[37] The lack of a Bulgarian military academy was a serious weakness in the system. It was not until 1912 that the Military Academy was founded in Sofia, and then the Balkan Wars and World War I disturbed the normal rhythm of education.[38] During the period under study there were no officers who had passed the course at the Bulgarian Military Academy.

Another important aspect of the education of officers was in-service training. A few basic goals were set for them: to master to perfection the elements of their job of the moment, to study and master the obligations of that job, and to absorb the military doctrine on the country's defense and on the development of its military. Before any such measures were taken, the information and the theoretical military knowledge of the officers had to be enriched. For that purpose the monthly magazine *Voenen Journal* was established and then, after 1892, the newspaper *Voenni Izvestija*.[39] Translated literature on military matters was published in *Ofitzersaka biblioteka*, established in 1893.[40] Thus, a variety of theoretical material was placed at the disposal of every Bulgarian officer.

The practical training of military units and staffs was refined as well. The training program was developed gradually after 1886, beginning with plans for the distribution of annual manuals for each branch of the service,[41] and after 1892 Russian instructions were replaced with Bulgarian ones. The manuals were based on the orders of the minister of war issued annually for that purpose, the regulations, the *Instruction for Tactical Knowledge* for officers and second officers, issued in 1904, the 1909 *Instruction for Practical Training*,[42] and especially the 1904 *Situations for the Guidance of Units*.[43] In these and other documents three basic parallel directions in the training of officers were stressed: lectures, practical exercises, and individual study of military matters. It was the practical exercises that were considered "the most important part of officers' training,"[44] and the *Instruction for Practical Training* treated the solution of tactical problems in detail and provided instructions in that connection.

The training exercises that had been developed by the time of the Balkan War were as follows:

1. The solution of tactical problems on a map, done weekly in groups.

2. Map maneuvers and war games led by the commanders of divisions and brigades and their staffs.

3. For the specialized branches, weekly accomplishment of special technical tasks.

4. Practical exercises in the field without troops, carried out under the direction of the respective commanders from company to division in June and December. The largest exercises of this type were carried out in the Stara Zagora area in 1905 under the leadership of the minister of war, and the results were deemed edifying.

5. Exercises in the field with officers of the general staff, carried out each summer under the staff's command. The exercises of 1909, around Sofia-Supnitza (now Stanke Dimitrov), and 1911, around Burgas, produced especially good results, among them unity in the views of the general staff officers.

6. Lectures. After 1905, about a third of the officers were working on topics in military history by critique and analysis of operations in a particular war.

7. Training at the summer camps of the troops, where the officers trained not only their subordinates but themselves as well.

8. Grand royal maneuvers, which took place in September and in which several divisions, supplemented by reserves, participated in order "to ensure training of the higher command and full harmony among the individual tactical units and the various types of weapons." Such maneuvers took place in 1888, 1896, 1902, 1904, 1905, 1906, 1910, and 1912.[45]

These various exercises testify to the existence of an effective program of in-service training, the results of which were apparent in the wars of 1912-18.

In 1893 staff officers' courses were established for infantry, artillery, and cavalry officers[46] with the aim of deepening their knowledge of their particular branch and preparing some of them for study in foreign military academies. On this foundation the Infantry, Cavalry, and Artillery Schools were founded in 1901, 1903, and 1906, respectively.[47] Their programs were differentiated by branch and included innovations in the tactical use of the different organizational units and the interaction of the different branches in battle. These schools prepared well-trained commanders of battalions, batteries, and squadrons.[48] The increase in the importance of the artillery led in 1907 to the establishment of an additional course in higher mathematics for second lieutenants destined to be assigned to the artillery after graduating from the Military School.[49] Generally speaking, the artillery was paid special attention, and its personnel was particularly conscientious in mastering new things.[50]

Analysis of the system of officer training reveals some weak points. Most important of these was the general character of the training at the Military School, which by 1909 had made it necessary to set up expensive additional units for the special training of the officers of the different branches. Senior officers had to study at foreign military academies, and this was financially disadvantageous, politically unjustified, and sometimes unsuitable from the point of view of the development of a unified Bulgarian military. In some aspects of the training the approach was too academic and theoretical, and in the initial decade of the period under study too much emphasis was placed on self-education and officers' personal ambition to master military knowledge. Because of financial problems, in-service training was often insufficient, and this led to some delay in the development of officers' skills in command and organization. It should be pointed out, at the same time, that new ideas and modern methods and forms of training were gradually developing. Most important, the number of trained active and reserve officers was being increased with a view to launching a war of liberation of the Bulgarians in Macedonia and Thrace. Although with some delay, the question of special training for officers of the different branches was eventually settled. From the beginning of the nineties the principle of unity of theory and practice was strengthened, and about half of the study time was devoted to practical exercises. All this brought the peacetime training of officers up to the level of that of the most advanced armies, enabling the officers to fulfill their functions successfully not only as commanders and leaders but also as teachers and trainers.

Estimates of the level of training were made periodically. In 1892 the Austro-Hungarian Ministry of War expressed its appreciation of the condition of the Bulgarian officer corps, and the conclusions in the reports made by the Austro-Hungarian attaché in Constantinople in 1894 and 1896 were superlative.[51] In 1899 a colonel on the Russian general staff stressed the high level of theoretical knowledge and practical skill of the Bulgarian officers, especially those of the general staff.[52] To various degrees, the estimates made by the Ministry of War were positive.[53] This was one of the reasons the political leadership decided to launch a war against the semifeudal Ottoman Empire.

In 1912 the Bulgarian army entered a new stage, and the training of officers in this period was carried out under wartime conditions. On the eve of the first Balkan War, the peacetime personnel of the army included 3,563 officers, of whom 2,476 (69 percent) were in the infantry, 494 (14 percent) in the artillery, 316 (9 percent) in the cavalry, 217 (6 percent) in the engineering and railway troops, and 60 (2 percent) in the navy.[54] This distribution reflects the contemporary conception of the roles of the various branches in the light of the peculiarities of the Balkan theater of operations. After mobilization, the officers in the active army numbered 6,839, and there was a shortage, based on wartime requirements, of about 40 percent.[55] The difficulty here was that the Military School had been closed. This error of the Ministry of War was not repeated during World War I, when the number of Junkers increased sharply.[56] During World War I, moreover, the school program drew upon the experience of recent military actions,[57] thus bringing the training of the young officers closer to the requirements of contemporary warfare. The great need for officers during World War I necessitated the opening of a second school for reserve second lieutenants in 1916 at Skopje under the command of Colonel Boris Drangov, an eminent military pedagogue. The organization of the programs at the schools for reserve officers was regularly revised and refined in accordance with current experience in the war.[58]

The Bulgarian army began World War I with 5,100 active officers distributed as follows: 3,503 (69 percent) in the infantry, 814 (16 percent) in the artillery, 386 (6 percent) in the cavalry, 317 (6 percent) in the engineering forces, and 80 (2 percent) in the navy.[59] During mobilization the total number of the officers rose to 15,700,[60] which represented a shortfall of 13 percent.[61] Although during the war the Military School trained 1,115 officers and the other schools 5,450 reserve officers,[62] their number was insufficient to replace the casualties. For example, on March 1, 1918, the officers of the active army were 3,885 in number (64 generals, 253 colonels, 412 lieutenant colonels, 449 majors, 1,130 captains, 282 lieutenants, and 695 second lieutenants), while on September 1 the army had 2,300 officers fewer than were required.[63] The data show that the high command was unable to solve the problem of reinforcements.

The rearrangement of the educational system after Bulgaria entered the war was done quickly and in good order.[64] Special attention was paid to providing students experience of military operations on the various fronts of the war, an opportunity to master the various types of engagements and the methods of fighting connected with them, and encouragement to analyze their own experience.[65] Training for defense against the enemy's balloons and airplanes, tactics against tanks, defense against poison gas, and other subjects were part of the course of study.[66] The officers were quick to adopt innovations and implement them in the training of their combat troops.

Because the goals of the Balkan War gave it the character of a popular war of liberation, Bulgarian soldiers and officers fought with extraordinary enthusiasm, ardor, and initiative, daring at the level of command, a constructive approach to the planning and leading of military actions, and an inflexible will to win.[67] The high level of training of Bulgarian officers was of particular significance for the eventual victory. As Lieutenant General Nikola Ivanov pointed out, "the conduct of hostilities was in the hands of the regimental and lower commanders."[68] It was the artillery officers that proved particularly well-trained.[69] An example of this is the assault on the Odrin fortifications. As early as 1911, a Bulgarian intelligence officer provided the battalion commanders and staff officers supervising the artillery with detailed information regarding the fortification system, and upon its analysis it was decided that the assault should be made on the eastern side.[70] This is in fact what was done in March 1913. The superiority of the Bulgarian army and its commanders was recognized by representatives of the Western European armies, by the press,[71] and even by the Turkish officers themselves.[72] Of special significance from the point of view of this study is the assessment of the German and Austro-Hungarian general staff, who, having made some critical remarks, called the Bulgarian officer "diligent, assiduous and zealous in his service, rational and unpretentious, stern with himself, self-controlled, bold and forward in spirit, and full of fiery love for his Fatherland."[73] The unanimity in these assessments by observers with diverse attitudes toward Bulgaria suggests that they can be considered objective and truthful.

During the Balkan War the Bulgarian army achieved some advances in the art of warfare. The Bulgarian general headquarters laid the groundwork for the development of large operations with commands for various fronts. They were responsible for a number of innovations in tactics — the formation of large artillery groups, the use of the fire shaft, fixed and flexible barrage, direct fire by artillery to render timely and efficient support to the troops, continuous fire support of infantry by artillery, concentration of artillery fire on a critical point, formation of special assault detachments when advancing toward reinforced positions and fortifications, utilization of the airplane not only for intelligence but for bombing, and others.[74]

World War I, in which Bulgaria had become involved through the ability of Tsar Ferdinand and the government of Vassil Radoslavov to avail themselves of popular sentiment with regard to the unsettled national problem, ended in a second national catastrophe. Unlike the Balkan Wars, which had unified Bulgarian society, this war split it on the basis of sympathy or antipathy toward the opposing blocs, while the Bulgarian communists and the peasants argued strongly for neutrality and nonparticipation in an imperialist war. The severe conditions both at the front and in the interior, the lack of food, clothing, and arms, the disloyalty of the allied countries, above all of Germany, the consciousness of the national character of the war, and the influence of the October Revolution created the climate for mutiny in a number of units, led by their commanders.[75] The culmination of the antiwar movements was the Soldiers' Uprising of 1918, which was cruelly crushed and suppressed.[76] For the most part, however, the officers continued obedient to the palace and the ruling class.[77]

Bulgarian soldiers and commanders fought with dignity in the conviction that it was not for conquest but for the liberation of Macedonia and Dobruja.[78] Even the enemy recognized their humanity and military skill.[79] Many officers personally led their soldiers into battle and paid for victory with their lives.[80] The experience of the Balkan Wars had strengthened the army, as was apparent in the successful operations in Serbia in the autumn of 1915, the storming of the Tutrakan bridgehead, the offensive against the Romanians in the autumn of 1916, and the ejection of the British and French from Macedonia. On the Balkan fronts as elsewhere, defense became important in theory as well as in practice, and here the Bulgarians were especially active and successful at Doiran in April 1917, at Mount Jarebichna in May, and at the bend of the Cherna and at Bitolja a year later.[81] Outstanding for its organization and execution was the Doiran operation of September 1918, for which General Vladimir Vazov, the commander of the defense, was awarded high honors by his erstwhile enemy, the commander of the British troops.[82] On the basis of the direct experience obtained during the military actions of the war, Bulgarian military thinking came to important conclusions regarding the importance of the officer during wartime.[83] According to Tenjo Tonchev, "the main and most characteristic trait of the Bulgarian officers was their sense of honor and dignity, their boldness and courage, their sublime patriotism and selflessness."[84]

When the breakthrough of the forces of the Entente, superior in manpower and especially in equipment and tactics, on the Bulgarian front in September of 1918 required the Bulgarians to capitulate, it was another national catastrophe because it required the handing over of additional Bulgarian territory — southern Dobruja, western Thrace, the western region — to Balkan neighbors, imposed enormous reparations, and made the country still more dependent economically on the Western European countries. The military aspects of the armistice destroyed the Bulgarian army and crippled the training of recruits after 1919. The Bulgarian army and its officers entered a new stage (1919-44) during which the principles, forms, and methods of training of officers were fundamentally altered in accordance with the army's function as support for the bourgeois ruling class and fascism.

NOTES

1. Hristo Hristov, *Osvobogdenieto na Bulgaria i politikata na zapadnite dargavi 1876-1878* (Sofia, 1968), p. 220.
2. *Bulgarska voenna istorija*, vol. 2 (Sofia, 1984), pp. 32-33.
3. Evlogi Bugashki, "Vaznikvaneto na burgoaznata politicheska sistema v Bulgaria," in *Bulgaria 1300: Institutzii i dargavna traditzija*, vol. 1 (Sofia, 1981), pp. 676-77.
4. Petar Stoilov, Momchil Ionov, and Ljudmil Petrov, "Bulgarskata armija kato institutzija (1878-1944)," in *Bulgaria 1300*, vol. 1, p. 372.
5. Stoilov, Ionov, and Petrov, "Bulgarskata armija," p. 375; Stojan Penkov, "Prinosat na general Parensov za utvargdavane na ruskoto i za ogranichavane na pruskoto vlijanie varhu bulgarskata armija sled Osvobogdenieto," *Voennoistoricheski sbornik*, 1969, no. 2, p. 9.
6. P.M.T."Ofitzeri za bulgarskata armija sled Osvobogdenieto," *Voennoistoricheski sbornik*, 1927, no. 5-6, pp. 60-61.
7. *Bulgarska voenna istorija*, vol. 2, pp. 73, 234-79; *Dargaven vestnik* no. 36, February 15, 1892.
8. *Bulgarska voenna istorija*, vol. 2, pp. 250-52; *Pologenie za slugbata i pologenieto na ofitzerite ot bulgarskata voiska* (Sofia, 1906); *Pologenie za povishenijata v chin i dlagnost na ofitzerite ot bulgarskata voiska* (Sofia, 1906); *Pologenie za slugbata i pravata na ofitzerite ot bulgarskata voiska* (Sofia, 1908).
9. *Parvi vipusk na Sofiiskoto voenno uchilishte* (Sofia, 1929), p. 12; *Bulgarska voenna istorija*, vol. 2, pp. 41, 53-54; Georgi Valkov, *Ruskite uchiteli na bulgarskoto voinstvo* (Sofia, 1977), p. 93; Ivan Dimitrov, "Ruskata pomosht za sazdavane i razvitie na bulgarskoto voenno uchilishte (1878-1885)," *Voennoistoricheski sbornik*, 1978, no. 3, p. 138.
10. *Bulgarska voenna istorija*, vol. 2, p. 57.
11. Ibid., pp. 92-93.
12. Ibid., pp. 74-75.
13. Tzentralen dargaven istoricheski archiv, fol. 3, op. a.e. 44, 1. 84.
14. Dimitrov, "Ruskata pomosht," p. 143.

15. Georgi Valkov, "Bulgarskite vaorageni sili v perioda na tjahnoto sazdavane (1877-1885)," *Izvestija na instituta za voenna istorija pri Generalnija shtab i na voennoistoricheskoto nauchno drugestvo* (hereafter *Izvestija*) 31 (1981):79-81.

16. Vassil Vassilev, "Za sotzialno-klassovata haracteristika na bulgarskata armija prez perioda 1877-1918," *Izvestija* 31 (1981): 59.

17. Valkov, *Ruskite uchiteli*, p. 126.

18. *Istorija na Srabsko-bulgarskata voina 1885* (Sofia, 1971), p. 89.

19. Boris Cholpanov, "Vlijanie na ruskoto i savetsko voenno iskustvo varhu bulgarskoto voenno iskustvo," *Izvestija* 2 (1966):50.

20. Elena Statelova, "Izgragdane na vaoragenite sili na Iztochna Rumelija," *Voennoistoricheski sbornik*, 1983, no. 6, pp. 14-29.

21. Radoslav Mishev, "Obuchenie na bulgari v ruskite voennouchebni zavedenija ot Osvobogdenieto do kraja na XIXv.," *Voennoistoricheski sbornik*, 1983, no. 6.

22. Mishev, "Obuchenie na bulgari," p. 54; Nikolai Mitev, "Roljata na ruskata armija i ruskoto voenno iskustvo za organiziraneto, obuchenieto i vazpitanieto na bulgarskata armija (1877/78-1912/13)," *Voennoistoricheski sbornik*, 1953, no. 4, p. 26.

23. Nikola Gekov, *Bulgarskoto voinstvo 1878-1928: Voennopoliticheski pogled barhu razvitieto i boinite dela na nashite vaorageni sili ot Osvobogdenieto dosega i tjahnoto badeshte* (Sofia, 1928), pp. 27-28; *Kratak obzor na boinija sastav, organizatzijata, popalvaneto i mobilizatzijata na bulgarskata armija ot 1878 do 1944* (Sofia, 1961), p. 26.

24. Podpolkovnik Blenkner, *Voennoistorichesko znachenie na Srabskobulgarskata voina: Strategichesko-takticheska studija* (Tarnovo, 1900), pp. 58, 104.

25. *Bulgarska voenna istorija*, vol. 2, p. 200.

26. *Plan za razpredelenie na godishnite zanjatija v armijata* (Sofia, 1892), p. 5; Stojan Penkov, *Boen primer i bratska pomosht* (Sofia, 1974), p. 129.

27. *Doklad do negovo velichestvo Ferdinand I, tzar na bulgarite, po sluchai 25-godishninata ot vazshestvieto mu na bulgarskija prestol, 1887-1912*, Ot Ministerskija savet (Sofia, 1912), pp. 352, 374; *Voennoto na N. V. Uchilishte ot osnovavaneto mu do dnes (1878-1934)* (Sofia, 1934), pp. 153-54; *Sistematicheski sbornik na zakonite ukazite, zapovedite i tzirkuljarite po voennoto vedomstvo, 1901-1907, I dopalnenie* (hereafter *Sistematicheski sbornik — I dopalnenie*) (Sofia, 1908), pp. 471, 483.

28. *Voennoto na N. V. Uchilishte*, pp. 192, 193; *Kratak obzor na boinija sastav*, p. 66.

29. Gekov, *Bulgarskoto voinstvo*, p. 107.

30. *Bulgarska voenna istorija*, vol 2, p. 283.

31. Ibid., pp. 319-21; *Pravilnik za Shkolata za podgotvjane na zapasni podporuchitzi v pehotata* (Sofia, 1901).
32. Gekov, *Bulgarskoto voinstvo*, p. 108.
33. *Bulgarska voenna istorija*, vol. 2, pp. 250-52.
34. Radoslav Mishev, "Bulgarsko-avstroungarski voenni otnoshenija (1879-1900)," *Voennoistoricheski sbornik*, 1985, no. 1, p. 71.
35. Geko Popov, "Politikata na vtoroto narodnoliberalno pravitelstvo sprjamo bulgarskata armija (1903-1908)," *Voennoistoricheski sbornik*, 1980, no. 4, p. 21.
36. Mitev, "Roljata na ruskata armija," p. 27.
37. Penkov, *Boen primer i bratska pomosht*, p. 161.
38. *Dargaven vestnik*, no. 164, July 23, 1912; *Bulgarska voenna istorija*, vol. 2, pp. 432-33, 452-60.
39. Nauchen arhiv na Bulgarska akademija na naukite (hereafter NA BAN), fol. 9, a.e. 2964, 1. 1-7; *Bulgarska voenna istorija*, vol. 2, pp. 282, 283-86.
40. *Bulgarska voenna istorija*, vol. 2, p. 287.
41. *Sistematicheski sbornik na zakonite, ukazite, zapovedite i tzirkuljarite po voennoto vedomstvo ot 1877-1878 do January 1, 1901* (hereafter *Sistematicheski sbornik*), 2 vols. (Sofia, 1901-2), pp. 947, 987, 1036, 1059, 1108, 1176, 1154-1155 et passim.
42. *Doklad do negovo velichestvo Ferdinand I*, pp. 387-88; *Sistematicheski sbornik — I dopalnenie*, pp. 871-73.
43. *Sistematicheski sbornik — I dopalnenie*, pp. 97, 105, 113, 123, 139, 150, 160, 168, 196-204, 205, 213, 215, 217, 249, 253, 271.
44. *Ustav za obuchenie i deistvie na pehotata* (Sofia, 1905), p. 168.
45. *Doklad do negovo velichestvo Ferdinand I*, pp. 391-96; *Sistematicheski sbornik*, pp. 1156, 1158; *Bulgarska voenna istorija*, vol. 2, pp. 403-4, 385-86, 372.
46. *Bulgarska voenna istorija*, vol. 2, pp. 286-87.
47. *Pologenie za Kavaleriiskata shkola* (Sofia, 1903), p. 5; *Sistematicheski sbornik — I dopalnenie*, pp. 512-14; *Bulgarska voenna istorija*, vol. 2, pp. 382-83.
48. *Bulgarska voenna istorija*, vol. 2, p. 405.
49. Jako Molhov, "Bulgarskata artilerija prez Balkanskata voina,"*Voennoistoricheski sbornik*, 1970, no. 6, p. 37.
50. *Sistematicheski sbornik — I dopalnenie*, pp. 517, 518.
51. Mishev, "Bulgarsko-avstroungarski," pp. 80-82.
52. *Obikolkata na N.Epanchin, polkovnik ot ruskija GSHT v Bulgarija prez esenta na 1899* (Pleven, 1901), p. 27.
53. Tzentralen voenen arhiv (hereafter TZVA), fol. 1, op. 5, a.e. 323, 1. 209, 418, 425, 428, 463, 582, 586; a.e. 322, 1. 68; a.e. 446, 1. 22, 128.

54. TZVA, fol. 7, op. 1, a.e. 206, 1. 147.
55. *Kratak obzor na boinija sastav*, p. 66.
56. *Voennoto na N. V. Uchilishte*, pp. 199, 200.
57. Ibid., p. 227.
58. *Pravilnik za Shkolata*, p. 119.
59. TZVA, fol. 7, op. 1, a.e. 206, 1. 147.
60. TZVA, fol. 40, op. 2, a.e. 482, 1. 556.
61. *Kratak obzor na boinija sastav*, p. 107.
62. Ibid., p. 113.
63. *Spisak na ofitzerite ot bulgarskata voiska (na deistvitelna slugba) kam 1 mart 1918* (Kjustendil, 1918), pp. 1-49; *Kratak obzor na boinija sastav*, p. 114.
64. *Zapoved no.4 po Deistvuvashtata armija ot 26 septemvri 1915*, Voennoistoricheska biblioteka, Sofia.
65. *Zapoved no. 113 po Deistvuvashtata armija ot 9 dekemvri 1915*, Voennoistoricheska biblioteka, Sofia.
66. TZVA, fol. 40, op. 2, a.e. 606, 1. 74-75; a.e. 787, 1. 238-41; fol. 48, op. 5, a.e. 232, 1. 134.
67. Kiril Kossev, *Podvigat 1912-1913* (Sofia, 1983), p. 210.
68. NA BAN, fol. 4, a.e. 10, 1. 355.
69. Jako Molhov, "Bulgarskata artilerija prez Balkanskata voina," *Voennoistoricheski sbornik*, 1970, no. 6, p. 50.
70. *Odrin 1912-1913*, Sbornik spomeni (Sofia, 1983), p. 41.
71. Kossev, *Podvigat 1912-1913*, pp. 210-11.
72. *Odrin 1912-1913*, pp. 142, 143, 156.
73. Stilijan Noikov, "Otzenki na germanskija i avstroungarskija generalen shtab za bulgarskata armija v Balkanskata voina 1912-1913," *Voennoistoricheski sbornik*, 1983, no. 2, p. 49.
74. Kossev, *Podvigat 1912-13*, p. 208; Molhov, "Bulgarskata artilerija," p. 50.
75. Gencho Kamburov, "Revoljutzionnijat podem v Bulgarskata armija sled Oktomvriiskata revoljutzija," *Voennoistoricheski sbornik*, 1967, no. 3, pp. 4-24; Joto Jotov, "Borbata na BRSDP (t.s.) protiv Parvata svetovna voina sred armijata na fronta," *Voennoistoricheski sbornik*, 1962, no. 1, pp. 111-18; idem, "Buntat v 27-i Tchepinski polk prez vreme na Parvata svetovna voina 1915-1918," *Voennoistoricheski sbornik*, 1956, no. 1, pp. 104-22; idem, "Antivoenni nastroenija i projavi sred visshi ofitzeri ot bulgarskata armija prez Parvata svetovna voina," *Izvestija* 32 (1981):53-54; V. Karaivanov, "Vlijainieto na Fevruarskata i Velikata oktomvriiska sotzialisticheska revoljutzija v Rusija varhu bulgarskata armija," *Izvestija* 3 (1967): 3-29.
76. Ivan Marinov and V. Karaivanov, "Voennoto organizirane i provegdane na Voinishkoto vastanie prez 1918," *Izvestija* 7 (1969):3-46; Ivan

Draev, "Boinite sili na Voinishkoto vastanie prez 1918," *Voennoistoricheski sbornik*, 1968, no. 4, pp. 11-28.

77. Iono Mitev, "Za istoricheskija pat na bulgarskata armija," *Izvestija* 31 (1981):90-91.
78. Mitev, "Za istoricheskija," p. 91.
79. NA BAN, fol. 57 k, a.e. 35, 1. 1; Tenjo Tonchev, *Svetovnijat pogar i Bulgaria* (Sofia, 1984), pp. 437-38, 463-65.
80. NA BAN, fol. 40 k, a.e. 58, 1. 98-100.
81. Tonchev, *Svetovnijat pogar i Bulgarija*, pp. 391-92.
82. Vladimir Vazov, "Kratki givotopisni belegki," 2 pts., Voennoistoricheska biblioteka, Sofia; Tonchev, *Svetovnijat pogar i Bulgarija*, p. 467.
83. Boris Drangov, *Pomni voinata* (Sofia, 1917), pp. 4, 35-36, 41.
84. Tonchev, *Svetovnijat pogar i Bulgarija*, pp. 447, 448.

The Selection and Education of Greek Officers from Independence to 1920

Thanos Veremis

From its turbulent birth in the aftermath of the War of Independence to the Tricoupis reforms of the 1880s, the Greek regular army was limited to buttressing the authority of the new state. The very formation of state-controlled troops was based on the principle of restraining the internecine strife among the war's irregulars and their defiant claims on the central government. By the last quarter of the nineteenth century, the state had eliminated rival sources of power and proceeded to transform the diminutive forces that had policed the countryside into a massive institution that would serve the irredentist cause in the field.

Throughout the last century of the Ottoman presence in Greece, the two dominant social groups on the periphery of the empire were the local landed notables functioning as a component of the Ottoman tax system and the armed chieftains entrusted with the protection of roads from brigands who might obstruct the traffic of goods and people on the mainland. The War of Independence reconciled the two only temporarily. When the prospect of a new central authority began to materialize, politicians and military men grappled for control of the emerging state. What the traditional elites failed to realize was that the state could make use of their services only if it secured their exclusive loyalty and ultimately their subordination to its will. In other words, political power could no longer remain fragmented on the periphery of the state, nor would the central state share its authority with the old order on a partnership basis.[1]

The defiant chieftains were eased out of state service with decorations and land and replaced by a state army made up mostly of Bavarian professionals. The regular army was from the outset faced with the task of quelling rebellions of forces resisting the centralizing process as well as the hostility of the idle warriors turned brigands who ruled the countryside. The new military was therefore divorced from the warrior tradition of challenging political authority while the defiant forces were isolated outside the law. The new army's service to the state was secured without any involvement of it in politics, but the rebel brigands were periodically employed by the state to support irredentist uprisings in Ottoman-held territories. Thus the revolutionary tradition was preserved and at the same time military employees were kept free of the virus of rebellion.[2]

Officer selection and education during the initial forty-five years of the Hellenic kingdom served the overriding priority of nation building. From the last quarter of the nineteenth century, important reforms in military education reflected political and social developments in the larger Balkan scene. Balkan nationalisms, an expiring Ottoman empire, and the redistribution of influence among the great powers constitute the background and cause of the Greek army's development up to the end of World War I.

The Military Academy was established at Nafplion, the first capital of liberated Greece, to provide the regular army with a professional officer corps. The intention of its founder, the Bavarian philhellene Colonel von Eydeck, was to encourage notables and warriors of the War of Independence to bring their sons into the service of the state. The local notables were, however, slow to respond to this appeal, and it was the uprooted former volunteers of the diaspora and refugees from territories in which the revolution had failed who initially grasped the opportunity that promised professional security. Native warriors feared that free tuition and board would ensnare their offspring into the service of the government or simply abhorred its disciplinary methods. Of forty-three students who entered the institution in 1928, only eight graduated three years later. The output of graduates remained comparably low until the last quarter of the century.[3]

The first president of Greece, John Kapodistrias, was preoccupied with the formation of a modern officer corps to command a regular army on the Western model. To this end he asked General N. Maizon, who had cleared the Pelopponese of the Egyptian occupation forces, to release French officers and noncommissioned officers for the use of the Greek military school, which was promptly restructured along the lines of the French Ecole Polytechnique. The goal of imitating the French prototype proved much too ambitious in view of the lack of the educational background that would enable cadets to pursue intensive training in the sciences. The ages of the cadets, ranging from thirteen to seventeen years, and the varying degrees of literacy among first-year students constituted formidable obstacles. Furthermore, the prospect of three years of strict discipline and hard work discouraged the sons of influential families who could secure positions in the officer corps through the back door of patronage. Kapodistrias therefore established yet another category of future officers, the Akolouthi, who acquired a brief acquaintance with principles of artillery and engineering and after passing examinations became lieutenants.[4]

The continuing reluctance of prominent members of society to enter the academy led Kapodistrias to seek recruits in other social strata. Thus in October of 1829 he turned to the orphanage of Aigina, whose boarders were mostly children orphaned during the War of Independence. This source of recruitment did not last long but yielded a crop of officers dedicated to the service with an esprit de corps that they passed on to their sons.[5]

The president's personal interest in the improvement of the academy promised to make the institution an important center for the dissemination of military as well as technical skills. However, a month after Kapodistrias attended the first graduation in July 1831, he was assassinated by political opponents. King Otto and the Bavarian advisors who came with him to Greece in 1833 altered the charter of the academy. According to the royal decree of March 3, 1834,

> Four junior and four senior classes are formed. The young men enter the lowest and pass a year in each, then, after undergoing an examination, are placed in the army . . . where they are bound to serve for at least four years. . . . At the end of the initial four years the pupils undergo an examination; those who pass advance into the senior classes, the others must quit the academy. . . . The studies of the four junior classes comprise ancient and modern languages, geometry, geography, calligraphy, algebra, history, drawing, dancing, gymnastic, swimming, fencing, surveying. . . . The instruction of the pupils in the four senior classes is suitably general and technical to fit them for the artillery and the engineers. Consequently, the higher branches and applications of mathematics, natural philosophy, chemistry, fortification, gunnery, the construction of roads and bridges, form the subjects of their studies.[6]

Full tuition was fixed at 1,000 drachmas a year (equivalent to the annual salary of an academy instructor), but only 14 percent of the cadets enrolled paid the entire sum. About 14 percent paid 750 drachmas, about 20 percent 500, and another 14 percent 250. A third of the places were reserved for the sons of civil and military employees who had rendered important services to their country and were therefore relieved of tuition fees altogether. Between 1834 and 1840 the annual number of entrants varied from 140 to 60, but the average fee paid indicated that most cadets were recruited from the well-to-do sector of society.[7]

The academy operated in Aigina for three and a half years. Many of its graduates supplemented their education in the artillery and engineering school at Metz and the Ecole Polytechnique in Paris. Others were given scholarships to study in Munich by King Otto's father, King Ludwig of Bavaria. Graduating cadets who had excelled in the more demanding courses were selected for the artillery and the engineering corps, while those of lesser qualifications entered the infantry. This method of officer selection for the three corps remained in force through the academy's time in Piraeus between 1837 and 1894.[8]

During the initial twelve years of its operation, the academy was run by foreign military instructors and directors. According to the Treaty of London, the king of Greece was empowered to raise a body of troops in Bavaria for the needs of the new kingdom. Between 1833 and 1835 close to fifty-five hundred Germans were employed in the Greek regular army, but after their four-year engagement these began to return home.[9] The hellenization of the army and its command coincided with the commission of Lieutenant Colonel Spyromilios, a hero of the War of Independence, as the first Greek director of the academy in 1840. In the meantime, as Otto secured internal order and stabilized his regime, he began to feel that great expenditure for the military was no longer necessary. The military budget was accordingly cut from nine million drachmas in 1833 to four million in 1838. The standing army was reduced from close to ten thousand in 1833 to six thousand in 1838, though it later rose again to eight thousand.[10] Forever changing its regulations, the academy cut the junior classes from four years to one and then to two when Spyromilios assumed command, while preserving the four-year duration of the senior classes. The six-year course lasted for the remainder of Otto's reign.

The 1843 political upheaval against Otto's absolute rule had a serious impact on the academy. Discipline among cadets declined, and teachers brought their politics into the institution or simply ceased to take an interest in its future. Between 1843 and 1846 the academy, then under Lieutenant Colonel Karatzas, reached its lowest point. The new director, seeking to restore discipline, ignored the academy's tradition of self-management and was ultimately faced with an armed rebellion. The government expelled the nine cadets considered responsible for the rioting and closed the institution for a year. The incident illustrates both the free traffic of politics and civilian values in military institutions and the tolerant treatment of disciplinary infractions by the state. In his report on the condition of the academy in 1851, Colonel Rainek, inspector general of the army, noted the liberty with which cadets voiced their criticism of the professional shortcomings of the faculty. According to Rainek, too many cadets were being forced by their families to enter the military school either because it was seen as a proper choice of career or because it was hoped that their term in the academy would reform their unruly characters. Perhaps more than the cadets' social backgrounds and idiosyncrasies, however, the political anomalies that accompanied the latter part of Otto's reign may bear responsibility for the decay of military education.[11]

During the long reign of King George I, which commenced in 1863, the education of officers was repeatedly altered both in form and in substance. In 1864 six years of studies were assigned to prospective officers of the artillery and the engineering corps and four years to officers of the infantry and the cavalry. The annual number of entrants was not to exceed sixty between the ages of fifteen and eighteen. In 1866 the course was fixed at five years for all corps, and in 1868 the regulation of the academy reverted to the charter of 1864, which remained in force until 1870. These frequent changes in regulations reflected the instability of the period and the inertia of an army whose peacetime force remained at its Ottonian level of eight thousand.[12]

During the first sixty years of its life the Greek state was entirely dependent on the military academy for the dissemination of sorely needed technical skills and education. Almost invariably the curriculum included arithmetic, algebra, geometry, stereometry, trigonometry, drawing, methods of construction, topography, building, and engine design. From 1870 theoretical subjects such as physics and mathematics were given during an initial five-year course and applied military education was concentrated in the last two years of the academy. The cadets with the highest grades in these subjects were selected for the technical corps, but there were always students whose chose to conclude their studies after completing an initial program of theoretical subjects and pursue a career in teaching or civil engineering. Thus the institution produced civilian architects, engineers, and teachers of theoretical sciences until the foundation of the Greek Polytechnic Institute in 1887. Officers of the engineering corps were often used by the Ministry of the Interior for the supervision of public works such as the construction of bridges, roads, and government buildings, and their services were employed not only by the state but by the private sector as well.[13]

The Bavarian captain of the engineering corps Frederik Tsetner promoted technical education by establishing a collection of tools and engines for the use of students and artisans. This collection, offering technical information and literature as well as equipment, was officially set up with government support in 1836. The military origin of technical education in Greece was obvious during the first decades of the Polytechnic Institute's operation because many of its professors were army officers.[14]

Between 1877 and 1897 a series of crises made the dismemberment of the Ottoman Empire appear imminent, a prospect which heightened the antagonisms among Balkan nations over the future distribution of the territorial spoils. The evolution and development of regular armies in other Balkan states was instrumental in reviving the Greek army from its inertia. Greek governments finally abandoned the convenient policy of utilizing irregulars to promote irredentist aspirations and realized that the final reckoning would take place on the field of battle.

The academy was animated by a series of reforms which began in the 1870s and reached their peak during the term of Harilaos Tricoupis. The reformer statesman aimed at bringing the education of officers into line with a new policy that viewed the regular army as the future champion of irredentist struggles. Between 1879 and 1882 universal conscription was put into effect and the standing army was modernized and increased to thirty thousand strong. However, the constant changes of governing regulations (in 1877, 1880, 1881, 1885, etc.) retarded the beneficial effects of reform.[15]

In 1882 the academy entered one of its best periods since its founding. It acquired a new set of regulations that lasted for thirty years and cut the course of study to five years, thus placing emphasis on military subjects rather than intermediate scientific education.

Entrance required a high-school diploma and therefore saved the institution the loss of young men who, having entered the school at a tender age, often dropped out along the way: of 576 cadets enrolled from 1828 to 1882, 303 (barely 53 percent) had become officers. The academy remained closed, however, to candidates below a certain financial level, since tuition, board, and other expenses exceeded 2,500 drachmas a year (the annual income of the average civil servant). The institution concentrated on theoretical scientific subjects and failed to provide practical experience to prospective officers of the technical corps. It completely neglected the needs of the largest branch and backbone of the army, the infantry.[16]

The tuition-free School for Noncommissioned Officers, founded in 1882, was designed to supply officers for the infantry and to a lesser extent the cavalry. An initial period of service as NCOs and three years of study gave candidates of moderate means the opportunity of entering the officer corps with seniority two months behind those who graduated from the academy at the same time. Since the early years of the operation of regular troops, the overwhelming majority of officers had risen from the ranks and, although, they possessed experience in ordinary military functions, conspicuously lacked military education and acquaintance with modern methods. The disparity between academy graduates and officers who had risen from the ranks was especially obvious in the almost exclusive presence of the former in the senior ranks. Most academy graduates, however, chose to be placed in the two prestigious technical corps (table 1), which were crowded because of their small size, thus undermining their prospects of rapid promotion. Hence, infantry officers often reached the middle ranks before their colleagues in the artillery but seldom rose above them.[17]

TABLE 1

Military Academy Graduates in Relation to the Total Number of Officers, of the Various Branches, 1891

	Officers	Academy Graduates
Infantry	924	10
Cavalry	110	5
Artillery	152	147
Engineers	79	79
◊ Total	1,265	241

The problem of improving the quality of infantry officers became a preoccupation of the Greek military after the ignominious defeat by the Turkish forces in 1897. Thus the entire academy class of 1900 was obliged to enter the infantry. The long-term trend, however, was toward change in the entire structure and orientation of military education. In his influential 1909 tract on the reform of the officer corps, M. Raktivan, an artillery lieutenant, insisted that the existence of two schools for officers and the lack of any schooling for the majority of them was responsible for the sorry state of the infantry and the lack of cohesion among officers. Raktivan proposed a single institution for the preparation of future officers, free of tuition, so that no economic hindrance would inhibit able candidates from entering. Furthermore, he urged that theoretical subjects and the length of the course should be restricted and emphasis placed on training in applied military science.[18]

The Balkan Wars of 1912-13 revolutionized military education and the recruitment of officers. After 1913 the academy abandoned its Ecole Polytechnique prototype and adopted Saint-Cyr as its model, concentrating mainly on preparing officers for the infantry and cavalry. The emphasis was shifted from mathematics and theoretical subjects to practical training, while the five-year course was reduced to three. Noncommissioned officers were allowed to graduate from the academy in two years, while civilians were obliged to pursue preparatory courses for a year before commencing a two-year program. In 1914 the charter of Evelpidon was revised to supply a large officer corps ready to take the field: 270 students entered the institution, almost equal to the number of its graduates throughout its initial fifty years of operation. Although admission quotas remained high until 1920, the proportion of academy graduates in the officer corps diminished markedly between 1912 and 1922 (table 2) because of the influx of reserve officers who had been granted regular commissions.

Tuition fees were abolished in 1917, but the social origin of cadets at the academy had been changing significantly since 1913. The large number of admissions had made the institution readily accessible to those who could afford it, and the traditional preference for prominent members of society had therefore given way to candidates who were socially less privileged. At the same time, prominent families were eager to send their children to the academy once the institution had lost its prestige and exclusiveness. Furthermore, the gradual growth

The Selection and Education

and diversification of the economy had increased the range of professional opportunities and therefore broadened the career options of young men. The academy with its free tuition attracted mainly those who could not afford to finance their own education.

TABLE 2

Military Academy Graduates in Relation to the Total Number of Officers, 1895-1925

Army List	Officers	Academy Number	Graduates Percent
1895	1,230	344	28.0
1900	934	330	35.0
1904	1,396	373	27.0
1909	1,229	359	29.0
1912	1,301	372	28.5
1914	2,627	369	14.0
1919	4,705	872	18.5
1925	3,287	700	21.0

Source: T. Veremis, *The Interventions of the Army in Greek Politics 1916-1936* (in Greek) (Athens, 1983), p. 80.

The school for noncommissioned officers was discontinued in 1915, and a new category of officers appeared during the wars in the Balkans. Reserve officers who had been granted regular commissions formed the largest group in the Army List of 1920. These were conscripts who at the end of their military service were offered the option of positions in the army. Most of them had completed their secondary education and a few had attended the university before being conscripted, and their decision to remain with the service was often dictated by lack of financial security. Their brief and superficial contact with military education and the circumstances under which they had entered the army determined the professional outlook of these officers. Their frequent involvement in politics and military societies reflected to a certain extent a measure of civilian behavior that they inevitably introduced into the service. For this they earned the contempt of academy graduates, who never accepted them as their equals either in character or in military education.[19]

The intense interest in military conspiracies shown by reserve officers who had been granted regular commissions can also be explained by their lack of professional security. The least stable group in the officer corps, they constituted a kind of thermostat of the corps: whenever the Army List was too crowded, they were the first to be retired. Their dependence on military and political patrons had therefore become a condition for professional survival. Since most regular commissions were granted between 1913 and 1920, especially during Eleftherios Venizelos's terms and his clash with King Constantine, there was a strong propensity among these officers to support the Liberal leader. When the "great schism" between followers of the charismatic Venizelos and the no less popular Constantine occurred, it was reserve officers who had been granted regular commissions rather than academy graduates who supported the former Venizelos, twice obliged to resign because the king refused to endorse Greece's entry into the war on the side of the Triple Entente, the summer of 1916 formed his own revolutionary government in Thessaloniki and summoned his followers to stand by him and his pro-Entente policy. It was reserve officers holding regular commissions who were the first to abandon their posts in significant numbers and rush to his side. Their vital role in the dispute between liberals and royalists eventually made these officers a radical elite in the army and the vanguard not only of Venizelism but also of antimonarchical currents. By 1920 this group of officers formed the most numerous category in the army.[20]

From the last quarter of the nineteenth century on, the efforts of Greek governments to create a professional officer corps that would command and modernize an augmented regular army resulted in the development of a corporate identity among the more prominent of the military. The reformed academy increasingly attracted an elite which by the first decade of the twentieth century had begun to voice both professional and national grievances. Between 1872 and 1895 the officer corps increased by over 240 percent, from seven hundred to eighteen hundred.[21] In the same period officers serving in Parliament constituted between 7 and 15 percent of the deputies, a significant overrepresentation of the military, and academy graduates were overrepresented among these deputy officers. Needless to say, lawyers commanded an even higher percentage of the total, but profession itself or achievement within it does not necessarily explain a representation disproportionate to the size of a professional group. The answer should be sought in the significance of the particular social class and the influence of its members in society. The fact that junior officers were usually more numerous in Parliament than their more accomplished seniors, even in terms of their relative numerical strength in the army, may verify this observation.

Between 1897 and 1909 it was the academy graduates who became the most vociferous critics of royal interference in military matters as well as the vanguard of military corporatism. The pronunciamento of 1909 against the monarchy and its political clients was spearheaded by the Military League, an organization almost exclusively made up of young academy graduates.

The expansion of a peacetime force of twenty-five thousand in 1900 into an army of a hundred fifty thousand at the outbreak of the First Balkan War in 1912 transformed the officer corps not only in size but in social background. Between 1912 and 1920 the corps became more representative of Greek society and less willing to accept the superiority of civilian rule. According to the revised constitution of 1911, officers were prohibited from running for Parliament, but the propensity for the military to become involved in politics by making use of mass coercion increased dramatically throughout the interwar period.

NOTES

1. The most vivid account of the new state's formative years is given by John Petropulos, *Politics and Statecraft in the Kingdom of Greece 1833-1843* (Princeton, 1968).
2. T. Veremis, "O taktikos stratos stin Ellada tou I9ou aiona" in D. Tsaousis, ed. *Opseis tis ellinikis koinonias tou 19 ou aiona* (Kollaros, Athens, 1984), pp. 165-176.
3. E. Stasinopoulos, *I istoria tis scholis Evelpidon* (Athens, 1954), pp. 35-38.
4. Ibid., pp. 43-44, 50-51.
5. Ibid., pp. 52-53.
6. Frederick Strong, *Greece as a Kingdom* (London, 1842), pp. 272-73.
7. Ibid., pp. 272-74.
8. D. Koromilas, an academy graduate studying at the Ecole Polytechnique in 1838, complained to the Ministry of Army Affairs that his monthly salary of sixty-eight drachmas was hardly enough to pay for his tuition, books, and board in Paris (Stasinopoulos, *History*, p. 72).
9. Strong, *Greece as a Kingdom,* pp. 280-81.

10. Ibid., pp. 259-62.
11. Stasinopoulos, *History* (1933 edition), pp. 78-79.
12. A Haralambis and K. Nider, *Istorikon ypomnima peri tou organismou tou taktikou stratou* (Athens, 1907), pp. 129-31.
13. Costas Biris, *Istoria tou Ethnikou Metsoviou Polytechniou* (Athens, 1957), pp. 13-16.
14. Ibid., pp. 265-66, 485-527.
15. Alexander Mazarakis-Ainian, *Istoriki meleti 1821-1897 kai o polemos*, vol. 1, (Athens, 1950), pp. 308-9.
16. Ibid., pp. 309-10; Haralambis and Nider, *Istorikon*, pp. 240, 268-70.
17. Haralambis and Nider, *Istorikon*, pp. 270-71.
18. M. Raktivan, *Mia meleti epi tou stratou mas* (Eleftheroudakis, Athens, 1909), pp. 17-48.
19. T. Veremis, "The Officer Corps in Greece 1912-1936," *Byzantine and Modern Greek Studies* 2 (1976): 116-17.
20. Ibid.
21. Christina Varda, "Politevomenoi stratiotikoi stin Ellada sta teli tou 19ou aiona," MNIMON, 8 (1980-82): 53.

The Ludovika Military Academy, 1802-1920

Kálmán Kéri

The need for Hungarian officer training became apparent in 1802, when Hungarian infantry and hussar regiments were battling against Napoleon under the standard of the House of Habsburg. When in 1808 King Francis I of Hungary, emperor of Austria, married Maria Ludovica, duchess of Modena-Este, the Hungarian nation made a coronation present of 50,000 forints to the new queen, who donated the sum toward the establishment of a Hungarian military academy. At the same time the king made available a building in Vác called the Terezianum after Queen Maria Theresa. By the time the Diet met in 1808, 662,000 forints had been donated for the purpose from various sources. The Diet decided to establish the Ludovika Military Academy,[1] and the enthusiastic estates subscribed 800,000 forints for it.[2]

The beginning of formal officer training in Hungary was, however, delayed by wartime difficulties and by the court Council of War in Vienna. Moreover, when the Napoleonic wars were over, the prospect of an extended period of peace reduced both the need for it and interest among young men in pursuing a career as an officer. Nonetheless, the palatine Archduke Joseph and the Diet continued to press for Hungarian officer training and the erection of a suitable building for it. With the king's approval, construction began in 1830 on the present site of the Ludovika, and officer training was to have begun there in 1836. However, the Diet took the view that Hungarian should be the language of instruction, a demand that the king, in line with the stance of the Council of War, rejected. The Diet thereupon adopted a wait-and-see attitude on the officer training issue[3] and contemplated establishing a technical university in the Ludovika building.[4]

The Revolution and War for Independence, 1848-49

Influenced by the revolutionary movements of 1848, in September of that year the monarch finally agreed to officer training in

Hungarian. An invitation to apply for admission appeared in the official gazette on November 23, and prospective students responded to it. However, despite the efforts of the Hungarian defense minister, Lázár Mészáros, instruction could not begin immediately because the imperial army, charged with wresting back all the gains made by the Hungarians in the revolution, was using the building as a military hospital.[5] The teachers and students therefore dispersed, some returning to their homes, some following the government to Debrecen, and some volunteering for military service in some unit or other of the *honvédség*, the Hungarian defense force. In the spring of 1849 the Hungarian National Assembly proclaimed the dethronement of the House of Habsburg. The combined Austrian and Russian armies eventually forced the *honvédség* to lay down its arms, thus bringing the War for Independence to an end, and the question of officer training in Hungary became moot.

Officer Training in the *Honvédség* under the Austro-Hungarian Monarchy

Among the reforms brought about by the Compromise of 1867 was the establishment of a new *honvédség*, which took on an increasingly important role in the armed forces of the Austro-Hungarian Monarchy.[6] This defense force of course needed both regular and reserve officers. The training of these officers may conveniently be considered in terms of five periods: 1869-73, 1874-83, 1883-1901, 1898-1913, and 1914-18.

The Initial Period, 1869-73

In the initial period, the officer corps included regular officers of the old imperial army, qualified retired officers who asked to be restored to the active list, reserve officers from the imperial army who had completed their terms, qualified officer trainees from the imperial army, and officers who had done military service during the War for Independence and were still fit to serve.[7] However, all these together were far from sufficient in numbers or quality. As a result, in the winter of 1869-70, the first officer training course was established to make up the shortfall.

Officers and noncommissioned officers from the imperial army had joined the *honvédség* in 1868 and the first basic training course for recruits had begun. When it was over, noncommissioned officers and privates who seemed suitable for promotion to officer on the grounds of training and character were detailed to attend a cadet course and then sent back to their units to take the cadet examination. Successful examinees were appointed reserve cadets. Of these, those who reported for active service attended the officer training course of 1872-73 and, having completed it, were commissioned on October 1, 1873, as regular second lieutenants in the *honvédség*.[8] Additional short periods of professional training brought swift promotion. For regular officers who lacked the required knowledge, a three-month officers' course and a separate three-month field officers' course were provided at the Ludovika.[9]

The Period of Development, 1874-83

Since the fund established for the support of the Ludovika Academy had, along with its building, been confiscated by the imperial War Ministry after the War for Independence and by 1870 had not yet been restored to the *honvédség*, the new officer training courses were temporarily held in buildings rented by the Hungarian Defense Ministry. After long negotiations the fund was handed over to the Ministry, sixty years after it had been established, along with the academy building.[10] Now both the money and the premises were available to take officer training a stage farther, but opposition from the imperial War Ministry prevented the establishment of an institution resembling the joint army's military academy or even its cadet schools.

A preparatory course was set up for 250 soldiers (*honvéds*) who had completed at least the first three or four years of secondary school, had had eight weeks' basic training, and had been recommended for officer training.[11] Application could also be made by noncommissioned officers who had proved themselves useful to their units and obtained high marks in an earlier examination. Those who completed the preparatory course with a mark of "good" or above (three or more out of a possible five) advanced to the officer training course in the following academic year.

The officer training course was open to soldiers, irrespective of origin or religion, who had earned good grades in the preparatory course or had had eight weeks' basic training and completed the eighth year of academically oriented secondary school (*gimnázium*) or the sixth year of scientifically oriented secondary school (*reáliskola*) with good grades and in addition done well in an examination before an examining board on the curriculum of the preparatory course.[12]

Including the preparatory course, the training program lasted two years, after which the three best students were promoted to second lieutenant and the others to cadet. The ranks of those admitted to the class of 1878-84 ranged from *honvéd* to sergeant. One student was Lance Sergeant Samu Kohn (later Hazai), who was promoted to cadet on September 1, 1874, served as defense minister with the rank of colonel general from 1910 to 1917, and by the end of the war was quartermaster general of the Monarchy's combined armed forces. At the top of the same course in 1884 was Acting Sergeant Sándor Szurmay, who was promoted to second lieutenant and later became an army commander, defense minister, and a knight of the Order of Maria Theresa.

Regulars and reservists in the *honvédség* were eligible for both the preparatory and the officer training course.

To the higher-officer training course were detailed twenty-five officer volunteers (twenty infantry and five cavalry) who had done at least two years' service with a unit as an officer, had been graded "very good" (four out of a possible five), and had passed an entrance examination. At the end of the academic year those with a mark of "excellent" (five) could count on promotion out of turn, while those with a mark of "good" were earmarked for service as adjutants.[13] From 1876-77 the students with the best results were sent to the joint army's war college in Vienna for general-staff training as special students.

The field officers' course, lasting five or ten months, was for longer-serving captains being considered for promotion.[14]

From the 1877-78 academic year, students were also sent to the Ludovika from the Gendarmerie.[15]

The Maturation of Officer Training in the *Honvédség*, 1883-1901

The next period brought a marked change, above all because soldiers of around twenty-one years of age chosen from among noncommissioned officers and men on active service gave way to youngsters of fourteen or fifteen placed under military discipline and training along the lines of the cadet schools of the joint army. During this period, the training of reserve and regular officers and in-service training of regular officers advanced to a higher level.[16]

The one-year reserve officer training course was for reservists directly recruited into the *honvédség* who showed special aptitude.[17] Its essential purpose was to turn out reserve cadets. The one-year Ludovika Academy volunteers' course was for recruits who had passed a secondary-school final examination or the equivalent.[18] It was aimed at ensuring sufficient numbers of adequately trained reserve second lieutenants and cadets. Volunteers for it were selected by their units and instructed at the academy from the 1883-84 academic year until 1889-90. By then the number of one-year volunteers had grown so much that training of them had to be transferred to the army's district command headquarters in Budapest, Szeged, Kassa, Pozsony, Székesfehérvár, Kolozsvár, and Zagreb. (In Zagreb the instruction was in Croatian.) Among those to take this course was the noted Asian scholar and researcher Aurel Stein, who was promoted to the rank of reserve second lieutenant in 1887.[19]

The regular-officer training course, like those of the cadet schools of the joint army, lasted four years.[20] The syllabus too was similar, but the course was conducted in Hungarian or Croatian. Admitted to the first year were sixty (from 1890-91 ninety) volunteers aged fourteen to sixteen who had passed an entrance examination. At the end of the fourth year the top two students were commissioned as second lieutenants, those with marks of "excellent" and "very good" as cadet warrant officers, and those graded "good" and "satisfactory" as lance corporals (after 1892, as cadet warrant officers) (table 1). Those completing one of these courses included Béla Kary, Aurel Stromfeld, Jenő Tombor, Vilmos Rőder, András Szepessy, Albert Bartha, Lajos Bartha, Károly Csáky, Imre Horváth, József Kerekes, Elemér Papp-Váry, Kálmán Révy, András Sipos, and Béla Szinay.

The higher-officer training course was, as before, designed to provide in-service training for young officers and prepared the best of them for attendance at the general-staff college of the joint army.[21]

The field officers' course continued as before.

TABLE 1
GRADUATES OF THE LUDOVIKA ACADEMY, 1873-1901

YEAR	TOTAL	LIEUTENANTS		CADETS			
		Infantry	Cavalry	Infantry	Cavalry	Gendarmerie	Audit
1873	68	67	1	-	-	-	-
1874	64	2	1	60	1	-	-
1875	165	3	-	150	12	-	-
1876	74	3	-	63	8	-	-
1877	79	3	-	67	9	-	-
1878	86	3	-	70	11	2	-
1879	100	3	-	90	5	2	-
1880	123	3	-	107	11	2	-
1881	131	3	-	112	9	7	-
1882		2	1	86	7	15	-
1883	80	3	-	57	11	9	-
1884	74	3	-	62	9	-	-
1885	-	-	-	-	-	-	-
1886	-	-	-	-	-	-	-
1887	60	1	1	44	14	-	-
1888	53	1	1	41	10	-	-
1889	56	2	-	42	12	-	-
1890	53	2	-	40	11	-	-
1891	67	2	-	46	19	-	-
1892	60	2	-	41	17	-	-
1893	59	2	-	42	14	-	1
1894	86	2	-	66	18	-	-
1895	76	2	-	58	16	-	-
1896	74	2	-	58	14	-	-
1897	83	1	-	67	15	-	-
1898	80	1	-	61	17	-	-
1899	77	2	-	65	10	-	-
1900	76	2	-	62	12	-	-
1901	82	2	-	69	11	-	-

NOTE: In 1873, cadets were trained by district headquarters. The term of the course was two years until 1884, four years after 1886.

The Prewar Period, 1893-1913

The *honvédség* had been growing steadily, and when in the mid-1890s it was decided to enlarge it still further it was necessary to increase the number of officers and their military knowledge. The officer corps was already 40 percent under strength. It was thought that the shortage could be made up by directing some of the one-year volunteers who had become reserve cadet officers into the regular army and transferring Hungarian-speaking officers from the joint army. The latter move, however, would have further reduced the already small number of Hungarian speaking officers in the joint army. Although 42 percent of the Monarchy's population was from Hungary, only 23 percent of the army officers were. To replace the older officers who had transferred from the joint army into the *honvédség*, the Ludovika Academy was obliged to allow officers who successfully completed their courses to volunteer for service in the joint army.[22]

Once opposition from the joint War Ministry and general staff and from the Austrian National Assembly and government had been overcome, two four-year infantry cadet schools were established, in Pécs and Nagyvárad, and a three-year military secondary school was set up in Sopron.[23] Meanwhile the Ludovika Academy attained the status of a three-year military academy after the pattern of the Theresian Military Academy at Wiener Neustadt. The lion's share of the arranging for the fulfillment of this old desire was done by the general-staff captain Sándor Szurmay at the Hungarian Defense Ministry. Mainly responsible for obtaining royal consent for it was General Géza Fejérváry, who had not initially been friendly to the idea but later gave it his full support and made use of the full confidence the king had in him.[24] From October 1898 until August 18, 1901, the academy contained both students of the old-style four-year officer training course and those of the new academy intake. The former studied at the level of a cadet school and the latter at that of a university. On August 18, 1901, two second lieutenants and eighty cadet warrant officers graduated from the officer training course and thirty-five second lieutenants from the academy course.

The academy had the task over three years of producing infantry and cavalry officers with advanced theoretical training and practical skills.[25] Future infantry and cavalry officers received the same training except that candidates for the cavalry also learned the use of weapons on horseback. There was an intake of one hundred each year, fifty of them eighteen-to-twenty-year-olds who had matriculated from civilian secondary schools and passed an entrance examination and fifty from the three-year military secondary school, including a few who had passed the third of cadet school with marks of "excellent." Their uniforms were like those of infantry officers. On their collars they wore the marks of their proficiency: one gilt stripe signified "good" or "satisfactory" and two "excellent." Little gilt buttons on the stripes, jokingly referred to as "scrambled eggs with buttons," meant outstanding academic achievement. The first- and second-year students wore bayonets, the third-year students swords.

At the end of the third year the students could apply to join one of the infantry or cavalry regiments of the joint army.[26] There were years in which more of the graduating cavalry second lieutenants joined hussar regiments of the joint army than joined those of the *honvédség* (table 2).[27] Thus it came about that between a third and a quarter of the second lieutenants and lieutenants in the hussar regiments of the joint army were officers who had trained at the Ludovika Academy, including seven of the fourteen full lieutenants of the 13th Imperial-and-Royal Hussars. Among the graduates of those years were Jenő Rátz, Vilmos Nagy, Géza Lakatos, Béla Miklós, Géza Heim, Gusztáv Jány, and Ferenc Farkas.

A central officers' course was held at the Ludovika Academy in 1904 to develop and extend the military knowledge of more senior infantry lieutenants and provide guidance for self-training.[28] From 1905 on, however, an officers' school with a curriculum similar to that of the schools of the joint army corps headquarters was formed in every *honvéd* district.

The higher-officers' course of in-service training for around thirty young officers at a time continued in the same form as before in a building erected next to the main academy building.[29] The top six to eight second or full lieutenants in each course were detailed to join the joint army's general-staff college in Vienna.

A field officers' course lasting ten months was set up to broaden the knowledge and capabilities of captains due for promotion to field officer.

TABLE 2
GRADUATES OF THE LUDOVIKA ACADEMY, 1901-18

LIEUTENANTS

YEAR	TOTAL	honvéd Infantry	Cavalry	Artillery	k.u.k. Infantry	Cavalry	ENSIGNS	OTHER
1901	35	24	6	-	4	1	-	1[a]
1902	38	20	10	-	2	6	-	-
1903	53	31	10	-	4	7	-	1[b]
1904	85	43	10	-	18	14	-	-
1905	81	56	14	-	4	7	-	-
1906	91	71	10	-	3	7	-	-
1907	92	62	12	-	4	14	-	-
1908	89	43	19	-	11	16	-	1[a]
1909	92	48	21	-	8	13	-	2[a]
1910	73	34	19	-	5	12	-	1[a]
1911	64	40	17	-	1	6	-	-
1912	75	44	13	-	7	9	-	2[a]
1913	72	50	15	-	-	7	-	-
1914								
August 1	76	50	15	-	3	4	-	4[c]
October 15	86	30	21	35	-	-	-	-
1915								
March 15	96	53	-	43	-	-	-	-
August 18	141	95	-	46	-	-	-	-
1916	199[d]	41[d]	-	-	-	158[d]	-	-
1917								
"Academy Class"	104	62	4	24	5	8	-	1
August 17	122	72	15	32	-	-	3[e]	-
1918	127	75	15	34	-	-	2[f]	1[a]

NOTE: The therm of the course was three years until 1914, variable afterward (see text).

a. Audit Office.
b. Local posting.
c. Commissariat.
d. Held back from earlier years.
e. Artillery.
f. Infantry.

Artillery-officer training was also given, the first academy artillery department being formed in the autumn of 1912.[30] In October 1914 it supplied 43 second lieutenants to the Hungarian artillery, which developed rapidly during wartime. By the end of the war it had raised the latter's complement by 138.

The War, 1914-18

On July 31, 1914, the mobilization of the Monarchy's entire armed forces, including the *honvédség,* was ordered.[31] To supply the increased officer requirements of the mobilized forces, students in the most senior years at the Ludovika Academy and the cadet schools joined active units immediately, the former as second lieutenants and the latter as ensigns. Thus students of the following classes were commissioned as second lieutenants: third-year men with three years' training on August 1, 1914 (76 men); third-year men with two years' training on October 15, 1914 (86 men); second-year men with eighteen months' training on March 15, 1915 (96 men); first-year men with ten months' training on August 18, 1915 (141 men); students in the combined course for those born in 1897, 1898, and 1899 after one year's training on August 18, 1916 (41 men); second-year men with two years' training on August 17, 1917 (122 men); second-year men with two years' training on August 17, 1918 (127 men). The 158 men enrolled during the final years of the cadet schools at Nagyvárad and Pécs, which had been merged with the Ludovika Academy, graduated as ensigns after three years' training on August 18, 1916. A so-called Academy Class was held at the Ludovika in the 1916-17 academic year for reserve ensigns and cadets who had been sent back from the front for training with a view to making them regular officers. From this course 104 students were commissioned as second lieutenants in the autumn of 1917.

Military Collapse and the Hungarian Democratic Republic

The Ludovika Academy was a passive observer of the revolutionary events that began on November 1, 1918.[32] Since the students had not been sworn into actual military service, they were not used as an armed force. Some students who were unable to endure this passive role left the academy on their own initiative and reported for duty with military formations operating in their districts. Some students were released from the academy at their parents' request, and the remainder undertook internal duties and attended occasional lectures.

On November 25, Lieutenant General Lajos Bartha handed over command of the academy to Colonel Aurel Stromfeld of the general staff, who retained it until January 15, 1919. In the early days of December, artillery and engineer academicians of the Wiener Neustadt and the Mödling engineers' military academies and students and academicians of the artillery cadet school in Traiskirchen marched in, led by their teachers under full discipline. Those from Traiskirchen brought all their textbooks and teaching aids and all their equipment apart from their weapons. The newcomers were placed in the appropriate academy classes, a special group being established for the engineers while the cadet-school students from Traiskirchen were placed in the artillery class. It was possible to resume regular instruction in early December, but matters were impeded by guard duty and other internal chores, the care of the horses, and the restlessness of the students. Uneasy about their future and about what was happening to their parents in areas now occupied by foreign forces, they felt helpless at not being able to prevent the armed occupation of their home districts. Mainly because of this unease, the commander of the academy granted everyone leave from December 7, 1918, until January 6, 1919.

The Dictatorship of the Proletariat

The War Commissariat of the Hungarian Soviet Republic formed on March 21, 1919, abolished the academy only on April 12, when the establishment of an officer training course for the Red Army was ordered.[33] According to the decree first-year students were dismissed forthwith, while second-year students were told to choose another career or join the Red Army. Those who did the latter had to complete their studies and say which infantry or cavalry division they wished to be posted to in less than two weeks. The decree ended with a very humanitarian stipulation:

> Those first-year students of the Ludovika Academy and those second-year students choosing other careers who, being from occupied areas, are unable to return to their homes and are, moreover, unable to provide for themselves, may temporarily remain

on the academy premises. The command shall make immediate arrangements for their separate board and lodging and submit a register of names on which the grounds for the provision and the length of time for which it is absolutely necessary shall appear as well.

Some two weeks later this ruling had been amended so that those who remained on the premises had to pay rent and provide some of their food. To do so they had to find work. Most of those who remained reported to the Red Army general headquarters in Gödöllő or to other headquarters, less out of need or conviction than because they were ordered to do so by Stromfeld. The majority of those who did so were appointed "comrade orderlies." They were cordially welcomed everywhere and well treated, being posted in most cases alongside staff officers or subaltern staff officers.

Although a training course for Red Army commanders was set up, an order came on the day it assembled for it to disband, partly because only fifty-one men had volunteered for it and partly because its students were needed at the front.[34] A military-college course beginning on June 15, 1919, was arranged in its stead, those ordered to attend being second-year Ludovika students, first-year men who had entered the academy from cadet schools, and fourth-year students of cadet schools which had been merged into the Ludovika.[35] Of the 270 men in the course, which was the last for two and a half months, 144 were fourth-year cadet-school students. The secret aim of the officers of the department at the Ministry that dealt with training was to have a guard unit at their disposal for an armed counterrevolutionary uprising that they were planning.

At noon on June 24, 1919, the commander of the academy paraded the students and announced that there would be an uprising on that day led by the city commandant, Jozsef Haubrich, to overthrow the present regime, if necessary by armed intervention in which selected units of the Budapest local guard would forcibly suppress the Red Army units that stood by the regime. For this armed action the students of the Ludovika were needed. Those who chose not to participate might leave without prejudice; those who remained under the leadership of their officers would have to be prepared for the possibility of armed conflict. Some two or three students withdrew; the rest took part in the armed action which followed during the course of the afternoon. A detachment went out and occupied the Józsefváros telephone exchange; the rest prepared to defend the academy until further orders and repelled two armed assaults during the afternoon.

The promised general uprising against the regime failed to materialize, however, and the Ludovika students were left on their own. Their commander turned to Haubrich, who instructed them to break off the action and the following morning ordered them to lay down their arms. Having realized that it was pointless to continue the battle, the teachers and students became prisoners of the Red Army and were locked into a large hall at the Maria Theresa Barracks in Üllői Street. They expected the same fate as the Moscow cadets, who had been executed, and this was hinted at by those guarding them.[36] The instructors were sentenced to death, while the students (myself among them) were taken before the revolutionary military court. Stromfeld, the former commander of the academy, who was chief of staff of the Hungarian Red Army at this time, interceded for them, as did the Italian Colonel Guido Romanelli of the Allied Military Mission in Budapest.[37] Subsequently, the death sentences of the instructors were commuted to prison terms of ten to fifteen years. After sixteen days of suspension, the students appeared before the president of the summary court headed by Miklós Kiss, Budapest's city commandant.[38]

Whereas the prosecutor demanded the severest sentences, one of the defense argued that the students had acted under orders and recommended in view of their youth that they be simply kept under strict guard and reeducated as communists. The presiding judge accepted the defense submission, and two days later we were escorted to the former Jesuit house, where for two weeks we attended lectures on Marxism, a view of the world unknown to us and, because of our upbringing, quite alien. There our commander and Ervin Sinkó, one of our lecturers who was a communist, treated us very kindly. From there we were taken to what had been the Ranolder girls' boarding school in Pest, where we were kept under strict guard.

In the meantime a new training course for commanders[39] had been started on July 10 at the Ludovika, on orders from the War Commissariat, for about two hundred men.

The National Government

The participants in this course dispersed when the Romanian forces arrived on August 3. On the very next day former teachers returned, and former students too reported in growing numbers. On August 5 the officers who had been sentenced arrived as well. The former cadet-school students from the schools in Budapest, Nagyszeben, and Temesvár who had taken part in the counterrevolution withdrew to the infantry cadet school at Hüvösvölgy in Budapest on August 12.

On September 18, 1919, the defense minister of the national government ordered the Ludovika Academy to resume functioning.[40] Academicians and students who had served in the Red Army were screened to assess their conduct under the Soviet Republic, particularly their service in the Red Army.[41] The conduct of only three academicians was found to be at fault. One of these went abroad, and the other two were dismissed from the academy. In October 1919 regular instruction began. The first-year class consisted of former fourth-year students at cadet schools and military secondary schools who had also been studying for a secondary-school certificate.[42] The previous first-year men became the new second-year men and the previous second-year men the new third, appointed honorary second-lieutenant academicians.[43] The syllabus for the first year was devised on the basis of a four-year course,[44] and this was the form in which the Ludovika Academy entered a new period in its history that was to last until the spring of 1945.

Of the commanders of the academy up to 1920, Lajos Bartha and Aurel Stromfeld were themselves former students of the Ludovika who had gone on to complete the general-staff training course at the war college in Vienna. The others had been trained in the joint army but had served in the *honvédség* for decades and entirely accepted the Hungarian national education laid down by the Defense Ministry in Budapest. The teachers, too, were until the 1890s drawn from the joint army; after that they were almost exclusively former Ludovika students.

The language of instruction was Hungarian, with an interesting exception which derived from the Hungarian constitution. Associated with Hungary was Croatia, which had a great measure of autonomy. Indeed, there was a separate *honvéd* district headquarters in Zagreb, and the official language of command and training in the four infantry regiments and the regiment of hussars from Croatia was Croatian. A separate class was set up on a regular basis at the Pécs cadet school for students from Croatia. There the various subjects were taught in Croatian, although the students also learned Hungarian and there were one or two German lessons every week as well. Hungarian students at the Ludovika had to learn Croatian, and this situation obtained right up to the collapse of the Monarchy in the autumn of 1918.[45] The famous Yugoslav writer Miroslav Krleza was among those in the Croatian class at the cadet school in Pécs, and from 1910 to 1912 he studied at the Ludovika Academy.[46]

The subjects taught, apart from the purely military subjects, always included the elements of a general education: history, geography, chemistry and physics, higher mathematics, descriptive geometry, legal and political studies, social studies and political economy, and a little French. There was not a word, however, about domestic political issues, the platforms of particular parties, trade unions, the agrarian question, emigration, class structure, or the minorities issue: "A soldier does not engage in politics; his entire conduct is determined by the rules of the service and the official obligations of his calling." Gymnastics, fencing, and sports in general were given suitable emphasis in the curriculum. Even the infantry students and academicians were taught to ride.

During the war the teaching process was impeded by overcrowding. Courses unconnected with the academy, a reserve hospital, in 1918 even a propaganda course, a school for reserve officers, and a volunteer one-year school for Hungarian hussars (attended by Count Mihály Károlyi, later president of the Republic) were all transferred to the Ludovika building.

Conclusion

By way of summary one can say that the Ludovika Academy fulfilled its declared function of providing officer training for a mere fifty years, from 1869 to 1919. It was a matter of developing an army out of nothing and of creating an officer corps out of individuals who represented the extremes of political experience, military knowledge, general education, and scholastic achievement and a wide range of social and religious backgrounds. For instance, officers who had fought on the Hungarian side in the 1848-49 War for Independence encountered officers who had served against them in the imperial army at that time. Officers with several years of college-level military schooling were thrown together with those who had completed only four to six years of primary school and done a military course lasting a few weeks or months. Men from the lower middle classes who had engaged in industry, commerce, or farming found themselves mixing for the first time with sons of the nobility, the officer corps, and high official circles. Followers of the majority Roman Catholic religion encountered practitioners of the Jewish faith. And yet, in the thirty years before World War I there developed an officer corps that could be considered unified. Much of the credit for this belongs to the Ludovika Academy, which increasingly became the intellectual foundation of the officers of the Hungarian army, irrespective of how and where its commanders and teachers had entered the *honvédség*.

All this was accomplished in the face of a top military leadership that feared for the unity of the Monarchy under a ruler who displayed only a gradually decreasing mistrust and within the framework of a paralyzing attitude on the part of the political powers in Austria. These ensured that initially the academy, an institution amounting to a college, could provide only training courses in a limited sphere of military knowledge, from 1884 operate at cadet-school level, and only from the turn of the century provide officer training to a college standard. Consequently it took thirty years for the military training of *honvéd* officers to attain the level of training required of joint-army officers, although the standard then became such that Ludovika graduates with postings in the joint army were considered among the best-trained officers of all: nine of the graduates later returned to command the academy, three became chiefs of the joint general staff, nine became minister of defense, four received the Order of Maria Theresa, and two became prime ministers.

The intellectual and political basis for the training at the Ludovika was dualism. A cardinal element of this was that the supreme commander of the *honvédség* to whom Hungarian soldiers swore allegiance was also the emperor of Austria, a fact that had to be noted, willy-nilly, in the training of its officers although wherever possible it was glossed over and the epithet "royal" given prominence. The text of the oath prescribed for soldiers of the *honvédség* added to the phrase "to fight in a brave and manly fashion wherever the will of His Majesty may desire" the formula "according to the sanctified laws of our country." The general expression "His Majesty" was always replaced by "the Hungarian king," an example being the motto "For King and Country" displayed on the cap. Of course, the idea of an independent Hungarian army was espoused in his heart of hearts by every Ludovika student.

It is staggering what education in fidelity to the king had managed to accomplish in half a century. In 1848 the Hungarian army had marched into battle to a song that begins, "Lajos Kossuth sent news/His regiments have run out./If he sends the same news again/We shall all have to go." Whereas until 1867 Francis Joseph had been the one who had crushed the Hungarian War for Independence, the one who kept the Hungarian people in slavery, and the executioner of the "Thirteen Martyrs of Arad," in 1914 the *honvédség* marched into battle to the same song but replacing Kossuth's name with Francis Joseph's. Despite all the difficulties, the Ludovika trained an enthusiastic, self-sacrificing corps of officers loyal to the king. These officers played a decisive role in ensuring that the troops of the Monarchy, so mixed in terms of national and social origin, stood up in battle for four years against an enemy superior in numbers and weaponry, although the casualties were extremely high. Once considered third-rate, the *honvédség* earned the sincerest praise from the senior commanders of the joint army. Having superciliously looked down on, ignored, or occasionally disparaged the units of soldiers from Hungary and Croatia, they now greeted those deployed near them or under their command amid the grave battles of World War I with the cry, "Thank God, here's the *honvéd*!"

NOTES

1. The basic sources used in the preparation of this essay include *A magyar királyi honvédség története 1868-1918* (hereafter *HT*) (Budapest, 1928-); *A magyar királyi honvéd Ludovika Akadémia története* (hereafter *LT*) (Budapest, 1930); Béla Szinay, "100 év, 10 év," *Ludovikás Levente* (19-30): 1-19; Gyula Kádár, "Ludovika Akadémia," *Budapest*, no. 10 (1979), pp. 14-15; Gábor Bona, *Tábornokok és törzstisztek a szabadságharcban 1848-49* (Budapest, 1983); Tibor Papp, "A magyar honvédség megalakulása a kiegyezés után," *Hadtörténelmi Közlemények*, 1967, pp. 697-708; Ervin Sinko, *Szemben a bíróval* (Budapest, 1983), pp. 47-49; Lajos Kiss, *Vörös város* (Budapest, 1959), pp. 313 and 321-27; József Bolony, *Magyarország kormányai 1848-1975* (Budapest, 1978); *Briefe Kaiser Franz Josephs an Kaiserin Elisabeth*, 2 vols., ed. George Nostitz-Rieneck (Vienna and Munich, 1966).
2. Act VII, 1808.
3. Archivum Regni, Box B, fasc. B ad I, 1829-41, National Archives, Budapest.
4. *1832-36 évi Országgyűlés irományai*, vol. 7/1, p. 447.

5. Memoirs of Lázár Mészáros in *LA*, pp. 289-336.
6. Acts IX, XI, XII and XLI, 1867.
7. *HT*, p. 65.
8. *LA*, pp. 339, 889.
9. Ibid., p. 361; *HT*, p. 72.
10. Act XVI, 1872.
11. *LA*, pp. 366, 374.
12. Ibid., pp. 368, 375.
13. Ibid., p. 372.
14. Ibid., pp. 339, 889.
15. Ibid., 399.
16. Act XXXIV, 1983; *LA*, pp. 366, 397, 398.
17. *LA*, p. 396.
18. Ibid., p. 398.
19. Ibid., p. 875.
20. Ibid., pp. 405-22.
21. Ibid., p. 401.
22. Ibid., p. 488.
23. Ibid., pp. 462-64, 487, 488, 525.
24. Ibid., pp. 472-74, 493, 534, 535, and 536; Act XIII, 1890; Act XIII, 1897.
25. Ibid.
26. Ibid., p. 488.
27. Ibid., pp. 928-43.
28. *HT*, p. 77.
29. *LA*, p. 505.
30. Ibid., pp. 537, 556-59.
31. Ibid., pp. 943-51.
32. Ibid., pp. 663-71.
33. Ibid., pp. 678-79.
34. Ibid., p. 680.
35. Ibid., pp. 688-96.
36. Kiss, *Vörös város*, pp. 313, 321, 326, 327.
37. Ibid., p. 329; *LA*, p. 715.
38. *LA*, p. 712.
39. Ibid., pp. 746-47.
40. Ibid., p. 765.
41. Ibid., p. 765.
42. Ibid., p. 765.
43. Ibid., p. 765.
44. Ibid., p. 760.
45. Ibid., pp. 359, 361, 367, 368.
46. *Briefe*, vol. 1, p. 368; vol. 2, p. 175.

Revolutionary Army, Professional Officers: Active Imperial-and-Royal Officers in the Hungarian Army in 1848-49[1]

Gábor Bona

In the spring of 1849 the Habsburg imperial forces suffered defeat after defeat in battles with the Hungarian revolutionary forces and had to retire to the western borders of Hungary. The military force of the Habsburg Empire was considered one of the strongest on the continent, and few had doubted its quick victory over revolutionary Hungary. Habsburg propaganda had strengthened and the results of the early military operations encouraged this expectation. The imperial divisions invading Hungary in December had had rapid and spectacular successes at the beginning and quickly occupied two-thirds of Hungary's territory. Pest-Buda, the capital, had fallen into Habsburg hands at the beginning of January 1849, and the bulk of the Hungarian army had had to retreat beyond the Tisza while the revolutionary government moved to Debrecen.

The European public had received the news of these events mostly from Austrian sources, as Hungary was almost completely isolated. The official *Army Bulletins* analyzing the events in the Hungarian theater of war not only reported the successes of the imperial army but announced that the Hungarian forces consisted of only a few thousand riffraff rebels. Field Marshal Alfred Windischgrätz, the commander in chief of the imperial forces operating in Hungary, had written in January 1849 that the dissolution of the Hungarian army would take but a few days, and the European press had accepted this opinion. However, it was soon proven wrong.

One of the main reasons for the Hungarian military successes that ensued was that the Hungarian *honvéd* army of 1848-49 was a regular, up-to-date military force organized and led by professional soldiers, former officers of the Habsburg standing army. Even the ethnic origins of these officers were quite curious — one-third of them were not Hungarian. In 1848, even professional officers were influenced by ideas in addition to loyalty to their nation.

In the spring of 1848, revolutions swept all over Europe, including the multinational Habsburg Empire, where bourgeois-democratic, social, and national ideas were spreading in German, Hungarian, Slavic, and Romanian. Habsburg state power was shaken to its foundations. Chancellor Metternich, who personified the absolute, bureaucratic state, had to flee Vienna, leaving chaos in his wake. An armed uprising broke out in the Italian provinces with the aim of a unified Italy. The government's promise to initiate a constitution kept the people of Vienna quiet for a time. A delegation of the Hungarian Diet three hundred strong appeared in Vienna demanding the promulgation of laws passed by the Hungarian legislature that transformed the feudal society into a pluralistic one and the government into a modern parliamentary regime. The court was forced to yield.[3] Ferdinand V, Austrian emperor and king of Hungary, promulgated the new Hungarian constitution in April 1848 and appointed the first Hungarian cabinet responsible to Parliament. It was independent in administration of Hungary's domestic affairs, and its seat was Pest-Buda.

Hungary itself was, however, a multinational country; only about half of its inhabitants were Hungarians. Its Serbian, Romanian, and Slovak inhabitants had their own demands: acknowledgment of their nationhood, a status similar to what the Hungarians were fighting for. The Hungarian government was willing to give to all citizens equal rights regardless of their national origins but wished to preserve the political unity of the state. The politicians of the national minorities were not satisfied with this solution.

The Serbian, Romanian, and, to a lesser degree, Slovak national movements gained strength. The April Laws, which emancipated even non-Hungarian peasants from serfdom, while granting full property rights to former serfs left the system of large estates untouched. As a consequence, seizure of lands occurred in some regions, and the Hungarian government had to employ the military to safeguard the ownership of land. In some places Hungarian and non-Hungarian peasants alike suffered under a Hungarian landowner in these incidents. In areas populated by non-Hungarians, the peasants' class struggle merged into a national one.

The Serbians of southern Hungary and the Serbian guardsmen of the Military Frontier rose up in arms to create an independent entity, the *voivode*, directly subordinate to the imperial government rather than to Hungary. This struggle had a social color too, as the guardsmen wanted freedom from their heavy compulsory military service and other feudal obligations. The Hungarian government sent units of the imperial military garrisoned in Hungary against the rioters. The April Laws made this possible, as they subordinated to the authority of the Hungarian minister of war all forces stationed in Hungary. The armed forces stationed in Hungary amounted to some fifty thousand, two-thirds of them recruited in Hungary. Approximately twenty thousand were deployed in southern Hungary. This number seemed, however, too small, since as early as July 1848 the Serbian rebels had thirty to forty thousand. Some two-thirds of the rebels were ex-servicemen, frontier guardsmen, and volunteers from Serbia. As a consequence, the Hungarian government mobilized part of the National Guard, a militia organized on the pattern of the National Guard of the French Revolution. The government also formed an army of ten thousand volunteers to be organized into ten *honvéd* battalions.

The officers of these ten battalions, organized between the end of May and mid-July, came almost without exception from the Habsburg standing army's active or, to a lesser degree, retired lists. To fill the approximately 260 vacant officer's posts, an announcement in the Hungarian newspapers on May 21 was specifically addressed to the Hungarian officers of the Habsburg army stationed in Hungary. In a few days several hundred applications were received.[2] Not only Hungarian but German, Austrian, Serbian, and Croatian officers of the Habsburg army joined the Hungarian volunteer battalions. Among their motives were having been born in Hungary, having a Hungarian wife, speaking Hungarian, and serving in a regiment of Hungarian recruits. As additional motivation conditions in the Habsburg army should be considered.

Between the end of the Napoleonic Wars and 1848, Austria had participated in no major wars. One of the characteristics of such long periods of peace is the slowing down of promotions and the maintenance of armies' effectives at a minimum level, and this had happened in the Habsburg Empire. The lack of jobs in the peacetime army had hurt many aspiring young men in Hungary, sons of the growing bourgeoisie who were seeking status through an army commission at a time when no new commissions were available. This was the case particularly with young men among the *honoratiores*, professionals without noble status, and the sons of the lesser nobility, a proportionately larger social stratum here than anywhere else in

Europe except parts of Poland. These young people looked to the army for permanent employment and social status to no avail.

More important, however, was the status of the young officer candidates within the army. At the lowest rank of the commissioned hierarchy were the "imperial-and-royal cadets," who, while on active service, had to wait years for a commission.[3] Even when they were appointed to the lowest grade of the officer corps, their salaries were extremely low. They were also subject to severe restrictions on their personal lives. Only one-third of the officers were permitted to marry, and these were required to find a bride whose family was willing and able to deposit the *caucio*, the commitment to pay the expenses required by the social status of the officer but not covered by his salary. Before 1848 it was possible to buy the next higher rank from the Treasury or a comrade for an officially prescribed price. This practice was abolished, but the system of patronage could not be eliminated and continued to breed discontent.

On the eve of the 1848 revolution, then, there was tension among the officers of the Habsburg army, especially the young ones, whatever their nationality, and a demand was being voiced for reform. This does not mean that the majority of the multinational officer corps would not have been loyal to the Habsburg dynasty. After all, these officers were themselves frequently the sons of officers, and at the military academies they had been taught in the same spirit. The emperor's person and the dynasty seemed pure and inviolable even in the eyes of most of those who were dissatisfied with their lot; it was not the monarch but the government that they blamed for their troubles. The main impetus to change was the increasing power of bourgeois and nationalist ideologies. Although not unknown in the army, until 1848 these ideologies had scarcely affected the loyalties of the officer corps. The dynasty had introduced countermeasures: thus, troops were stationed not in their native countries but in other provinces of the Empire, and units were almost always on the move from one garrison to another. This system precluded friendly relations between the army and the local inhabitants or the officer and local political movements and leaders, on the time-honored *divide et impera* principle of tyrants. In the event of a social or national uprising, troops of another nationality would be ready to act. Although during the thirties and forties some revolutionary organizations — Polish, Pan-Slavic, Italian — had been uncovered among a few dozen young officers, they had not affected the army as a whole.

In May of 1848, however, several hundred Habsburg professional officers asked for transfers to the Hungarian army then being formed. Yet this did not necessarily represent any revolutionary change. The new army was being formed under the supervision of the Hungarian government and with the monarch's permission, and to join it officers required only the permission of the Ministry of War in Vienna. Often they were commissioned at higher ranks and received higher salaries. It was known that this new military force would be Hungarian in character and sworn to defend the Hungarian constitution at the same time as the monarch. This situation was not unique, for in Vienna and all over Austria at the time there were organized volunteer rifle [*Jaeger*] battalions whose officers also came from the Habsburg army. Those who joined the *honvéd army* might have thought that they were going to fight against the Serbian uprising, which was regarded as a revolt even by the court in Vienna.

By September the political situation changed dramatically. Field Marshal Radetzky had defeated the Italians, and Windischgrätz had suppressed Prague revolt. The Viennese court, encouraged by these victories of the counterrevolution, moved to curtail the democratic reforms that Hungary had achieved in April. It knew very well that the abolition of the feudal system could not be undone, but it wanted to limit the wide-ranging civil rights and the rather substantial domestic autonomy of the country and was determined to use military force if necessary. The powerful camarilla, consisting of the Habsburg archdukes, leading generals, and various court officials, took control. It charged Josip Jelačić, governor of Croatia, with the defeat of the Hungarian "revolutionary party" by military force. To the same end the Habsburg court concluded alliances with the leaders of the Romanian, Slovak, and Serbian national movements within Hungary, promising them certain rights for their national minority groups. The camarilla acted in complete secrecy. The court had to reckon with the moral aspect of its covert actions; after all, the monarch had promulgated the Hungarian April Laws and taken an oath on the new constitution. These historical facts could not so soon be openly repudiated. Jelačić's possible defeat also had to be taken into account. Nonetheless, in September the counterrevolution was launched against Hungary.

In mid-September, Jelačić invaded Hungary with an army of forty thousand consisting of Habsburg troops stationed in Croatia and a great number of frontier guardsmen. The Hungarian government sent regular troops against the aggressors: two *honvéd* battalions and various national guard units were dispatched. A curious situation evolved: the combatants were troops and officers of the same sovereign. The perplexity was greater in the Hungarian camp than among Jelačić's troops. The leader of the Hungarian contingent, Count Ádám Teleky, was a general in the standing army. He sent a special military envoy to Jelačić to ask about his aims and his credentials. At the same time, two officers of the 60th Wasa Infantry Regiment were sent to Vienna to clarify the orders of Theodor Latour, the minister of war. But these actions did not solve any problems. The two officers were not admitted to see the minister; Jelačić received the Hungarian envoys and hinted that he had followed the command of an even higher authority when he crossed the border of Hungary but refused to demonstrate the authenticity of his orders.

The numerical superiority of Jelačić's forces and the political uncertainty forced Teleky to withdraw without a fight. The Hungarian government urged him and his successor in the theater, Lieutenant General János Móga, another Habsburg army general, to be faithful to their oaths and stop the invaders. This order was reconfirmed by Archduke Stefan, palatine of Hungary. Shortly thereafter, the palatine fled to Vienna, and Móga could do nothing else but deploy his troops in a defensive position on September 28 at Pákozd, 40 km west of Budapest. On September 29 Jelačić was defeated in the Battle of Pákozd and retreated in the direction of Vienna.

Unaware of his defeat, the court endorsed his action, and royal decrees of October 3 ordered the dissolution of the Hungarian parliament and ministry and appointed Jelačić governor of Hungary with full powers. Drafted by the camarilla, these ordinances were rejected as unlawful by the Hungarian parliament. This response was revolutionary. A new government with absolute powers was created by election from among the members of the parliament with Lajos Kossuth as president. It was he who began preparations for the defense of the country.

The main task was to organize an effective army to block the expected attack by the Habsburg army. Besides the existing ten *honvéd* battalions, the basis of this Hungarian revolutionary army was to be that part of the Habsburg army that would come over to the revolutionary side. Some of these standing army units were garrisoned on and recruited from Hungarian territory, while others, responding to the call of the fatherland, had returned home from Bukovina, Galicia,

Bohemia, and Austria. The total of these regular troops was twenty-three battalions of line infantry, four Székely frontier battalions, and nine hussar regiments. The effectivenes amounted to approximately thirty thousand. Among them were two battalions recruited from northern Italy. The rest of the troops who sided with the revolutionary government were predominantly Hungarians whose new loyalties may be easily understood. It is interesting that of about fifteen hundred professional officers of the Habsburg army, 15 percent arrived at the same decision.

To trace the evolution of these officers' motivations, it is necessary to refer to the events. By October of 1848, they had fought first against the Serbian rebels and then against Jelačić for nearly six months under the command of the Hungarian minister of war. They had shed their blood, received decorations, and been promoted to higher ranks as rewards for their gallantry. They had done their best to defend the prerogatives of the sovereign as well as the rights of Hungary and the unity of the Empire. Generally they had nothing to do with politics and did not know that Jelačić and the Serbian rebels were supported with money and supplies by the Ministry of War in Vienna. Honest and loyal, they could not follow the political maneuvers of the court. During these last six months these professional officers of the standing army had become comrades-in-arms of the officers and men of the Hungarian National Guard, *honvéd*, and volunteer units, themselves mostly former professional Habsburg officers. All hated the common enemy and most of all the Serbian volunteers, whose cruelty was felt by the civilian population as well.

These officers could not understand why a proclamation of the emperor at the beginning of October declared them rebels and their enemies the emperor's friends. This, in their eyes, was far from honest, and therefore even if a shift to the left had occurred in Hungary they would have obeyed the orders of the revolutionary government. But the Hungarian parliament was also loyal to the crown, and no one was yet talking about dethroning the monarch or establishing a republic and independence. Even Kossuth himself blamed the camarilla rather than the sovereign for the confrontation. The behavior of the highest-ranking officer had a very important effect on the state of mind of the officers. The Hungarian minister of war remained in office after October, as did two of the four leaders of the Hungarian high district command. A great many divisional, brigade, and other commanders also remained with the revolutionary army.

The Habsburg court waged a massive disinformation campaign to mislead the Hungarian officers. Thus, after the October break, the sovereign sent an order-of-the-day to his "favorite Hungarian minister of war," and this meant that the minister's activities were acknowledged as legal. This fact was widely publicized in the press. Even in the highest Hungarian circles it was thought that if the minister, Mészáros, was proclaimed legal the whole Hungarian government could claim to be legal as well. The officers hoped for a peaceful agreement between the monarch and the government and did not want to give up their positions in the *honvéd* army. Most of them indeed remained in it; only a few hundred obeyed the call to return to the imperial flag. In remaining, the Hungarian officers were motivated by national sentiments, while the Germans, Poles, and Italians thought that the events in Hungary would help in the formation of their own nation-states as well.

The outbreak of the Vienna revolution on October 6, 1848, prevented the imperial government from launching a new attack against the Hungarian revolution until December. During this period, a *honvéd* army of approximately one hundred thousand was organized. Units that had come over from the imperial army formed the nuclei of the new battalions. The training camps, the drill sergeants, and most of the officers also came from the imperial standing army. The rapidly growing Hungarian army offered opportunities for promotion and for the use of their knowledge and abilities, neither of which advantages was available for them in the Habsburg army. The Hungarian *honvéd* army was organized under the direction of officers of the Habsburg army and on the model of that army. These officers were not only well trained but experienced in everyday military practice. Thus the problem of professionalism common to new revolutionary armies was solved. At the same time, an army fighting for a new social and political order and for national aims must alter the thinking of officers from the old army.

In Hungary the revolution had been led by the liberal gentry. Its purposes — the buorgeois transformation of society without severe harm to the financial and political status of the nobility and autonomy for Hungary within the Habsburg Monarchy — had already been attained. Most of the nobility wished to stop the revolution at this stage. So far as the war was concerned, they considered it only self-defense, the protection of their achievements against Jelačić in September and against Windischgrätz in December. They did not envisage a revolutionary war or a war for independence. They wanted to win only to force the sovereign to recognize the April Laws and had not the slightest intention of seceding from the Empire. This program was readily accepted by the former officers of the imperial army. Problems arose, however, when the leftists of the revolution began to come to power. Following the offensive of Windischgrätz in December, the press and the public began to urge social reforms, the overthrow of the Habsburg dynasty, the establishment of a republic, and separation from the Empire. These ideas were dreaded by these officers because of their loyalty to the dynasty, their education, and their family background. This fear — combined with the defeats on the battlefield — 'as the main motivating force behind the resignations at the end of December and at the beginning of January 1849 of approximately one-third of the former imperial officers, some five hundred men. In order to put an end to the resignations, which could have caused the total disintegration of the army, General Görgey had to issue a proclamation explaining the legitimacy of Hungary's defensive war and denouncing all premature republican hopes. It was mostly due to Görgey's action that the thousand remaining ex-imperial professionals in the Hungarian *honvéd* army remained loyal to the end to the cause of liberty and independence.

The Constitution of Olmütz was imposed by Francis Joseph I in March of 1849. It suppressed the constitution and autonomy of Hungary and decreed it a province of the Empire. The Hungarian parliament responded by dethroning the Habsburg dynasty and proclaiming the country's independence. Thus was the war transformed from a struggle of self-defense into a war of independence. The revolution now abandoned its emphasis on "legality." Those officers who had previously served in the imperial army lost the legal basis of their service in the Hungarian one. The proclamation of independence meant that the dual oath of the officers of loyalty to the monarch and the Hungarian constitution was finally destroyed because it contained an irreconcilable contradiction. The internal logic of events caused soul-searching among the officers and resulted in quick changes of mind. The majority could not accept the dethronement but had no choice but to continue the struggle. A quantitative assessment of the officer corps of the Hungarian revolutionary army (table 1) shows that 992 former regular Habsburg officers fought through the entire revolutionary war. They constituted approximately 10 percent of the army's officers, two-thirds of its generals, and half of its colonels, lieutenant colonels, and majors. (Forty percent of the higher-ranking *honvéd* officers, from majors to generals, were either retired regular officers or officers who had left active service before the revolution of 1848.)

TABLE 1

RANKS OF FORMER HABSBURG OFFICERS IN THE HUNGARIAN ARMY AND PROPORTIONS OF TOTAL

	Rank in the Habsburg Army	Rank in the Hungarian Army	Total of Said Rank in Hungarian Army
General	2	22	34
Colonel	1	56	105
Lieutenant Colonel	6	76	190
Major	12	230	523
Captain	177	441	2,200
1st Lieutenant	238	62	?
2d Lieutenant	556	5	?
◊ Total	992	992	App. 9,000

TABLE 2

NATIONALITIES OF FORMER HABSBURG OFFICERS IN THE HUNGARIAN ARMY

Nationality	Number	Percent
Hungarian	645	65.1
German and Austrian	179	18.0
Serbian and Croatian	38	3.8
Polish	18	1.8
Italian	13	1.3
Other	42	4.3
Soldier dynasty	33	3.3
Unknown	24	2.4
◊ Total	992	100.0

The nationality distribution of the 992 (table 2) shows that nearly two-thirds of them were Hungarians. Of those of German origin, two-thirds were born in Hungary; with the exception of the Saxons of Transylvania, the Germans of Hungary were ardent supporters of the Hungarian War for Independence. One-third of the Germans and Austrians were born in Austria, Bohemia, and Galicia and in various parts of Germany. It is very interesting that more than twenty of this latter group belonged to the aristocracy, including Count Károly Leiningen-Westerburg, Baron Emil Uchtritz-Fuger, Baron Ernő Hugel, Count Károly Buttler, Count Arthur Scherr-Thoss, Baron Arthur Meerscheid-Hülessen, and Baron Albert Leutsch. Most of them had family connections in Hungary, such as a Hungarian wife or an estate or both; the majority were zealous supporters of the unification of Germany, and this is why they joined the Hungarian — anti-Habsburg — revolution. On October 20, 1848, at the time of the Vienna revolution, Count Leiningen wrote, "Vienna is the place where Germany's fate will be decided, and I am overjoyed that, in contrast to others, I do not have to fight against my fatherland."[4]

The relatively large number of Serbian and Croatian regular officers in the Hungarian revolutionary army can be explained by the fact that one-fourth of the officer corps of the imperial army were South Slavs. Many of them recognized that the real enemy of their own national movements was not the Hungarian revolution but Viennese absolutism. The main motivation of the Italian and Polish officers was the affinity of the Hungarian revolution with their own national movements and antimonarchistic sentiment. Alessandro Monti, commander of the Italian legion in the Hungarian War for Independence, had been a cavalry captain in the imperial army who had gone over to the side of the Italian insurgents in the spring of 1848 and had come to Hungary as special military envoy of the Piedmont government.

A very interesting group of former Habsburg officers of the *honvéd* army was a characteristic outgrowth of the Monarchy. This is the group of officers from so-called soldiers' dynasties. This term covers officers whose nationality is impossible to determine. For example, the son of a Hungarian officer and an Italian mother born in Galicia and educated in the military academy at Graz was completely unable to say what his nationality was; he could choose on the basis of which of the influences he met with was the stronger. Such cases were common in the Empire for some two hundred years. This stratum of society — soldiers and administrators — had been gradually developing since the middle of the eighteenth century, and the standing army, with its institutionalized training of officers, was its breeding ground. Thousands of officers and officials knew as their fatherland the Monarchy as a whole rather than one or another of its component countries. Their mother tongue was German, and for them patriotism was loyalty to the ruling dynasty. In 1848, when the power of the Habsburg Monarchy was shaken and the center of interest shifted from Vienna to Pest-Buda, this stratum lost its footing, and many of its members sided with the Hungarian revolution.

NOTES

1. This paper is a summary of my book *Tábornokok és törzstisztek a szabadságharcban 1848-1849* (Budapest, 1983). Bibliography and archival sources can be found in that book.
2. The surviving applications for leave are in the custody of the National Archives, Military Council of the National Guards 1848.
3. On the basis of the *Militär Schematismus für des k.k. Heer* (Vienna, 1825-48).
4. Henrik Marczali, *Gróf Leiningen-Westerburg Károly honvéd tábornok levelei és naplója 1848-1849* (Budapest, 1900), pp. 30-31.

Social Origins, Selection, and Training of the Officer Corps in Hungary after the Ausgleich, 1867-82

Tibor Hajdú

It is commonly held that the Hungarians have always been a nation of proud warriors, born to ride and fight on horseback and little inclined to settle down and work hard. While this may have been true of them in the past, after the Turkish danger had diminished and artillery and infantry had become more important than light cavalry, the military profession gradually became less and less attractive even to the traditional noble warrior class. Certain social changes fostered this tendency. In eighteenth-century Hungary, depopulated and devastated by the Turkish wars, a nobleman could easily obtain land. When Hungary became an integral part of the Habsburg Monarchy, there was no longer any independent Hungarian government or army in which Hungarian boys could have military careers in a national context.[1] The military profession simply no longer appealed to Hungarian youth.

At the outbreak of the revolution of 1848, there was a great shortage of officers.[2] After the suppression of the revolution, the number of Hungarian officers diminished even further. By 1860, only 6.6 percent of the generals and 6 percent of the colonels on active service in the Habsburg army were Hungarians, while among the retired officers these proportions were 6.7 and 8.5 respectively.[3] In the same year, in the hussar regiments, the typically Hungarian branch, as many as 28 percent of the officers were Hungarians. In the infantry regiments, however, they amounted to only approximately 6-7 percent, and in the special branches such as artillery and engineers the proportions were even smaller. The decline in the number of Hungarian officers was due more to the misgivings of the Hungarians vis-á-vis the dynasty than to discrimination.[4] The nationality of two well-known generals who joined the Habsburg army in the fifties, Baron Géza von Fejérváry and Anton von Galgótzy, for example, did not hinder their extraordinary advancement.

In the year prior to the *Ausgleich* of 1867, 7 percent of the generals and 6 percent of the colonels on active service (and 6.4 percent of the generals and 8.7 percent of the colonels on the retired list) were Hungarians. Thus the number of Hungarian officers had reached its nadir about 1860 and remained stabilized for the coming decade. Approximately 33 percent of the hussar officers were Hungarians, but their increase was counterbalanced by the very low percentage even in the other cavalry regiments (*Kürassier* and dragoons).

After the *Ausgleich*, a slow reconciliation took place between the emperor and the Hungarian nation as the hopes of the *Ausgleich*-makers — Deák and Andrássy — were subjected to a long series of accommodations.[6] The old Hungarian dream of an independent army was formally realized but at first took a distorted form. A national army without artillery or technical branches, without a military academy (not even military bands were allowed), openly treated as a second-line force, and supervised by the hostile Vienna generalcy remained in its first decade anything but an object of national pride:

> . . . the joint defense minister, Franz von John, sent a circular instructing the military commands to ignore orders from the Hungarian ministry; on the day of Andrássy's appointment, Archduke Albrecht, commander in chief of the Monarchy's military forces, issued an order stating that all endeavors to separate the regiments on a nationality basis should be decisively thwarted. Thus the Hungarian Ministry of Defense was established, but it remained unclear how far its authority extended, what kinds of matters it could decide upon, and, most important, whether it would have command of any forces.[7]

Andrássy, severely criticized both by the generals in Vienna and by patriotic Hungarians, did his best for the *honvédség* (a name inherited from the 1848 revolutionary army). Before drafting his plans he consulted the *honvéd* commanders of 1848-49: General György Klapka, Major I. Ivánka, and others. He would have liked to have Klapka as his minister of defense, and Klapka indeed helped him by taming the parliamentary left during the army debates. The Austrian generals, however, would not hear of Klapka. Friedrich Prinz von Liechtenstein, commander of all troops in Hungary, announced that he would retire if "the traitor" were appointed to any rank.[8] In the end Andrássy kept the Ministry of Defense for himself, until 1871 endeavoring to give it a national character. Under him its staff was predominantly civilian and thus depended more on the parliament in Pest than on the generals in Vienna.[9] His successors remained civilian politicians up to 1884, when with the appointment of General Fejérváry a new, non-"48" officer era began and the Ministry of Defense became more integrated with the military administration of the Monarchy.

The numerous *"honvéd* associations" organized by officers of the *honvéd* army of 1848 demanded commissions and a decisive role for revolutionary veterans in the new *honvéd* army. The Andrássy cabinet forbade them to interfere in military matters, politics, or anything else beyond their legitimate charitable function.[10] To disarm the manifest popular aversion to the new army, Andrássy did commission as many revolutionary officers as possible, but he could not recommission generals. Two or three years after the *Ausgleich* he retired most of the old lieutenants, who, being on the average fifty years old, were not very useful for commanding platoons in any case. In its first years, the *honvéd* army had only two generals on active service: Eduard Gräf, commander of the Kolozsvár *honvéd* district (one of seven such districts), a *Kaisertreu* Transylvanian German nobleman, and Archduke Joseph, a thirty-five-year-old lieutenant general who was appointed commander in chief of the *honvéd* army by Francis Joseph I and remained in the post until 1905. Of active colonels, 7 were from the revolutionary army of 1848 and 4 from the Habsburg army. Of 14 lieutenant colonels, 11 were revolutionary veterans, as were 42 of the 71 majors. Of 88 captains 1st-class, 35 were revolutionary veterans, while 39 came from the Habsburg army and 14 from the retired list. Similarly, of 29 captains 2d-class, 18 were veterans, of 176 first lieutenants, 65, and of 189 sub-lieutenants, 56.[11]

The *honvéd* army contained officers who had once fought against each other. Several of the colonels had been imprisoned after the revolution and spent six or seven years in Olmütz prison or elsewhere; among these were János Máriássy, János Horváth, and Eduard Czillich. Andrássy himself had been a colonel in 1848-49 and was hanged in effigy. His adjutant, Major Count Schweinitz, had served in 1849 as a young lieutenant and guarded the imprisoned freedom fighters in the Arad fortress, where many of them had been hanged.[12] This strange situation did not cause major friction. Those who joined the army took the reconciliation with Francis Joseph as seriously as did the latter himself.

Approximately 10 percent of the *honvéd* officers were Croats. In autonomous Croatia the *honvéd* units served under Croatian command and with Croatian as the language of command. Of the senior officers, about a third were Germans or of German origin. Some of the latter were veterans of the revolution, such as Czillich, or were part of the Hungarian gentry. Approximately 4 percent were middle-class Slovaks, among them Sztanko, Janik, and Halmay-Holoska. Only half of the senior *honvéd* officers were of Hungarian nationality. Whereas men of Romanian, Serbian, and Ruthenian nationalities together composed a quarter of the enlisted men, only a few of the officers were of these nationalities.

All these factors, combined with poor equipment and deficient training, made the *honvéd* army neither equal with the imperial forces nor popular in Hungary. Although Hungarian aristocrats did not seek *honvédség* commissions for their sons, there were many aristocrats among the senior officers. Major Count L. Vay, Archduke Joseph's adjutant, had fought in 1848 under the national banner and after 1849 had been exiled for many years. The gentry, having played a prominent role in 1848, had its share of the new *honvéd* army during its first years, when it constituted the majority of the senior officers.[13] After a few years, however, there were remarkable changes in the *honvéd* officer corps. The old veterans of the revolution faded away, and the influx of officers from the joint army was reduced because of a shortage of officers in that army. Therefore, throughout the seventies, rather liberal methods in the selection and training of *honvéd* officers prevailed.

Until 1872-73, young *honvéd* officers were trained in six-week courses organized at the headquarters of the district commands. The nobility showed less and less interest every year in a *honvéd* officer's career, and this was true of the Austrian nobility as well. Even the members of the lesser gentry competing for civil service posts were not inclined to send their sons to serve in the *honvéd* army, for military salaries compared unfavorably with their equivalents in the civil service. Whereas in Austria the middle class filled the positions abandoned by the nobility, in Hungary the industrial, commercial, and professional middle classes were not interested in military careers. Men of ambition and talent had so many opportunities in civilian life after the *Ausgleich* that they did not choose to invest the time and effort even to become reserve officers by attending the same six-week training courses.[14] Consequently, the *honvéd* authorities had to accept as an officer candidate almost anyone who wished to become an officer and had the minimal qualifications to do so. Troop commanders were ordered to identify the recruits who seemed suitable for officer training.[15] On the one hand, this system was more democratic than the previous one; on the other hand, it was difficult to obtain satisfactory results with such mixed groups of candidates as the *honvéd* academy in Pest had in its first one-year course in 1872-73. The academy was not yet the well-organized and well-run institution of higher learning that the Ludovika Academy became.[16] The cadets were mostly grown men who, having failed to finish high-school, were trying in vain to secure for themselves some gainful employment. Even in the academic year of 1879-80, of the 141 entering cadets only 27 had had a full high-school education, and 7 had had only a few years' education in a village elementary school.[17]

In 1873, an eight-month preparatory class, including some German-language instruction, was established for candidates who had not finished high school. Only 60-80 percent (and sometimes fewer) of the cadets passed the preparatory school examination.[18] In 1880, the commander of the academy had to ask the *honvéd* district commands not to nominate for admission "youngsters who have had fewer than four high-school classes or have barely an elementary-school education and are mostly artisans' apprentices, except when they have shown outstanding talent and comportment during long service and have the character appropriate to an officer." To do otherwise "would undermine officer corps authority and alienate the cultivated classes from an officer's career."[19] Three years later, Francis Joseph I himself summoned a conference on the improvement of *honvéd* officers' training. The minister of defense, G. Ráday, admitted that "the question of officers' replacement is one of the darkest questions of the future" and that, in contrast to the joint-army academies, "the Ludovika Academy is full of sons of shopkeepers and artisans, and there are even seventeen or eighteen peasant boys." In answer to Francis Joseph's question why the *honvéd* cadet level was lower than that of the Austrian *Landwehr*, the minister said simply, "In Hungary there is no middle class."[20] After that meeting, changes were made in *honvéd* officer selection and training under Francis Joseph's personal supervision.[21]

The late seventies were the most difficult years in *honvéd* officer selection and training; the revolutionary veterans had retired, and neither the new officers nor those transferred from the joint army were the best material. These years offered an opportunity for talented outsiders too. The later Minister of Defense (1910-17), General Samu Hazai, son of a Jewish liquor manufacturer, was recruited for a *honvéd* battalion, sent to the Ludovika Academy, and graduated in 1824. Later only a small number of Jews were commissioned, both in the *honvéd* and the Joint Army, not on racist grounds — for it was still possible for them to be reserve officers — but because they were thought inapt for professional and social reasons.

During these years the *honvéd* army included only a thousand to eleven hundred professional officers, many fewer than the twelve thousand on the active list of the joint army, which after Königgrätz was transformed into a mass army based on general conscription on the Prussian model. In fact, the joint army had more officers of Hungarian nationality (nearly a thousand) than the *honvéd*. Although research in this field is not yet complete, it is safe to say that no more than seven hundred of the *honvéd* army's officers (70 percent) were native Hungarians. In the joint army, however, the percentage of Hungarians rose only slowly, in 1911 reaching 9.7 percent,[22] not much more than the 6-8 percent of the sixties.

The overwhelming majority of the Hungarian boys of noble origin who joined the army in the 1870s went to the joint-army academies and cadet schools. Poorer Hungarian boys were admitted to these schools less frequently than to the *honvéd* schools. Approximately half of the thousand Hungarian officers served in the cavalry, especially in the joint-army hussars, where even at the end of the nineteenth century 62 percent of the officers were noblemen while only 22 percent of the whole professional joint-army officer corps was of noble origin.[23] Advancement was more rapid in the cavalry than in any other branch except of course, the staff.

The Habsburg military leadership did not discriminate against Hungarians, but while the majority of hussar lieutenants and captains were Hungarians, among senior officers they remained in the minority. This was not, however, because of bias. It was embarrassing to the army command and the government that seven out of ten officers were Germans and only one Hungarian. The regime wished to attract more Hungarian noblemen to the army, at least to fill the posts in the hussar regiments, where they did not even have to learn the *Regimentssprache*. But Hungarians were inclined to quit the army after they had served the obligatory twelve years to marry and to assume the distinguished title of retired or reserve hussar captain or first lieutenant. (One might wonder, however, whether the comparatively small number of higher-ranking Hungarian officers was the cause or the effect of this early retirement.) The greater numbers of Hungarians in the joint-army schools and academies compared with those who continued in service also testify to this fact. In 1872-75, 13-14 percent of the cadets at Wiener Neustadt and in the technical academy were Hungarians.[24]

A Hungarian gendarmerie was organized in 1881 as a part of the *honvéd* army.[25] At the start (1881-86), not counting Croats, 70 percent of the gendarme officers were Hungarians and 20 percent of German origin. Only 2.2 percent were Romanians, Slovaks, and Ruthenians. A number of former noncommissioned officers were commissioned in the gendarmerie, a practice rare in the other branches at the time. In fact, 24 percent of the gendarme officers belonged to this group and some of them advanced to the rank of colonel. On the other hand, almost 40 percent were of noble origin.[26] The commissioned former noncommissioned officers were mostly Germans, the nobles mostly poor Székely from Transylvania or other parts of the country.

In the *honvéd* army active and reserve officers were trained together, and their social backgrounds were similar. In the joint-army officer corps, however, after the one-year reserve officer training course was instituted in 1869, there was a great difference in social background and status between active and reserve officers. In the initial years of 1869-75, 27 percent of the reserve officers of the joint army came from Hungary, more than half of these certainly being Hungarians. The proportion of Hungarians among the reserve officers rapidly came to surpass that among active officers.[27] A striking difference developed between the proportions of Jewish active and reserve officers. While Slavs and Romanians were underrepresented even in the reserve officer corps, their proportion in the reserve was greater than in the active officer corps.[28]

NOTES

1. For more details, see Tibor Hajdú, in *East Central European Society in World War I*, ed. Béla K. Király, Nándor F. Dreisziger, and Albert A. Nofi (New York, 1985), pp. 112-23.

2. See Gábor Bona in this volume and his book *Tábornokok és törzstisztek a szabadságharcban 1848-49* (Budapest, 1983).

3. *Militär-Schematismus der Österreichischen Kaiserthumes für 1860-61* (Vienna, 1861).
4. Julius von Lustig-Prean, *Zur Geschichte der Neustadter* (Vienna, 1926), p. 7.
5. *Militär-Schematismus der Österreichischen Kaiserthumes für 1866* (Vienna, 1866).
6. For a recent summary of Andrássy's fight for a Hungarian army, see Gunther E. Rothenberg, "The Military Compromise of 1868 and Hungary," in *The Crucial Decade: East Central European Society and National Defense, 1859-1870*, ed. Béla K. Király (New York, 1984), pp. 519-32.
7. Zoltán Szász, "The Founding of the *Honvédség* and the Hungarian Ministry of Defense, 1867-70," in Király, *The Crucial Decade*, p. 535.
8. Ede Wertheimer, *Gróf Andrássy Gyula élete és kora*, vol. 1 (Budapest, 1910), p. 429.
9. Vera Székely, ed., *A központi államigazgatás tisztségviselői a dualizmus korában*, vol. 1, *Magyar Királyi Honvédelmi Minisztérium* (Budapest, 1979).
10. Endre Kovács, ed., *Magyarország története*, 10 vols. (Budapest, 1979), 6:792, 815.
11. Based on the data of Zsigmond Mikár, ed., *A magyar királyi honvédség schematismusa* (Pécs, 1870).
12. Ödön Egervári, *M. kir. honvéd törzstisztek albuma* (Pest, 1870); Bona in this volume.
13. Egervári, *Honvéd törzstisztek albuma*; Bona in this volume; official rank lists.
14. Tibor Papp,"A magyar honvédség megalakulása a kiegyezés után 1868-1890," *Hadtörténelmi Közlemények*, 1967, no. 2; Tibor Hajdú, "Az értelmiség számszerű gyarapodásának következményei az első világháború előtt és után," *Valóság*, 1980, no. 7. Fejérváry even voiced this opinion in his parliamentary speech on January 26, 1889 (quoted in the official biography published in Pozsony in 1901 for the fiftieth year of his career as an officer, p. 139).
15. Papp, "A magyar honvédség."
16. See Kálmán Kéri in this volume.
17. Papp, "A magyar honvédség"; cf. Pál Biró, *A m. kir. Honvédelmi Minisztérium működése az 1877-1890 években* (Budapest, 1891). Biró served as head of section in the Ministry of Defense.
18. Biró, *Honvédelmi Minisztérium*, p. 65; cf. László Dezséry Bachó, ed., *A m. kir. Honvéd Ludovika Akadémia története* (Budapest, 1930).
19. Bachó, *A Honvéd Ludovika Akadémia*, p. 383.
20. Ibid., p. 392.

21. Hajdú, "Az értelmiség számszerű gyarapodásának következményei," p. 25.
22. *Militär-statistisches Jahrbuch für des Jahr 1911* (Vienna, 1912).
23. Karl Kandelsdorfer, "Der Adel im k.u.k. Offizierscorps," in *Streffleurs Militärische Zeitschrift* (Vienna, 1897), p. 249.
24. *Militär-Statistisches Jahrbuch für das Jahr 1875* (Vienna, 1878), pp. 131-135.
25. Loránd Preszly, *A csendőrség úttörői* (Budapest, 1926).
26. Ibid.
27. *Militär-Statistisches Jahrbuch*, pp. 121-27.

The Training of Polish Officers, 1765-1830

Jerzy Cytowski

The first proposals for institutions for military training appeared in Poland as early as the sixteenth century in the writings of Andrzej Frycz-Modrzewski, Szymon Marycjusz, and many others, among them Łukasz Górnicki, Bartosz Paprocki, Józef Wereszczyński, Piotr Grabowski, Jan Tarnowski, and Błażej Lipowski.[1] The great Polish writers Jan Kochanowski and Mikołaj Rej also advocated the preparation of youth for the defense of their country. In the course of the seventeenth century, the need for a military training system gradually gained wider acceptance in the light of the numerous wars of the period, changes in the organization of foreign armies and in the conduct of warfare, and the establishment of the first military schools in many other countries.[2]

The proposal of the establishment of a military school in Poland was included in *pacta conventa* of a series of elected kings beginning with Henryk Walezjusz,[3] and some of them, for example, Sigismund II Waza, Władysław IV, and Jan III Sobieski, tried without success to implement it. Both electors of Saxony, August II and August III, committed themselves to establish such a school but failed to do so. It was only the banished king Stanisław Leszczyński who, in 1737, founded at Lunéville, in France, a military academy in which Poles were given an opportunity to enroll.[4] But Lunéville was too distant and the number of Polish and Lithuanian graduates (167) too small for the school to have any influence on the standards of training of Polish officers. At the same time, in 1740, Stanisław Konarski founded the Collegium Nobilium in Warsaw, which, under the patronage of August III, fulfilled the function of a military academy.[5] Because of its very selective admissions policy, however, it was not in a position to influence the qualifications of the officer cadre in any significant way.

The Knights' School, 1765-94

The first military school in Poland, the Knights' School, was found in Warsaw in 1765 by Stanisław II August Poniatowski. In the *Articuli pactorum conventorum* issued by the king on September 7, 1764, he stated that "we decide to establish a knights' school for the young and to see that it trains them well," and this did not remain merely a promise.[6] The school was named His Majesty's and the Polish Republic's Academy for the Noble Cadet Corps or The Knights' School for His Majesty's and the Polish Republic's Cadets,[7] and the duality of its name found its reflection in both the curriculum and the educational process. The school prepared young nobles for military service and, especially after 1768, equipped them with the knowledge necessary for the performance of civic duties as well. The king was the head of the school and Adam Kazimierz Czartoryski its commandant; August Sułkowski was vice-commandant until 1768 and was succeeded by Count Fryderyk Moszyński. John Lind was the first general director for education, Krzysztof Pfleiderer the second, and Mikołaj Hube the third.

The parliamentary constitution of 1766 provided for a total enrollment of two hundred,[8] but this figure was never reached. In 1769 the number of cadets fell to a hundred and after that to sixty. The Knights' School trained the sons of nobles. At the outset it provided a three-year program for sixteen- to twenty-one-year-olds. Under the educational reform introduced in 1768 the period of instruction was extended to seven years and the age at enrollment was fixed at between seven and twelve years. The Knights' School admitted youths from all parts of the Kingdom of Poland, from Lithuania, and even from Pomerania and Silesia, which were not then part of the territory of the Polish state. According to a 1780 resolution of the Sejm, one-third of the cadets were to come from Great Poland, one-third from Little Poland, and one-third from Lithuania.[9] The structure of the school was twofold. Each cadet belonged to one of eight (later seven) grades. Cadets were also subdivided into brigades and divisions, the numerical strength of which was closely related to the number of cadets enrolled and was constantly changing.[10] Cadets wore uniforms and were under strict military discipline.

The principal aims of the educational program were defined in the *Réglement général* and various documents compiled mainly by Czartoryski with the assistance of the officers and teachers of the school.[11]

The school was designed to train good citizens well-prepared for military service and various public posts for the good of the country. Cadets were expected to distinguish themselves by harmonious intellectual and physical development, excellent manners, encyclopedism, unblemished rectitude, humor, and a passion for their homeland. In the early years of the school its curriculum placed great emphasis on the development of these qualities. The Collegium Nobilium was like the military schools of France, Austria, Germany, and England in stressing military subjects at the expence of liberal education. In addition to mastery of weapons, drill, topography, cartography, and field training, cadets there were taught arithmetic and geometry, the history of Poland and the modern world, geography, literature, drawing, and French and Latin. The curriculum worked out for the Knights' School by Lind, introduced in the 1769-70 school year and, with some minor alterations, remaining in force until the close of the school, consisted of five years of liberal education and two subsequent years of solid preparation in either engineering or law.

Since at that time the Knights' School admitted boys of seven to twelve, reading, writing, and arithmetic formed the core of the curriculum in the first two years. The elementary period was a novitiate, after which the corps council decided whether a cadet would be permitted to continue. In the subsequent years pupils took mathematics, ancient and modern history, the history of Poland, Polish linguistics and poetry, drawing, geography, foreign languages (Latin, French, German, and English), civil law, military and civil architecture, drill, horsemanship, fencing, and dancing. For some time cadets were instructed in administration as well. Subsequent changes in the curriculum increased the proportion of time allotted to subjects that increased a cadet's knowledge of his country: the history of Poland, literature, public law, and Polish civil law. Cadets who chose military service were made acquainted with military engineering and took part in military exercises.

In the early years of the Knights' School a considerable proportion of the classes were conducted in German or French. Only as foreign teachers were gradually replaced by Poles did Polish become the main language of instruction. Modern instructional methods were employed.[12] The former system of rote memorization of information from textbooks and lectures was abandoned, and cadets were encouraged to develop their intellectual abilities through reasoning and discussion. Considerable time was devoted to demonstrations, and wide use was made of teaching aids provided in laboratories equipped with collections of minerals, illustrations, and drawings. Cadets were given ample opportunity for individual work and the study of literature, the general practice being to stimulate ambition and rivalry.

The modern curriculum and teaching methods required new textbooks and reference works, initially brought from abroad. These were eventually replaced by the textbooks used in civilian (mainly Piarist) schools and books published in Poland by the Society of Writers Founded to Publish the Best and Most Useful Books for the Country, the National Education Board, and the Society for Elementary Books. The Knights' School took pride in the fact that in 1768 it assumed the operation of printing house of Wawrzyniec Mitzler de Kolof, which became its property in 1778 and served its purposes till 1798.[13] In a very short time the school library had grown to some ten thousand volumes. Next to the collection at the Main School of Poland in Cracow, the library was one of the finest in Poland and one of the best in Europe for military literature.

Much attention was paid to examinations.[14] Once a week the director for education was obliged to visit each class, which in itself was considered a kind of examination for cadets and their teachers. Every month so-called common examinations were held, and once a year — usually in August — there were general examinations on all levels to determine each cadet's suitability for admission to the next grade. Great importance was attached to all examinations and to the general examinations in particular. The king himself was a member of the examination panel. On July 29, 1791, for example, he was present at the examination in theory and afterward watched field training. The best cadets were awarded prizes by him and had their names written on a golden board. Many officers and teachers were also cited.[15]

The Knights' School was the first in Poland to implement such a broad program of liberal education. Cadets, especially after 1768, were given an opportunity to acquire elementary knowledge in the earlier grades and secondary-school education with some elements of a contemporary university course in the later ones. A considerable proportion of graduates acquired profound knowledge of the military sciences, particularly military engineering, as well. An interesting feature of the program was the emphasis placed on preparation for intelligent citizenship and military service. Most of this rested with civilian teachers and tutors, whose task was, first of all, "to enlarge minds," and with officer teachers who "nurtured hearts." Selection of subject matter and methods was one of the basic duties of the commandant, teachers, and class masters. Such subjects as modern history, the history of Poland, natural law, ethics, and international law were considered appropriate for developing good citizenship and patriotism.

Moral education was entirely secular in nature. Religious fanatism and bigotry of any kind were forbidden. The teaching of religion, limited to instruction in catechism, was carried out by clerical directors. Some religious elements were incorporated into school rituals, but the main aim of the program was to develop in cadets the qualities that would help them to serve their country, among them honor, rectitude, and honesty.[16] Of great importance for this education for good citizenship were two works by Czartoryski, *Moral Catechism for Pupils of the Cadet Corps* and *Various Definitions through Questions and Answers*, the latter being an extension of the ideas and principles discussed in the former. These works defined the model cadet and outlined the educational program. A cadet was expected to "love his homeland above all and therefore attempt to equip himself with the general skills and knowledge that will enable him to serve it." He was to "respect authority, be charitable and affectionate toward his peers, and show solicitude for the humble."[17] Cadets were obliged to obey their superiors and expected to show kindness, helpfulness, and respect for their classmates. The program aimed to develop in cadets such virtues as honesty, gratitude, truthfulness, courage, and contempt for cowardice, quarrelsomeness, and gambling. Other explicitly stated educational ends included a proper attitude toward women, discretion, and good form, rationalism, honor, and responsibility for one's actions.[18] Education for good citizenship was encouraged by poetry. Ignacy Krasicki's poem "Our Bounden Duty to Love Our Country" was not only a patriotic song but also the school anthem, and cadets knew it by heart. Understanding of contemporary events, both at home and abroad, was another aspect of the program. Senior cadets stood guard at the palace, took part in sessions of the Sejm, and watched military parades and other ceremonies.[19]

Cadets grew up in a community regulated by orders-of-the-day. There were rules for behavior in school and out, covering matters of deference to teachers and schoolmates and comportment in the classroom and in the dormitory. The institution of lance corporal was important in the development of self-discipline. One of the best cadets in a brigade would be appointed lance corporal, whose duty it was to keep records on cadets in a special book and both reprimand them and report on their offenses to the school authorities. He was expected to set a good example in every respect.[20] About 1770 *dekuria* — five-member groups of cadets probably appointed by the school authorities with the approval of the lance corporals — were established to examine sanctions and problems connected with the training of cadets and make recommendations to the school command.[21]

The elaborate military rituals also served educational purposes. Even admission to the Knights' School was marked by ceremony.[22] A cadet was admitted into the school after two years' probation (the so-called novitiate) and with the approval of the corps council. Cadets of exceptionally good conduct might have their probation period shortened. If the corps council pronounced the novice to be "worthy of the honor of wearing a uniform," the "taking of the veil" ceremony took place.[23] In the presence of the school personnel, the cadet received his uniform, sword, musket, and cartridge pouch and confirmed his commitment to the requirements of army discipline with an oath. In the evening of the same day a reception was held for newly admitted cadets. Graduation was an equally festive occasion. The cadet wrote in a special book his pledge to cherish the honor of the school, expressed his gratitude for the skills and knowledge acquired, and promised to observe the rules of good conduct. Afterward the senior officer handed him a certificate with the words, "Remember that you were once honored to be a cadet."[24] The corps council assessed his attainments and conduct, and on the grounds of his performance his name might be inscribed on a gold, a silver, or a blue board. When a cadet became a behavior problem, his name would be written on a special black board and his exemption deferred, and he would be obliged to apologize to his superiors and schoolmates in a special black book.

The Knights' School endured until the end of 1794. During that period it graduated 650 "fund" cadets (whose fees were paid by the state) and about 300 "extramural" cadets (whose fees were paid from private sources). Its graduates distinguished themselves by their patriotism, civic virtues, democratic and very often radical social views, and extensive liberal knowledge. For example, when the Kościuszko Insurrection began in Warsaw on April 17, 1794, every cadet able to bear arms took part. Among the most famous graduates of the Knights' School were Tadeusz Kościuszko, Jakub Jasiński, Julian Ursyn Niemcewicz, Stanisław Fiszer, Józef Sowiński, Michał Sokolnicki, Karol Sierakowski, and Karol Kniaziewicz. Many other outstanding officers, writers, political activists, and contributors to the national cultural output were recruited from the ranks of graduates. The achievements and traditions of the Knights' School benefited and enriched all the other Polish educational institutions of its time.

As early as 1767 Prince Karol Radziwiłł had founded a private engineering and artillery school known as the Cadet Corps in Nieśwież[25] that enrolled the sons of the gentry between the ages of ten and twelve. It was originally intended for forty-eight boys, though this figure was never attained. Cadets were given the opportunity to learn general subjects in the ordinary schools of Nieśwież and military ones in the Cadet Corps. The course of military studies included applied geometry, planimetry, civil and military architecture, topography, artillery, mechanical drawing, and surveying. (The Cadet Corps in Nieśwież seems to have closed in 1784.) At the same time Prince Karol established another school in Nieśwież, this one a naval school called the Sailor Cadet Corps.[26] A five-year course included the history of Poland, the Polish language, rhetoric, Latin, physics, ballistics, mechanics, trigonometry, arithmetic, theoretical and practical geometry, physical and political geography, astronomy, geology, engineering, drawing, boat building, and one foreign language chosen from among French, German, English, and Italian. The king allotted to the school twenty-four launches, each equipped with four cannon. The idea of establishing a strong Polish fleet was inculcated in the cadets.

The Lithuanian treasurer Antoni Tyzenhaus established a cadet corps in Grodno in 1777. It was moved to Vilnius in 1782 and its name changed to His Majesty's Corps of Vilnius Cadets. The Corps was supported by the king and trained twenty-four cadets before its founder's death terminated its existence.

In 1780-81 the Main Artillery School and its associated Engineering School were established in Warsaw. Both were state-aided, with General Alojzy Brüll as their protector. The artillery school had forty-two cadets, either recruited from artillery companies or volunteers, and survived for ten years.

In 1783 Prince August Sułkowski founded a cadet corps in Rydzyń in which a dozen or so young noblemen studied general and military sciences. Four years later the crown grand chamberlain Wincenty Potocki established a cadet corps in Niemirów in Podolia.

Finally, in 1789 the Engineer Corps School was founded in Vilnius. The curriculum included military and technical subjects such as mathematics, fortifications, tactics, pyrotechnics, mechanical drawing, geography, and topography. In 1792 civil architecture, French, hydraulics, and sappers' training were added. The program emphasized exercises in draftmanship and the building of field and permanent fortifications.

In 1795 the Third Partition of Poland took place; the territory of the Polish Republic was annexed by Russia, Prussia, and Austria. The Polish state and armed forces ceased to exist, and with them the military educational system.

Officer Training in the Grand Duchy of Warsaw, 1807-14

The Grand Duchy of Warsaw was set up in 1807 on a part of the Polish territory that had been annexed by Prussia. Polish patriots believed that this would give them a head start in rebuilding the Polish state. The emerging army needed a substantial number of officers. Officers from the Polish legions in Italy and the pre-Partition Polish army were scarce, and their qualifications were in any case ill suited to the new kind of warfare. It became necessary to train a new officer corps to satisfy the needs of an ever-growing Polish army.

The Grand Duchy of Warsaw inherited from Prussia two cadet corps: one in Chełm, founded in 1776, and the other in Kalisz, founded in 1794. Both corps were lower-level military schools designed to prepare youths of Polish and German origin for study in the cadet corps in Berlin and, incidentally, to Germanize the Polish youths. When the Grand Duchy of Warsaw was established, the cadet corps in Chełm and Kalisz came under the supervision of the Governing Commission and were subordinated to the general corps commandant, General StanisUaw Kostka Potocki.[27] He dismissed all the officers, teachers, and tutors of German origin and appointed Colonel Wincenty Podczaski, a graduate of the Knights' School, and Captain Hilary Wierzejski commandant and vice-commandant of the cadet corps in Kalisz and Colonel Ignacy Cebulski and Captain Mikołaj Borkowski their counterparts in Chełm.

After some organizational alterations and curriculum changes, the number of cadets was fixed at eighty.[29] The school recruited young men of all estates between the ages of ten and sixteen. The sons of military men who had died or had been honorably discharged from the service, the sons of civil servants and of regular officers, and boys of special intellectual ability were given preference in admissions. As the number of applicants increased, twenty-four additional cadets were allowed to enroll in each class from 1809 on, with their schooling entirely dependent on fees paid by their parents or patrons. They lived outside the school, paid twelve hundred złotys a year, and were called "boarders" as opposed to the "fund " pupils provided for by the state.

From 1810 on, former pupils of the cadet schools made individual decisions with regard to choice of career. The curriculum, requiring only elementary knowledge of military subjects, was similar to that of six-grade departmental schools. Pupils were taught fortifications, fencing, and drill. Graduates choosing to stay in the army received their assignments with a regiment and only upon completion of several years of service were promoted to officer. Some of them continued studies at the Applied School.

The educational system incorporated some of the traditions of the Knights' School in its new moral catechism, its reward-and-punishment system, and its elaborate ritual. General Kostka Potocki was the author of a *Catechism for the Cadet Corps* that answered the question "What are the reasons a cadet should fulfill his military and civic duties?" with "Love of his homeland, its welfare and fame, and a desire to be respected by his fellow citizens and glorified by his descendants. Other less noble reasons are the avoidance of disgrace to a citizen, a soldier, a Pole, and all the more a cadet who is being prepared by his motherland to be her son."[30]

The ritual developed at the Knights' School was used for admission to the corps, the bestowal of uniforms and weapons, the conferring of decorations, the end of the school year, and graduation. After the general examination cadets received from the corps commandant honorary gold and silver medals with an eagle on them or silver marks of distinction with a wreath that they wore pinned to a green ribbon. A cadet might be decorated with a gold medal for "the particular virtue of constant diligence in studies and model conduct." Cadets' attainments and conduct were assessed by the corps council of officers and teachers. The council also decided on which board a cadet's name should be inscribed: white, blue, grey, or, for cadets dismissed from the corps or deserving of punishment, black. The honored cadets took special seats in classrooms and in the dining room.[31] At graduation, the commandant, the officers, and the other cadets bade farewell to the graduates with the words: "Remember that you were once honored to be cadets. Live and die for king and country!"[32]

The cadet corps of the Grand Duchy of Warsaw produced many good citizens and great patriots. About seventy infantry and cavalry officers were recruited from among the graduates of the Kalisz Corps in the period 1808-13.[33]

In 1808 the Artillery and Engineering School was founded in Warsaw. It remained under the supervision of a board of directors headed by Lieutenant Colonel Rydel until he was replaced by Lieutenant Colonel Mallet in 1810. The board decided on curriculum and teaching methods. The school enrolled forty-eight carefully selected students, most of them soldiers. Civilians were admitted only as day students for an annual fee of two hundred złotys. The course lasted three years. Gifted pupils were given the opportunity of having extra lessons in mechanics, hydraulics, physics, and astronomical geography. The school program included arithmetic, applied geometry, solidometry, trigonometry, algebra, mechanical drawing, topography, civil and military architecture, permanent and field fortifications, theoretical artillery, pyrotechnics, French and Russian, history, and geography. Public examinations were held every six months. The subject matter, forms, and methods were spelled out in *Annotations and Obligations of Artillery and Engineering School Cadets*, published in 1811.[34] Love of country, honor, sense of duty, and good fellowship were among the main virtues instilled in cadets. School ritual was, again, modeled on the traditions of the Knights' School.

In 1809 the Applied School of Artillery and Engineering was established in Warsaw to train higher-level commanders.[35] (Some time afterward, the existing School of Artillery and Engineering was renamed the Elementary School of Artillery and Engineering.) Its structure imitated that of the French school in Metz. Lieutenant Colonel Mikołaj Rouget was appointed commandant. The school admitted both civilians and soldiers. To be accepted a candidate had to pass a special competitive examination in arithmetic, geometry, trigonometry, algebra, statistics, and mechanics. Good grades in the examination enhanced the chances of promotion to second lieutenant and adequate pay. The school trained only twelve cadets. The one-year course covered descriptive geometry, mechanics, higher mathematics, drawing, architecture, permanent and field fortifications, artillery, and foreign languages. Many outstanding officers were graduates of the Applied School, among them Józef Bem, Ignacy Prądzyński, Wojciech Chrzanowski, and Klemens Kołaczkowski.

The medical personnel for the army of the Grand Duchy of Warsaw were trained at the Military Surgical School, founded in Warsaw in 1808, which produced surgeon's assistants, and the Academic Faculty of Medicine, established in Warsaw in 1809, which trained physicians and pharmacists. When in 1809 the University of Cracow found itself within the boundaries of the Grand Duchy of Warsaw, its premises were also used for training a military medical cadre.[36] Military medical schooling was under the Main Council of the Polish Army Health Service. Graduates of the military medical schools served as army surgeons, physicians, and pharmacists.

Officer Training in the Polish Kingdom, 1815-30

By decision of the Congress of Vienna in 1815, some of the territories of the Grand Duchy of Warsaw became the Polish Kingdom, linked to Russia by personal union. The Russian tsar, Alexander I, became its king, and his brother, the Grand Duke Constantine, was chosen commander in chief of the Polish army. The constitution of the Polish Kingdom established the character and structure of its armed forces. Formal education of career army officers was provided by the Cadet Corps in Kalisz, the Infantry Cadet Corps and the Cavalry Cadet School in Warsaw, the Applied School of Artillery and Engineering in Warsaw, and the Winter School of Artillery in Warsaw.

The Cadet Corps in Kalisz, inherited from the Grand Duchy of Warsaw, was originally under the Governmental Commission for Religious Beliefs and Public Education and from 1820 on under the supervision of the Governmental Commission for War. Colonel Józef Regulski was its commandant from 1814 to 1820, General Józef Wasilewski in 1820 and 1821, and General Ignacy Mycielski afterward. In 1820 General Maurycj Hauke, the commander of the Artillery and Engineering Corps, was appointed the general commandant of cadet schools. Cadets were accepted to the corps on the same basis as in the period of the Grand Duchy of Warsaw. Priority was given to sons of meritorious military men and civil servants. Some 30 to 40 cadets aged twelve to thirteen were admitted. Between 1815 and 1830 from 104 to 300 cadets were regularly enrolled in the corps.[37]

Initially the Kalisz Cadet Corps offered a four-year course; later it was lengthened to six. The educational program included mathematics, physics, chemistry, natural history, modern history and the history of Poland, logic, the constitution, calligraphy, drawing, religion, and languages (Polish, French, German, and Latin). The 1818-19 syllabus added military subjects: the history of the Polish army, military organization, tactics, fortifications, artillery, surveying, civil engineering, and military drawing. Later, drill, fencing, singing, and dancing were introduced.[38] Important changes in the curriculum occurred in 1820. At the expense of liberal subjects such as modern history, the history of Poland, the constitution, logic, and the history of the art of war, the hours of instruction in military subjects were increased and summer field training was arranged. New regulations were issued limiting the choices open to a cadet with regard to his career. Much attention was given to self-instruction, the demonstrative method of teaching, and laboratory experience.

Moral education was viewed from a secular perspective as preparation for citizenship, cultivation of love of country, responsibility, and courage to fight for the integrity of the national culture. Everyday educational activities involved training in neatness, decency, and good manners. Much attention was given to the development of habits of obedience and military discipline. The system of rewards and punishments and school ritual evolved from the traditions of the corps in the period of the Grand Duchy of Warsaw.[39]

Selected honor graduates of the Kalisz Cadet Corps were admitted to the Applied School. Most of them were promoted to noncommissioned officer and assigned to a regiment for further advancement to officer.

At the outbreak of the November Insurrection in 1830, the majority of officers employed in the corps, including the commandant Mycielski and the director for education Colonel Franciszek Koss, joined the insurgents. Many senior cadets took part in the insurrection. Major Grabowski, appointed commandant of the corps, reported to the minister of war: "Neither reprimands nor the most rigorous sanctions could alter the revolutionary fervor of the youths."[40] After the collapse of the insurrection the former cadets did not return to the corps, and a number of the cadets who had remained at school no longer wished to do so. Under the circumstances Tsar Nicholas I closed the Kalisz Cadet Corps on March 24, 1832. Some cadets were sent home while others joined the Russian cadet corps in Petersburg or Moscow. Among the best-known graduates of the Kalisz Cadet Corps were Ludwik Mierosławski, Juliusz Falkowski, Ignacy Marceli Paszkowski, Leonard Wasilewski, and Ludwig Sztyrmer.

The School of Infantry Cadets was opened in Warsaw in July of 1815.[41] Lieutenant Colonel Józef Paszkowszki was its first commandant, and he was succeeded by Colonel Ksawery Olędzki and, before the November Insurrection, by General Stanisław Trębicki. The manner in which the school approached its responsibility to prepare officers submissive to Grand Duke Constantine was patterned after the experiences of the Russian army. The school enrolled about two hundred cadets, after 1826 three hundred. It offered a two-year program, but initially, with the dismissal of some of the officers of the army of the Grand Duchy of Warsaw, cadets were promoted to second lieutenant upon completion of one year's schooling. Subsequently the course was lengthened to six years and more because of the lack of officer vacancies in regiments.

The educational program was entirely military. Cadets were taught regulations and practiced drill and field service. They went through a period of basic training and some form of specialized training while assigned to a platoon, company, battalion, and regiment. They were also made acquainted on a theoretical level with the combat organization of brigades and divisions. Emphasis was placed on the manner of issuing orders and detailed knowledge of interior service.[42] This situation was unsatisfactory to cadets who wanted individual study for the purpose of intellectual development. In 1824 they were allowed to learn foreign languages — French, German, and Russian — and from 1828-29 on instruction in tactics, mathematics, strategy, and topography was incorporated into the syllabus.

In spite of strict injunctions to avoid contact with others, the cadets maintained relations with the inhabitants of Warsaw and their friends on active duty with the regiments stationed in the capital. They were very active members of the clandestine military plot organized by Second Lieutenant Piotr Wysocki, a school instructor. On the night of November 29, 1830, 161 of the 196 cadets present that day decided to take part in the insurrection. It was they who urged the soldiers and inhabitants of Warsaw to fight, with the cry "Those who love the homeland, to arms!"[43]

In the period 1815-30, 680 graduates of the School of Infantry Cadets were given regular commissions. After November 29, 1830, all 200 cadets were promoted to the rank of second lieutenant.[44] Many of the cadets and graduates were conspicuous for their bravery and heroism during the insurrection.

Contemporary with the School of Infantry Cadets was the School of Cavalry Cadets, established in 1815, also in Warsaw.[45] Lieutenant Colonel Franciszek Czarnowski was its commandant. Its enrollment was half that of the Infantry School. Drill was the most important and almost the sole subject of instruction. Cadets devoted considerable time to the grooming of horses and riding. Orderliness and exemplary cleanliness prevailed. In the period 1815-30, 127 graduates were commissioned.[46]

The highest military school in the Polish Kingdom was the Applied School of Artillery and Engineering, founded in Warsaw in 1820 to replace the reorganized Artillery and Engineering School.[47] Colonel Józef Sowiński, a graduate of the Knights' School, was appointed commandant. Initially sixteen cadets were trained there, but from 1821 on their number increased to twenty-four. The school admitted mainly honor graduates of the cadet corps, officer candidates, and noncommissioned officers on the basis of competitive examinations.

The course originally lasted two years, later lengthened to three and, starting with the academic year 1829-30, to four. Based on that of the French *écoles d'application*, it consisted of mathematics, physics, chemistry, construction, artillery, permanent and field fortifications, topography, geodesy, and foreign languages — Russian, French, and German. Standards in mathematics, physics, and engineering were very high. A considerable amount of time was allotted to laboratory experience and work in the library. Practical exercises included visits to Powązki and tours around the country to acquaint cadets with the armaments industry and topography. In Zamość cadets carried out some surveying and sappers' exercises.

From 1830 on the Applied School of Artillery and Engineering graduated about a hundred cadets.[48] They were assigned duties of artillery, engineering, and sapper second lieutenants. Notable among them were Józef Henke, Józef Waligórski, Tomasz Potocki, Ludwik Rzewuski, and Władysław Czetwertyński.

The Winter School of Artillery was founded in Warsaw in 1825.[49] There cadets and noncommissioned officers studied theoretical and practical rules of ordnance. Colonel Valentin d'Hauterive was the commandant, and many experienced officers served as instructors. Teaching standards were very high. The course consisted of artillery, fortifications, mathematics, and infantry. By 1830 fifty-four cadets had completed the course.

Physicians and pharmacists for the military services of the Polish Kingdom were educated at the Medical Faculty, which in 1817 was joined to the newly founded University of Warsaw. In the period 1818-31 there was a school for surgeons' assistants, affiliated to the Main Military Hospital in Ujazdów in Warsaw.[50] The Medical Department of the Governmental Commission on War was in charge of the educational program.

In the November Insurrection of 1830-31, the military schools suspended work and their staffs, senior cadets, officer cadets, and students took part in combat operations. Short-term courses and new military schools such as the School of the Academic League, founded in Warsaw in December 1830, and the similar school established at Telsze in Lithuania, replaced the closed ones. After a short period of training graduates of these schools were promoted to second lieutenant and assigned to regiments.

With the failure of the November Insurrection, the Polish army and military educational system ceased to exist. The experiences and traditions of the Knights' School and of the military schools of the Grand Duchy of Warsaw and the Polish Kingdom proved to be an important heritage of the Polish educational system in general and of the military educational system in particular. Graduates of the schools honorably fulfilled their duties to their country and to the Polish nation.

NOTES

1. A. F. Modrzewski, *O poprawie Rzeczypospolitej* (Warsaw, 1953 [1551)]; Sz. Marycjusz, *O szkołach, czyli akademiach,* trans. Danysz Antoni (Wrocław, 1955), J. T. Głębocki, *Wywód o szkołach rycerskich czyli wojskowych w Polsce w ciągu dziejowym* (Cracow, 1866); J. Tarnowski, *Consilium rationis bellicea* (Cracow, 1858); B. Paprocki. *Hetman czyli konterfekt hetmański* (Cracow, 1578); A. Knot; *Z przeszłości szkolnictwa wojskowego w Polsce* (Poznań, 1928).

2. In 1555 the Spanish king Charles V founded an artillery school in Burgos. In 1587 Cardinal Mazzarini established the first military school in France. In the German states, military schools were opened in Berlin in 1563, in the Rhine country in 1616, in Saxony in 1692, in Prussia in 1717, and in Bavaria in 1765. In Holland a military school was founded in 1735, in Piedmont in 1736, in England in 1741, and in Paris the famous Ecole Royale Militaire was established in 1752. In Russia Peter the Great opened a navigation school, later converted into a naval academy, in 1702, an artillery school and an engineering school in 1712. Catherine I organized the cadet corps for young gentry in 1766. The Austrian Military Academy was established in 1752 and the Berlin Military Academy in 1765.

3. Knot, *Z przeszłości szkolnictwa*, pp. 3-4.

4. P. Boyé, *La cour Polonaise de Lunéville (1733-1766)* (Nancy, Paris, Strasbourg, 1926), chap. 5.

5. St. Konarski, *Pisma pedagogiczne* (Wrocław-Cracow, 1959), p. 357.

6. Volumina legum. 8:101.

7. M. Miterzanka, *Działalność pedagogiczna Adama ks. Czartoryskiego, generała ziem polskich* (Warsaw, Lvov, 1931), p. 26.

8. Volumina legum. 8:302.

9. Diariusz sejmu walnego ordynaryjnego warszawskiego sześcioniedzielnego r.p. 1780 . . . , Warsaw.

10. K. Mrozowska, *Szkoła Rycerska Stanisława Augusta Poniatowskiego (1765-1794)*, (Wrocław, Warsaw, Cracow, 1961), p. 28.

11. Réglement général, Manuscript No. 2808, Czartoryski Library (Microfilms of Military Political Academy); A. K. Czartoryski, *Katechizm rycerski* (Warsaw, Lublin, Łódź, Cracow, 1916).

12. Miterzanka, *Działalność pedagogiczna*, p. 35.

13. J. Szczepaniec, Drukarnia Mitzlerowska Korpusu Kadetów w Warszawie, Library Annals II,b, 1-2, 51-93.

14. Mrozowska, *Szkoła Rycerska*, p. 102.

15. *Gazeta Narodowa i Obca*, no. 64 (August 10, 1791).

16. Réglement général.

17. Czartoryski, *Katechizm rycerski*, p. 20.

18. Czartoryski, *Katechizm rycerski*; also Réglement général.

19. S. Bukar, *Pamiętniki* (Dresden, 1871), pp. 13-14.

20. "Powinności gefrejterów w brygadzie," in Mrozowska, *Szkoła Rycerska*, p. 124.

21. "Przepisy dla dekuriów," in J. Cytowski, *Wychowanie wojskowe w okresie Komisji Edukacji Narodowej* (Warsaw, 1973), pp. 105-23.

22. Formularz przyjmowania kadetów do nowicjatu," in ibid., pp. 123-26.

23. "Formularz obleczenia kadeta w mundur korpusowy," in ibid., pp. 127-30.

24. "Formularz abszytowania kadetów," in ibid., pp. 130-33.
25. Knot, *Z przeszłości szkolnictwa,* p. 11.
26. K. Kubik, *Psychologia i dydaktyka* (Gdynia, 1970), p. 8..
27. W. Gorzycki, *Oświata publiczna w Ksiestwie Warszawskim, organizacja władz i funduszów,* vol. 1, pt. 2 (Warsaw, 1921), pp. 64-65.
28. W. Lisowski, *Polskie Korpusy Kadetów 1765-1956* (Warsaw, 1985), p. 103.
29. B. Gembarzewski, *Wojsko Polskie: Księstwo Warszawskie 1807-1814* (Warsaw, 1905), p. 227.
30. Katechizm dla korpusów kadeckich, The Army of the Grand Duchy of Warsaw, No. 942/C, Polish Army Library Museum.
31. Gembarzewski, *Wojsko Polskie: Księstwo Warszawskie,* p. 230.
32. Ibid.
33. Ibid., p. 233.
34. Ibid., pp. 235-39.
35. Ibid., pp. 239-41.
36. Ibid., pp. 241-42; S. Wojtkowiak, J. Taler, W. Majewski, and F. Piotrowski, *Zarys dziejów wojskowej słuzby zdrowia* (Warsaw, 1974), p. 119.
37. Lisowski, *Polskie Korpusy Kadetów,* p. 112; B. Gembarzewski, *Wojsko Polskie: Królestwo Polskie 1815-1830* (Warsaw, 1903), pp. 149-50.
38. W. Tokarz, *Armia Królestwa Polskiego (1815-1830)* (Piotrków, 1917), p. 271.
39. Gembarzewski, *Wojsko Polskie: Królestwo Polskie,* pp. 147-51.
40. Lisowski, *Polskie Korpusy Kadetów,* p. 117.
41. Gembarzewski, *Wojsko Polskie: Królestwo Polskie,* p. 161.
42. St. Rutkowski, *Zarys dziejów polskiego szkolnictwa wojskowego* (Warsaw, 1970), p. 47.
43. W. Tokarz, *Sprzysiężenie Wysockiego i Noc Listopadowa* (Warsaw, 1925), p. 17.
44. *Zarys dziejów wojskowosci polskiej do roku 1864,* vol. 2 (Warsaw, 1966), p. 386.
45. Gembarzewski, *Wojsko Polskie: Królestwo Polskie,* pp. 161-64.
46. *Zarys dziejów wojskowości polskiej,* p. 386.
47. Gembarzewski, *Wojsko Polskie: Królestwo Polskie,* p. 151.
48. Ibid., pp. 160-61.
49. Ibid., p. 164.
50. Wojtkowiak et al., *Zarys dziejów wojskowej służby zdrowia,* p. 124.

V. PARAMILITARY OFFICERS' TRAINING

Maria Theresa's Noble Lifeguards and the Rise of the Hungarian Enlightenment and Nationalism

László Deme

At the 1741 Diet the Hungarian nobles enthusiastically offered their "lives and blood" in defense of Maria Theresa. For the remainder of her long reign, the queen was grateful for their loyalty in her hour of need: "I am a good Hungarian. My heart is full of gratitude to that nation," she wrote toward the end of her life, and her reign was replete with measures beneficial to Hungary.[1] Hungarian historians have tended to view her favorably. Mihály Horváth, the most influential nineteenth-century liberal nationalist historian, characterized her age as "the period of the reestablishment of confidence between the nation and the ruling house" and believed that she surpassed all the other Habsburgs in royal virtues.[2] Gyula Szekfű, a noted twentieth-century Hungarian historian, thought that the queen's extraordinary personality was responsible for a reign that was "one of the most remarkable periods" in Hungarian history.[3] Even recent Marxists associate "Habsburg-Hungarian compromise" with her rule.[4]

Despite occasional friction over taxes and tariffs, it was an era of good feeling and essential harmony between the queen and the Hungarians. Her appreciation for their service to the crown was probably a significant motivating factor in the establishment of the Hungarian Noble Lifeguards (Praetoriana Nobilium Turma Hungarica) in 1760.[5] The importance Maria Theresa attributed to the Guard is well illustrated by the fact that she spent 100,000 forints a year for its upkeep at a time when the total revenue from Hungary amounted to 3.2 million.

The Guard was an elite cavalry unit of the Habsburg army commanded by a senior general and led by three additional officers from the high aristocracy. The 129 Lifeguards came from the well-to-do and influential segment of the Hungarian lesser nobility, and each held at least the rank of second lieutenant. When it was first established, the officers and men of the Guard were assisted by four professionals (a chaplain, a judge advocate, a quartermaster, and a surgeon) and 81 enlisted men. The length of service was intended to be approximately five years, but many served longer.

The duties and functions of the Guard were in part decorative and ceremonial. Their splendid uniforms recalled traditional Hungarian military dress. They wore fancy high riding boots, red trousers, tunics heavily braided with silver, short tiger-skin cloaks over one shoulder, and tall headgear and were armed with ceremonial silver swords and carbines. There can be no doubt that their presence greatly contributed to the baroque magnificence of the imperial court.

In addition to their decorative function, the Guard's duties resembled those of the Secret Service of an American president. Jointly with the German Imperial Guard (Arciéren Leibgarde), they were charged with guaranteeing the personal safety of the head of state and the most important members of her entourage. They guarded the apartments of the queen, Emperor Francis I, the crown prince, and his wife and accompanied members of the imperial family to church functions, on errands in Vienna, and on excursions to the provinces. During Maria Theresa's reign twenty-six Guardsmen also served at the ducal court in Milan, and, perhaps more appropriately, another detachment did duty at the palatine's court in Pozsony (Pressburg) between 1766 and 1781.

The Guardsmen enjoyed a high social standing at court, far above that of ordinary junior officers. Each of them was personally introduced to the queen and leading dignitaries of the court. They also were privileged to attend court receptions and balls closed even to generals of the regular army. Viennese high society also welcomed them, and they appeared regularly in the palaces of the great court aristocracy and at foreign embassy receptions.[6]

Their social success was partially due to the careful selection process. Initially, one-third of the Hungarian Lifeguard was recruited from the junior officers of the regular army. The remainder were civilians recommended by their respective county congregations from all parts of Hungary, including Croatia and Transylvania. Thus, with a few exceptions, the Guard represented the best the country nobility had to offer, probably in terms both of local wealth and influence and of intellectual ability. Geographic diversity and the importance of the Guardsmen in their home communities were important prerequisites for the accomplishment of Maria Theresa's political purpose in creating the Hungarian Lifeguard. Even contemporaries recognized that the empress-queen had established the Guard not only to show her appreciation to the Hungarians but also "with the political intention of increasing confidence between the Hungarian and German nations."[7]

In view of the queen's general policies toward the Hungarian nobility, her political purpose seems paramount. In the eighteenth century the Hungarian nobility comprised about four hundred families of high aristocracy and approximately twenty thousand families of lesser or untitled nobility. The aristocrats (princes, counts, and barons) owned large estates and could personally participate in the legislative work of the upper house of the Diet. The untitled nobility had smaller landholdings but through the county congregations controlled local administration and had representation in the lower house. Together the aristocrats and lesser nobles had a monopoly on internal political power in Hungary. The queen's aim was to change this nobility's life-style and orientation. Many aristocrats who lived on their estates in Hungary and spoke Hungarian at home were induced to establish permanent residences in Vienna, where they often married Austro-German ladies and started speaking German and French in their homes. Attracted by the pleasures of the glittering imperial court and the many favors the queen bestowed upon them, they lost much of their Hungarian national character. From an independent territorial nobility they developed into an imperial court aristocracy.[8]

This system of *douce violence* was extremely effective.[9] According to Horváth, Maria Theresa exerted far more control over Hungary with her gentle ways, tact, and benevolence than her predecessor had been able to through oppression and bloody violence.[10] It should be noted, however, that the queen's primary purpose was not to denationalize any of her subjects but to found a modern supranational cosmopolitan state in which German was used more for administrative convenience than as an instrument of national policy.[11] Loyalty was expected to the dynasty and the Habsburg state rather than to any particular nationality.

Nevertheless, an important instrument of the queen's general policy toward integrating her empire was the Habsburg army. A special unit like the Hungarian Lifeguard had even greater potential as a "centripetal force" than regular troops. The literature conceptually connects the Lifeguard with the Theresian Academy, the queen's elite school for diplomats, civil servants, and officers.[12] One scholar even asserts that the Hungarian Noble Lifeguard should be seen primarily as a college-like institution the purpose of which was to provide useful knowledge and the advantages of the Viennese melting pot to young men who desired a career in state service. An appointment to the Lifeguards exposed them to contemporary Western culture which was unavailable in provincial Hungarian educational institutions.[13] This paper will attempt to show the extent to which the founding queen's intentions with the Lifeguard were realized during her reign. It will also examine the intellectual and political orientation of the most important Guardsmen and outline their influence on subsequent cultural and political developments in Hungary.

In many respects the Lifeguard was a success. Its establishment was greeted with enthusiasm in Hungary, and to a great extent it became a symbol of goodwill between the ruling house and the nation. The Guard also definitely fulfilled its ceremonial and security functions. Hungarian Guardsmen are credited with saving the queen from bodily injury at least once and Crown Prince Joseph on two separate occasions.[14] As a training school for civil servants the Guard was perhaps less successful; few of its veterans rose to prominence in the imperial bureaucracy. Service in the Lifeguard did, however, tend to further military careers; many Guardsmen who transferred to regular army units upon completing their tour of duty rose to high rank and achieved distinction.

The Guard's greatest impact, however, was on Hungarian intellectual life. It seldom happens that military service acts as a catalyst for new literary or philosophical trends. In Hungarian literary and intellectual history, however, the Enlightenment starts with the literary work of Guardsmen in the queen's service.[15] In the late 1760s and 1770s a literary circle developed among the Hungarian Lifeguards. Its members can be credited with at least three major contributions: (1) translating many current popular works of French, German, and English poetry and fiction into Hungarian, (2) transmitting the ideas of the Enlightenment to the Hungarian reading public, and (3) applying Western progressive ideas to Hungarian cultural and national needs and founding Hungarian linguistic and cultural nationalism.

Hungarian literature was in great need of enrichment with translations of foreign works. The few outstanding individual writers and poets in Hungarian literary history tended to be isolated individuals, and there was no real cultural center of Hungarian intellectual life. The country lacked an academy of sciences, national theater, or national museum. The few books published attracted a very limited reading public. Intellectual and literary progress was also greatly impeded by the continued use of Latin in scholarly publications, the legislature, the judiciary, and the schools.

Service in the Lifeguard prompted literary activity and equipped many to become translators. Exposure to Viennese polite society, concerts, theater, and the cosmopolitan intellectual atmosphere of the court stimulated literary pursuits, and familiarity with foreign languages was easy to acquire and even a necessity. Guardsmen were required to attend German and French language classes as part of their duties. A review of their conduct reports indicates that by 1774 most Guardsmen spoke two or more foreign languages.[16] Unfortunately, the books they chose to translate were not the great masterpieces of French, English, or German literature but books of little literary merit. Sándor Báróczi (1735-1809), a Transylvanian nobleman, for example, attracted attention in the 1770s with his translations of works such as *Cassandre*, a ten-volume heroic romance by Gauthier de La Calprenéde, a royal guardsman and gentleman in ordinary at the court of Louis XIV. Báróczi offered La Calprenéde's pseudohistorical novel, with its endless tales of princes and princesses declaiming high-flown emotions, primarily for its entertainment value. He considered his translation a sort of patriotic accomplishment, however, in that it added to the very few books available to the Hungarian reading public and helped to cultivate the much neglected Hungarian language.[17]

Báróczi was particularly successful in this with his translation of the *Contes moraux* by Jean Francois Marmontel, a contemporary French *littérateur* and member of the French Academy. Marmontel's short stories were noted for their delicacy of style. Báróczi's translation closely approximated the original in beauty and elegance and long remained an outstanding example of Hungarian literary prose. Even Marmontel seems to have been pleased with Báróczi's work. After being informed about the Hungarian translation of the *Contes moraux*, he expressed great pleasure that henceforth the "ladies of the Crimea" would also be able to enjoy his work in their own language.[18]

Other Hungarian Lifeguards translated popular contemporary French sentimental plays and short stories by Baculard d'Arnaud, Claude Joseph Dorat, and others.[19] Hungarian opinion of their work was favorable because they encouraged literary activity in the Hungarian language. In retrospect this attitude appears reasonable in light of the backwardness of Hungarian intellectual and literary life at the time. Although today these translations are no more read in Hungary than the originals are in France, at that time they were significant in exposing Hungarian readers to a more advanced mode of literary expression and contemporary Western style. Along with original plays, poems, and pamphlets, these translated works mark the beginning of the Enlightenment in Hungarian literary history.

The most prominent Hungarian writer of this new epoch was György Bessenyei (1747-1811).[20] In many respects Bessenyei was typical of the young Hungarians who served in the Lifeguard. He came from a moderately wealthy but influential noble family. As with most others of his class, his earning a living by a trade would have been unthinkable, and since his family owned enough land, there was no need to acquire even legal training, the customary education for young Hungarian noblemen. His formal education, therefore, comprised five years in a boarding school and an additional year of private tutoring at home. His instruction was very limited. He learned a little about religion and acquired a superficial familiarity with Latin and the classical authors. Without his appointment to the Guard he would probably have led a rather provincial existence looking after his land and serfs, socializing with neighboring landowners, hunting, and possibly participating a little in county politics.

Bessenyei served in the Guard from 1765 to 1773 and continued to live in Vienna until 1782. According to his conduct report, he read a great deal and continuously improved upon his knowledge of foreign languages.[21] Of this period in his life he wrote that after "coming to Vienna it occurred to me that I should study because it is good to know things," and he certainly made up for the lack of his early education.[22] He studied the writers of the French and English Enlightenment: Alexander Pope, John Locke, Edward Young, Charles Louis de Secondat, Baron de la Bréde et de Montesquieu, and — above all — Francois-Marie Arouet de Voltaire. He confessed having read a thirty-six volume collection of Voltaire's works several times[23] and was also influenced by other contemporary French historians and political scientists. The idea of "general welfare" (*Allgemeine Wohlfahrt*) popularized in Vienna at that time by Karl Anton Martini and Joseph von Sonnenfels made such an impression on him that he coined the Hungarian phrase for it and used it extensively in his own writings. As a playwright he was influenced by Johann Christoph Gottsched and Philippe Néricault Destouches.[24]

Bessenyei's ideas on creation and God and on man's relationship with the world show the strong imprint of Pope's *Essay on Man*, which he twice translated into Hungarian. Under Pope's influence, he accepted God as the creator but rejected conventional religious and revealed truth. He believed in the interdependence of all things in the "great chain of being." [25] Pope's idea that "whatever is, is right," however, seems to have made less of an impression on him, for much of his literary work aimed at changing the mode of thinking and cultural conditions in Hungary.

In a philosophical-historical treatise entitled *A magyar néző* (The Hungarian Spectator) and in other writings, Bessenyei argued against the irrationality of religion and attributed its origins to primitive man's need to explain natural phenomena he did not understand. Thunder and lightning, day and night, and the change of seasons were believed to be acts of God, and harmful events were blamed on evil spirits.[26] Those few who desired power recognized early that to speak in the name of God was the easiest way to control others. After spending time in remote forests and caves, they would claim to have communed with the deity and then proceed to give laws to their people as if by divine command.[27] Bessenyei was aware that laws and belief systems widely differed with time and place and took great delight in describing the worshippers of the sun or the moon, the believers in reincarnation, the faiths of India, or even the religious requirements of the Old Testament. Ostensibly, his descriptions were always of the errors of non-Christians, and, probably with an eye on the censor, he repeatedly stated that humanity found the real truth with Christianity. But the thrust of his message was clearly against all religion. Bessenyei suggested that religion was born out of ignorance and described its harmful effects in considerable detail. Most particularly, he objected to the fact that "with religion goes conversion, the means of which were beating, burning, promises, gifts, intimidation, and women." He decried the historical practice of converting pagan princes through marriage with Christian women. He considered conversions prompted by miracles (like that of Emperor Constantine) unsound because "the nature of miracles cannot be defined with certainty" and noted that with the progress of human knowledge they tended to decrease in number. He was also highly critical of the use of violence in the name of religion, from the bloody methods of Charlemagne converting the Saxons to the Crusades to the jihads of Islam.[28]

Bessenyei also held a negative view of the history of mankind. Influenced by Voltaire's philosophy, he saw the past only as a series of endless brutal wars, violence, bloodshed, and cruelty. Ancient Egypt, Persia, Alexander the Great, and the Roman Empire all aspired to conquest which resulted in human suffering.[29] Going even farther than his master, he judged Alexander a cruel conqueror who shed blood because he enjoyed battle.[30] He observed, with dismay, that nothing had changed with the advent of Christianity and that Christian princes too were constantly at war.

Opposition to war on principle is a rather unusual attitude to be held by a man who was, after all, an officer in the imperial army. But Bessenyei was not alone. Others among his fellow Guardsmen held similar views. Occasionally, the contrast between profession and philosophy was even more marked. Ábrahám Barcsay (1742-1806), for example, the most talented poet among the Guardsmen, left the Guard to join a cavalry regiment in 1767 and as a professional army officer spent most of his life in various garrison towns of the Monarchy. He fought in several campaigns and rose to the rank of colonel but as a poet exalted peace. In one of his odes peace appears as a personified deity whose glorious crown confers calm upon the nations of the earth and under whose reign Hungarians will prosper.[31] War is characterized as the ultimate evil. Barcsay blamed war on the kings of Europe; in a poetic letter to a friend he wrote that they sacrificed everything to their own caprice and that he would like to take away their toys. Their wars brought misery and destruction everywhere in Europe: "There are more fighters than workers on the land, more priests and parasites than merchants." He accused the monarchs of ruling the "children of the earth with trickery" and of enslaving their subjects.[32] Nor did he glorify the life of the soldier:

> The youth of the world should learn
> That military service is only elaborate misery.
> What Mars promises is only foolishness,
> Smoke and waning shadow and finally beggary.[33]

It was irrational, he believed, that in the service of their kings tens of thousands would kill others who could be recognized only because their uniforms were a different color and their standards bore a "different eagle."[34] The reference to the struggle of eagles is a clear reference to Austro-Prussian conflicts, but Maria Theresa was always excluded from criticism even in poems addressed to personal friends and not intended for publication. Barcsay wanted only a "thousand blessings" and marble monuments for this "great queen of the Hungarians."[35]

Bessenyei was equally loyal. He dedicated several of his works to Maria Theresa and thought of her with quasi-religious devotion even decades after her death. Personal loyalty, however, did not prevent Bessenyei in 1772 from examining the relationship between monarch and subjects in a play entitled *Ágis tragédiája* (The Tragedy of Agis). Using Plutarch and probably Gottsched as sources, he dramatized the struggle of two nobles in ancient Sparta to free the people from taxes, accumulated debts, and the tyranny of the rich. In the play Agis and Cleombrotes demand from King Leonidas the restoration of equality of means: the Law of Lycurgus. Under pressure, Leonidas orders the burning of the people's debt certificates. Although he recognizes the high motives of Agis and Cleombrotes, he demands they accept the responsibility for the rebellion and apologize. They both refuse. Cleombrotes professes only that he was faithful to the country. In his final message to the king, he says he was acting in the king's interest in attempting to ameliorate the people's misery. Agis exclaims even more proudly, "May Jupiter's thunderbolt strike me, but I admit no guilt whatsoever in Sparta." They are both condemned to death. Despite his defiance, Agis's dying words are a warning that the usual fate of rebels is death.[36] But the play not only seeks to discourage rebellion but suggests that the king should be a benevolent father and should secure his subjects' welfare and social harmony. Recent research in Hungary has stressed the influence of contemporary Viennese political theory on Bessenyei and emphasized that natural-right philosophy as advocated by Martini and Sonnenfels aimed at justifying Habsburg absolutism.[37] But it can also be noted that *The Tragedy of Agis* was written only a few years after Maria Theresa's *Urbarium*, which greatly improved the circumstances of the Hungarian serf. Therefore, it was possible to see the monarchy as the guarantor of *salus publicus* not only theoretically but on the basis of Hungarian social reality as well.

Bessenyei remained a monarchist all his life, but under the influence of the writings of John Locke he abandoned absolutist ideas for the concept of limited constitutional monarchy. Inspired by Locke's *Two Treatises on Government*, he wrote a pamphlet entitled *A törvények útja* (The Way of the Law) in which he rejected the idea of a benevolent absolute monarchy and explained the origin of the state on the basis of a social contract. People are born free, he argued, and only one's real father should have paternal power. Originally, people combined their individual liberties to create a "great and powerful liberty" and security for themselves. Consequently, "royal power, law, and liberty are always the heritage of the people," and the "supreme powers of the king can extend only to the limits established by the people." He further advocated equality of taxation and the separation of legislative and judicial powers, and he rejected the divine origin of kingship.[38] These were most advanced ideas for the 1770s in Vienna and Hungary, but the author did not succeed in publishing them. In Bessenyei's words, "this work, too, was prohibited by the honorable censorship whose task is to prevent people from gaining knowledge."[39] Thus, the pamphlet remained merely a document of the author's own development and the maturing of his political philosophy.

Bessenyei was most effective as a proponent of Hungarian cultural nationalism and cultural reforms. In many respects his work can be characterized as "the enrichment of a particular culture by importing values and patterns from other cultures."[40] In addition, Bessenyei also demonstrated impressive creative insight into contemporary Hungarian national and cultural needs. Between 1778 and 1781 he developed a comprehensive program for national and cultural revitalization in two pamphlets, *Magyarság* (Hungarianness) and *Egy magyar társaság iránt való jámbor szándék* (Pious Intention in regard to a Hungarian Association). As a true son of the Enlightenment, he considered knowledge "one of the most important means for the happiness of the country." The more widespread knowledge became, the happier the country. "Language, in particular the native language of each country, is the key to knowledge."[41] He stressed that in the past every nation had become cultivated through the use of its native language, never a foreign one.[42] It was his view that Hungarians had not progressed because everything had been written in Latin in Hungary since the eleventh century. In order to move ahead, Hungarians would have to "translate" the knowledge of the world into their native language. No other language would suffice, because "as long as the serfs speak Hungarian, the lords cannot forget it either."[43] To use a foreign language always reduce the borrowers to an inferior status.

According to Leonard W. Doob, at the early stages of their movement, nationalists tend to emphasize the need for the "development of potentiality" for their group.[44] Bessenyei was an early defender of the Hungarian language against those who suggested that it lacked power, depth, and flexibility to describe beauty and to express complex ideas. He compared the language to a mountain filled with gold ore which becomes valuable only when mined.[45] His prescription for the development of the potential of the Hungarian language included creating new words, defining existing terms through interpretive dictionaries, and using grammar books written by native speakers. He also urged the translation of foreign classics for the improvement of Hungarian literary life.[46]

With these reforms Bessenyei expected the betterment of the lot of the common people. With the remarkable naïveté characteristic of the intellectuals of the Enlightenment, he thought that if the works of Montesquieu and other important writers were available in Hungarian, everyone would be eager to read them. Even petty-bourgeois women in small towns would have more knowledge and understanding than the learned scholars of his own times.[47] Imitating the French, Bessenyei also wanted to see a Hungarian encyclopedia written by a group of experts. Such a work would spread knowledge not only in the arts and sciences but in various handicrafts that could not previously be learned in Hungarian.[48]

Bessenyei envisaged a Hungarian Academy of Sciences on the model of the Académie Francaise to carry out a program of cultural development and reform. The academy's highest priority would be the cultivation of the Hungarian language. Members would be selected from all parts of the country, regardless of religion, and "the introduction of equality would not be improper." The academy would organize scholarly activity, provide critical evaluation of scholarly works in its journal, keep copies of all books published in Hungary in its library, and publish award-winning works through its own press. Bessenyei expected the academy to be established with the help of the government and addressed the *Pious Intention* to the Hungarian magnates. In an obvious effort to please, he stated that "among the magnates were the greatest patriots" and they should use the prestige and power they had received from king and country to benefit the nation. Again, arguing from a utilitarian point of view, he stressed that the greatest benefit of the academy would be that "with the development of language, knowledge would spread among inhabitants belonging to all classes." Since poverty and ignorance went hand in hand, he expected to see material conditions improve as the population became better educated. Even the selection of civil servants would be facilitated as learned men made their knowledge and abilities known through publications supported by the academy.[49] During his visits from Vienna to Pest, he tried to organize a group of intellectuals into a scholarly association, but his plans did not materialize.[50]

Bessenyei's reform plans were motivated by deeply felt Hungarian patriotism. Reinforced by the example of past heroic deeds, he considered love of country and constructive efforts on its behalf a sacred obligation. He was also capable, however, of departing from long-held traditions. For instance, unlike most of his contemporaries, Bessenyei did not seem to hold the view that the nobility alone constituted the Hungarian nation. Not surprisingly for an early nationalist, his writings also contained a little boasting about the superiority of his people. He wrote, for example, that "no nation on earth surpasses the moral capabilities of the Hungarians, and if they would apply themselves they could be greater than anyone in learning, crafts, and military virtues.[51] But the Hungarians were not glorified at the expense of others. His purpose was rather to urge and encourage his compatriots to make vigorous efforts to advance the public welfare. Repeatedly, he stressed the usefulness of innovators in correcting the dangerous ignorance and backwardness of his times. His program for Hungary can be best summarized with the final admonition in one of his pamphlets: "We should not adhere to the old ways, because to follow them means only to desire ignorance. It is better for us to follow the great world."[52]

In retrospect, the significance of the literati of the Noble Hungarian Lifeguard is not primarily an aesthetic one. Their literary work did not stand the test of time, and the books they chose to translate were not representative of the best of the period. The student of literature cannot help but feel that instead of Calprenéde and Marmontel they should have translated Corneille, Racine, and Moliére. We should also note that Bessenyei was a poor dramatist and that his long philosophical poems are often dull and lack poetic force. The significance of the literati in the Guard lay in the impact of their ideas on their times and on successive generations. Although they personally remained faithful to their queen and the Monarchy, by propagating progressive enlightened Western ideas they undermined the prevailing atmosphere of baroque harmony among Hungarians and prepared the way for the intellectual ferment of the coming decades. They also provided new direction and a comprehensive framework for the development of a modern Hungarian national culture. Most of Bessenyei's ideas were realized through the efforts of cultural and political leaders of the next two generations. Hungarian cultural life did "follow the great world." In the first two decades of the nineteenth century, Hungarian literature was enriched and vitalized by the appearance of many foreign classics in Hungarian. At the same time, through the efforts of many scholars and writers, the Hungarian language was modernized, its vocabulary enlarged, and its grammatical structure clarified. Hungarian nationalists concentrated on making Hungarian the official language of the country and kept the language question at the center of public attention until the 1840s. Bessenyei's most important concrete proposal also materialized when István Széchenyi, a liberal aristocrat, founded the Hungarian Academy of Sciences at a session of the Diet in 1826.

In light of these developments it appears that Maria Theresa's intentions in founding the Noble Hungarian Lifeguard were realized only in part. The Guard fulfilled its immediate functions but did not accomplish its political purpose. The culture and learning its literati acquired at the imperial court were used not to promote centralism and the interests of the *Gesammtmonarchie* but to foster Hungarian cultural nationalism, which ultimately became a disintegrating force and a serious challenge to the Habsburg dynasty.

NOTES

1. Adam Wolf, *Aus dem Hofleben Maria Theresia's*, 2d ed. (Vienna, 1859), p. 353. Similarly, Maria Theresa wrote to her daughter-in-law, Maria Beatrix of Modena, in 1771, "I feel so deeply obliged to the Hungarian nation that I cannot commend it enough" (Eugen Guglia, *Maria Theresia: Ihr Leben und ihre Regierung*, 2 vols. (Munich, Berlin, 1917), 1:116. On Maria Theresa's reign, see further Alfred von Arneth, *Geschichte Maria Theresia's*, 10 vols. (Vienna, 1863-69); Heinrich Kretschmayr, *Maria Theresia* (Gotha, 1925). On the life of Maria Theresa's court, the diaries of her chief court official are especially valuable; see Rudolf Khevenhüller-Metsch and Hanns Schlitter, eds., *Aus der Zeit Maria Theresias: Tagebuch des Fürsten Johann Josef Khevenhüller-Metsch, 1742-1776*, 7 vols. (Vienna, Leipzig, 1907-25). For useful biographies in English, see Constance Lily Morris, *Maria Theresa, the Last Conservative* (New York, 1937); C. A. Macartney, *Maria*

Theresa and the House of Austria (London, 1969); and William J. McGill, *Maria Theresa* (New York, n.d.).
2. Mihály Horváth, *Magyarország történelme*, 2d ed., 8 vols. (Budapest, 1873), 7:209, 461.
3. Bálint Hóman and Gyula Szekfű, *Magyar történet*, 8 vols. (Budapest, 1928-34), 6:243.
4. Ervin Pamlényi, ed., *A History of Hungary* (London, Wellingborough, 1975), p. 181.
5. The earliest history of the Guard was written by a learned participant-observer Guardsman: Sándor Báróczy, *Feljegyzései a magyar nemesi testőrség életéből 1760-1800-ig* (Budapest, 1936). For a somewhat old-fashioned secondary work, see Aladár Ballagi, *A magyar királyi testőrség története, különös tekintettel irodalmi működésére* (Pest, 1872). The establishment of the Guard is well-described by János Illésy, "A magyar királyi nemes testőrség felállítása 1760-ban," *Hadtörténelmi Közlemények* 8 (1895): 367-94, 522-46. For the best and most recent scholarly account on the Guard, see Kálmán Hellebronth, ed., *A magyar testőrségek névkönyve* (Budapest, 1939). Hellebronth compiles an enormous amount of information including individual biographies of each Guardsman, summary tables of service years, geographic distribution of membership, etc. The volume also includes valuable introductory essays.
6. On the organization, uniforms, duties, and social position of the Guard, see Báróczy, *Feljegyzései*, pp. 13-23; Illéssy, "A magyar királyi nemes testőrség," pp. 532-46; Hellebronth, *Magyar testőrségek*, pp. 11-19.
7. Báróczy, *Feljegyzései*, p. 12.
8. On denationalizing trends, see Alajos Mednyánszky, "Hazafiúi gondolatok a magyar nyelv kiterjesztése dolgában," *Tudományos Gyűjtemény*, January 1822, pp. 7-10; Horváth, *Magyarország*, pp. 287-97.
9. For the characterization of Maria Theresa's treatment of the Hungarians as *douce violence* we are indebted to Oscar Jászi, *The Dissolution of the Habsburg Monarchy*, 2d ed. (Chicago, 1961), pp. 61-65.
10. Horváth, *Magyarország*, p. 289.
11. Henrik Marczali, *Magyarország története III Károlytól a bécsi kongresszusig* (Budapest, 1898), p. 369.
12. Horváth, *Magyarország*, pp. 296-97.
13. Hellebronth, *Magyar testőrségek*, p. 32.
14. Báróczy, *Feljegyzései*, pp. 51, 24, 36.
15. József Waldapfel, *A magyar irodalom a felvilágosodás korában* (Budapest, 1954), p. 7. See similarly Pál Pándi, ed., *A magyar irodalom története 1772-től 1849-ig* (Budapest, 1965), pp. 5-53.
16. Hellebronth, *Magyar testőrségek*, p. 47.
17. As I have said (n. 5), Báróczy was the author of the first history of the Guard. On his literary role, see Jenő Pintér, *Magyar irodalomtörténete*, vol. 4, (Budapest, 1931), pp. 680-84; Pándi, *Magyar irodalom*, pp. 63-64; János

Horváth, "Báróczy Sándor," *Budapesti Szemle* 107 (1901):92-113, 193-221.
18. Pándi, *Magyar irodalom*, p. 64.
19. Pintér, *Magyar irodalomtörténete*, pp. 681-89.
20. For a recent biography and analysis of Bessenyei's work, see József Szauder, *Bessenyei* (Budapest, 1953). Long introductory interpretive essays by the editors are included in József Szauder, ed., *Bessenyei György válogatott művei* (Budapest, 1953), and László Vajthó, ed., *Bessenyei válogatott írásai* (Budapest, 1961). See further the relevant chapters of the already cited literary histories by Pintér, Waldapfel, and Pándi.
21. Hellebronth, *Magyar testőrségek*, p. 93. Bessenyei also had a reputation for studiousness among his peers. A fellow Guardsman advised him in a poem to leave his books for a while and take a pretty girl to a dance (Ábrahám Barcsay, *Költeményei* [Budapest, 1933], pp. 65-66).
22. Szauder, *Bessenyei válogatott művei*, p. 235.
23. Ibid., p. 14.
24. On foreign influences, see Pintér, *Magyar irodalomtörténete*, pp. 350, 365, 369, etc.; Pándi, *Magyar irodalom*, pp. 27-28.
25. Szauder, *Bessenyei*, pp. 20-27.
26. György Bessenyei, *Magyarság*; *A magyar néző* (Budapest, 1932), p. 20. Bessenyei's two pamphlets, originally published in Vienna in 1778 and 1779, were republished in one volume in 1932.
27. György Bessenyei, *A törvények útja* (Budapest, 1930), p. 39.
28. For Bessenyei's views on religion, see *A Magyar néző*, pp. 22-27, 35-43, 51-53.
29. Ibid., p. 29.
30. Vajthó, *Bessenyei válogatott írásai*, p. 109.
31. Barcsay, *Költeményei*, pp. 38-40.
32. Ibid., pp. 24-25.
33. Ibid., p. 43.
34. Ibid., p. 83.
35. Ibid., pp. 23-24, 119-21.
36. Szauder, *Bessenyei válogatott művei*, pp. 59-123, quotation on p. 121.
37. János Bruckner, "Bessenyei és kora politikai filozófiája 1772-1780," *Irodalomtörténeti közlemények*, 1954, pp. 21-42.
38. Bessenyei, *A törvények útja*, pp. 17-19, 32-35, 38-40.
39. Ibid., p. 43.
40. Florian Znaniecki, *Modern Nationalities* (Urbana, 1952), p. 145.
41. György Bessenyei, *Egy magyar társaság iránt való jámbor szándék* (Budapest, 1931), p. 14. The "pious intention" in the title was for the establishment of the Hungarian Academy of Sciences; in declaring language the key to knowledge Bessenyei was probably under French influence. Jean

de La Bruyére (1645-96) wrote in *Les Caractéres,* "Les langues sont la clef ou l'entrée des sciences."
42. Bessenyei, *Magyarság,* p. 11.
43. Ibid., p. 12.
44. Leonard W. Doob, *Patriotism and Nationalism: Their Psychological Foundations* (New Haven, London, 1964), p. 63.
45. Bessenyei, *Magyarság,* p. 9.
46. Bessenyei, *Jámbor szándék,* p. 25.
47. Bessenyei, *Magyarság,* p. 17.
48. Bessenyei, *Jámbor szándék,* pp. 26-27.
49. Ibid., pp. 27-37.
50. Denis von Silagi, "Zur Geschichte der ersten madjarischen gelehrten Gesellschaft," *Südost-Forschungen* 20 (1961):204-24.
51. Vajthó, *Bessenyei válogatott írásai,* p. 44.
52. Bessenyei, *Magyarság,* p. 17.

BIOGRAPHICAL INDEX

Albrecht, Bernhard (late eighteenth century)
Painter, drawing-master in the Military Academy in Wiener Neustadt in the 1790s.

Alexander I (1777-1825)
Emperor of Russia, 1801-25.

Arnaud, Baculard d' (1718-1805)
French playwright and poet.

August II Fryderyk [Frederick Augustus II] (1670-1733)
Elector of Saxony and Polish king.

August III Fryderyk [Frederick Augustus III] (1696-1763)
Elector of Saxony and Polish king.

Barcsay, Ábrahám (1742-1806)
Royal Hungarian Lifeguard and poet; retired from the Imperial Army as colonel.

Báróczy, Sándor (1735-1809)
Royal Hungarian Lifeguard; author, translator; retired from the Imperial Army as colonel.

Bartha, Albert (1877-1980)
Hungarian officer. Graduated Ludovika, 1895; Defense Minister in Mihály Károlyi government, November 9— December 12, 1918; in Turkey, 1922-25. Bourgeois politician, 1940-43; Smallholder's Party politician, 1945. Col. Gen., 1945, Defense Minister, Aug. 21, 1946—Mar. 14, 1947. Emigrated to U.S., 1948.

Bartha, Lajos (1869-1946)
Hungarian officer. Graduated Ludovika, 1888 as 2nd Lt. Commanded an infantry regiment, 1914; a brigade, 1915; the Ludovika Academy, March 19, 1915—Nov. 1918. Retired, 1922.

Belitska, Sándor (1872-1939)
Hungarian officer. Graduated Ludovika, 1890 as 2nd. Lt. Defense Minister, Dec. 16, 1920—June 28, 1923. Retired 1923. Promoted General of Infantry, 1925.

Bem, Józef Zachariasz (1794-1850)
General of the Polish Army. Commander in chief of the Hungarian insurgent army in 1849.

Benedek, Ludwig August, Ritter von (1804-1881)
Austrian general, Master of the Ordnance; commanded the Austrian forces defeated at Königgrätz/Sadowa in 1866.

Bessenyei, György (1747-1811)
Royal Hungarian Lifeguard; poet, playwright, translator, and pamphleteer.

Blaskowitz, Johannes (1883-1948)
German Colonel-General, World War II period

Blomberg, Werner von (1878-1946)
German Field Marshal and War Minister, World War II period.

Borkowski, Mikołaj
Captain of the Polish Army; Vice-Commandant of the Cadet Corps in chełm.

Bradley, Omar Nelson (1893-1981)
American General in World War II.

Brauchitsch, Walther von (1881-1948)
German Field Marshal, World War II period.

Bronsart von Schellendorff, Paul (1832-1891)
German General, War Minister.

Bruhl, Alojzy Fryderyk (1739-1793)
General of the Polish Army.

Cebulski, Ignacy
Colonel of the Polish Army; Commandant of the Cadet Corps in Chełm.

Charles (1887-1922)
Ruler of Austria-Hungary, 1916-18; I as Emperor of Austria; IV as King of Hungary.

Chrzanowski, Wojciech (1793-1861)
General of the Polish Army; Chief of the General Staff in the Sardinian Army in 1849.

Clausewitz, Karl von (1780-1831)
Prussian general, military theorist.

Closca (Ioan Oarga) (1747-1785)
Leader of peasant uprising in Transylvania, 1784-1785.

Constantine I, Gluksbourg (1868-1923)
King of Greece, 1913-1922.

Corneille, Pierre (1606-1684)
French dramatist and poet.

Crisan (Marcu Giurgiu) (1733-1785)
Leader of peasant uprising in Transylvania, 1784-85.

Csáky, Károly (1873-1945)
Hungarian officer. Graduated Ludovika, 1891, as cadet warrant officer. Defense Minister, June 28, 1923—Sept. 10, 1929. Lieutenant General, 1924; General of Cavalry and retired, 1927.

Czarnowski, Franciszek (?-1870)
Officer of the Polish Army.

Czartoryski, Adam Kazimierz (1734-1823)
Prince, General of Poland, Commandant of the Cadet Corps.

Czetwertyński, Władysław
Officer of the Polish Army.

Daun, Leopold Joseph Reichsgraf und Herr von und zu Daun (1705-1766)
Habsburg *General-Feldzeugmeister*, president of the *Hofkriegsrat*; adviser of the Empress Maria Theresa. Commanding officer of the Military Academy in Wiener Neustadt, 1752-1766.

Destouches, Philippe Néricault (1680-1754)
French playwright.

Dorat, Claude-Joseph (1734-1780)
French poet and writer.

Einem, Karl von (1853-1934)
German Colonel General, War Minister.

Eisenhower, Dwight David (1890-1969)
American General in World War II; President of the United States, 1953-1961.

Eugene of Savoy (1663-1736)
Imperial general; commanded the Habsburg armies in several wars against the Ottomans and in the Wars of the Spanish and Polish Succession.

Falkenhorst, Nikolaus von (1885-1968)
German Colonel-General.

Falkowski, Juliusz (1815-1892)
Writer, emigration activist.

Biographical Index

Farkas, Ferenc (1892-1944)
 Hungarian officer. Graduated, Ludovika, 1912, as 2nd Lieutenant. Commander, Ludovika Academy, Oct. 1, 1939—August 20, 1943. Col.-General 1944, in exile in Munich.

Fejérváry, Géza (1833-1914)
 Austro-Hungarian officer and official. Graduated, Wiener Nuestadt Military Academy, 1851, as 2nd. Lt. Maria Theresa Order for bravery at Solferino; trusted aide of Francis Joseph. Defense Minister, Oct. 18, 1884—April 27, 1903. Col. General of Engineers, 1887. Prime Minister, June 18, 1905—April 8, 1906.

Fiszer, Stanisław (1769-1812)
 General of the Polish Army.

Francois, Herman (1856-1933)
 German Lieutenant General in World War I

Franz [Francis] I. (1708-1765)
 Duke of Lotharingia [Lorraine], husband of Maria Theresa. Holy Roman Emperor, 1745-1765.

Franz [Francis] I (1768-1835)
 Habsburg Holy Roman Emperor as Franz II, 1792-1806, Emperor of Austria as Franz I, 1804-1835

Franz [Francis] Joseph I (1830-1916)
 Habsburg. Emperor of Austria and King of Hungary, 1848-1916.

Friedrich III (1415-1493)
 Habsburg. "King of the Romans" from 1440, Emperor of the Holy Roman Empire, 1452-1493.

Friedrich Wilhelm of Brandenburg (1620-1688)
 Elector of Brandenburg, 1640-1688.

Friedrich Wilhelm I of Prussia (1688-1740)
 King of Prussia, 1713-40.

George I., Gluksbourg (1845-1913)
    King of the Hellenes, 1863-1913.

Goltz, Colmar, Baron von der (1843-1916)
    German Field Marshal.

Górnicki, Łukasz (1527-1603)
    Humanist, political writer.

Gottsched, Johann Christoph (1700-1766)
    German author, playwright, and professor of poetry at the University of Leipzig.

Grabowski, Karol (1790-1840)
    Officer of the Polish Army, Commandant of the Cadet Corps in Kalisz.

Grabowski, Piotr (?-1625)
    Priest, author of works on economy.

Griewank, Karl
    German historian.

Guderian, Heinz (1888-1954)
    German General, Chief of the General Staff late in World War II.

Haig, Sir Douglas, the Earl (1861-1928)
    British Field Marshal.

Hammerstein-Equord, Kurt, von Freiherr (1877-1943)
    German Colonel-General.

Hanke, Jozef Ludwik (1834-1871)
    General of the Polish Army.

Hanke, Maurycy (1773-1830)
    General of the Polish army.

Haubrich, József (1883-1939)

Hungarian Social Democratic politician. Budapest city commandant and people's commissar, 1919. Probably knew of June 24 attempt at a counterrevolutionary putsch. Defense Minister in Social Democratic government of August 1-6, 1919, after fall of HSR. Condemned to death by counterrevolutionary court, but sent to USSR under exchange of prisoners, became steelworker.

Haugwitz, Friedrich Wilhelm Graf (1702-1765)

Adviser of the Empress Maria Theresa; president of the *Directorium in publicis at cameralibus*, Chancellor.

Hazai, Samu (1851-1942)

Hungarian officer. Graduated Ludovika, 1874, as cadet under the name Kohn. Father, a practicing Jew, ran a small distillery. Hazai completed six years of academic secondary school. As an officer became Hungarianized, took the name of Hazai and converted to Roman Catholicism. HOTC 1879; SC in Vienna 1881; then staff appointments chiefly in MOD. General of Brigade 1907. Defense Minister Jan. 17, 1910—Feb. 19, 1917. General of Infantry, Aug. 1, 1914; Col. General, Nov. 1, 1916. Quartermaster General for all the Monarchy's armed forces, Feb. 19, 1917 until end of war. Enjoyed full confidence of Francis Joseph. Much credit is due him for development of the *honvédség* and Ludovika Academy. After retirement lived highly respected in Budapest until his death.

Heck, Josef (1908-1959)

Colonel, Commanding officer of the Theresian Military Academy in Wiener Neustadt, 1958-1959.

Heeringen, Josias von (1850-1926)

German Colonel General, War Minister.

Heideck, Karl Wilhelm (1788-1861)

One of the three regents during King Otto's initial reign as a minor Bavarian (1833-1836)

Heim, Géza (1888-1942)
　Hungarian officer. Graduated, Ludovika, 1909, as 2nd Lt. Order of Maria Theresa, May 8, 1916, for action at San Martino del Carso. Taught at the Ludovika, 1928-34. General, 1940.

Henryk III Walezy (1551-1589)
　King of Poland and France.

Heye, Wilhelm (1869-1947)
　German Colonel-General; Commander of *Reichswehr*.

Hindenburg, Paul von (1847-1934)
　German Field Marshal; *Reichspraesident*.

Horea (Vasile Ursu Nicola) (1730-1785)
　Leader of peasant uprising in Transylvania, 1784-1785.

Horvath, Imre (1866-1936)
　Hungarian officer. Graduated, Ludovika, 1881, as cadet warrant officer. Order of Maria Theresa in Galicia, 1916. General of Brigade, 1923. Retired, 1924, as Lieutenant General.

Hube, Michal Jan (1737-1807)
　Director of sciences in the Knights' School.

Hunyadi, János (1407/9-1456)
　Voivode of Transylvania and Regent of Hungary.

Hutier, Oskar (1857-1934)
　German Lieutenant General.

Ibrahim Pasha (1789-1848)
　Viceroy of Egypt.

Jan III Sobieski (1629-1696)
　Military commander and Polish king.

Biographical Index

Jany, Gusztáv (1883-1947)
Hungarian officer. Graduated, Ludovika, 1905, as 2nd. Lt. Commander, Ludovika Academy, Oct. 1, 1931-Aug. 21, 1936. Commanded an army on the Don 1942-43. Col. General, resigned from the regulars, Oct. 1, 1943. Moved to Austria, April 1945, but returned voluntarily 1946; sentenced by a People's Court to die by firing squad.

Jasiński, Jakub (1759-1794)
General of the Polish Army, revolutionist poet.

Johann of Austria (1782-1859)
Archduke of Austria. Commanding officer of the Military Academy in Wiener Neustadt, 1805-1849.

Joseph II (1741-1790)
Maria Theresa's son, Holy Roman Emperor, 1765-1790.

Joseph Anthony (Josef Anton, József Antal) (1776-1847)
Archduke, palatine. Son of Emperor and King Leopold II. Successfully interceded between king and nation, supported the plans of reformer statesman Count István Széchenyi. Worked toward establishment of the Ludovika Academy. Founded the School of Industry, ancestor of today's Budapest Technical University.

Joseph Charles (Josef Karl, József Károly) (1833-1905)
Archduke, palatine. First commander in chief of the *honvédség* and a great believer and assistant in developing the Ludovika Academy. Wounded and decorated in Austro-Prussian War of 1866.

Kapodistrias, John (1776-1831)
First President of the Greek State, 1828-1831.

Karatzas, George (1803-1882)
Director of the Military Academy (1844-1862).

Károlyi, Mihály (1875-1955)
Hungarian left-wing politician, elected president of the republic, Dec. 13, 1918.

Kary, Béla (1875-?)
Hungarian officer. Graduated, Ludovika, 1894, as 2nd. Lt. Retired 1926 as Lieutenant General.

Kerekes, József (1880-1961)
Hungarian officer. Graduated, Ludovika, 1898, as cadet warrant officer. Instructor at Ludovika Academy. Commanded 1st Division of the Republican Army in 1919; toward the end of the Hungarian Socialist Republic Commanded a training course held on the Ludovika premises. Afterwards stripped of rank. Appointed retired Colonel General after 1945.

Kinsky von Wchinitz und Tettau, Franz Joseph Graf (1739-1805)
Major-General, commanding officer of the Wiener Neustadt Military Academy, 1779-1805.

Kiss, Lajos (1888-1943)
Hungarian revolutionary. A printer, he was member of the Budapest Central Workers' and Soldiers' Soviet in 1919, city commandant of Budapest and presiding judge at the trial of the Ludovika cadets. Sentenced to eight years, imprisonment after fall of the Hungarian Socialist Republic, he was sent to USSR in an exchange of prisoners.

Kluge, Guenther von (1882-1944)
German Field Marshal.

Kochanowski, Jan (1530-1584)
One of the most outstanding Polish poets.

Kniaziewicz, Karol Otton (1762-1842)
General of the Polish Army.

Kołaczkowski, Klemens (1793-1830)
General of the Polish Army.

Kornanski, Stanisław (1700-1773)
Political writer, publicist, pedagogue, educational reformer, poet, and dramatist.

Konstanty Pawlowica (1779-1831)
Great prince of Russia, Tsar Alexander I's brother, commander in chief, Army of the Polish Kingdom.

Korais, Adamantios (1748-1833)
Greek writer.

Kościuszko, Andrzej Tadeusz Bonaventura (1746-1817)
Polish national hero, General of the Polish Army and the army of the United States of America; insurrection leader in Poland in 1794.

Koss, Franciszek (1792-1841)
Director of Sciences in the Cadet Corps in Kalisz.

Kossuth, Louis (Lajos) (1802-1894)
Hungarian revolutionary leader.

Krasicki, Ignacy (1735-1801)
Poet, novelist, comedy writer.

Kruszewski, Ignacy Marceli (1799-1879)
Colonel of the Polish Army, Belgian general.

La Calprenéde, Gauthier de (1614-1663)
French novelist; served in the Regiment of Guards in Paris and became gentleman-in-ordinary in the royal household.

Lakatos, Géza (1890-1967)
Hungarian officer. Graduated, Ludovika, 1910, as 2nd Lt. Rose to Colonel General and army commander by Aug. 1, 1943. Prime Minister, Aug. 29-Oct. 15, 1944. Died in Australia during visit to relations.

Lehar, Anton (1867-1962)
Colonel of the Austro-Hungarian General Staff; won the Order of Maria Theresa and the Gold Medal for Valor in World War I.

Lenin, Vladimir Il'ic (Uljanov) (1870-1924)
Russian revolutionary and statesman.

Leonidas (third century B.C.)
In his play Bessenyei probably referred to Leonidas II, King of Sparta, 252-236 B.C.

Leszczyński, Stanisław (1677-1766)
Polish king, 1704-1709.

Lind, John (Linde, Jan) (1737-1781)
Director of sciences in the Knights' School.

Lipowski, Błażej (seventeenth century)
Author of the first infantry regulations in the Polish language.

Locke, John (1692-1704)
British philosopher and political theorist.

Louis XIV (1638-1715)
King of France, 1643-1715.

Ludendorff, Erich (1865-1937)
German Lieutenant General, First Quartermaster-General.

Ludovica, Maria, Duchess of Modena-Este (1787-1816)
As wife of Francis I became queen of Hungary, Jan. 6, 1808. Received coronation gift of 50,000 forints from Hungarian estates and donated it for the establishment of a Hungarian officer training school.

Ludwig A, Wittelsbach (1786-1868)
King of Bavaria, father of King Otto of Greece.

Lycurgus (ninth century B.C. ?)
Political reformer in Sparta; probable founder of Spartan constitution.

MacArthur, Douglas (1880-1964)
American General.

Mallet
Officer of the Polish Army.

Manstein, Erich von (1887-1973)
German Field Marshal.

Mao Tse-tung (1893-1976)
Chinese revolutionary and statesman.

Maria Theresa (1717-1780)
Queen of Hungary and Bohemia, Archduchess of Austria, 1740-80.

Marycjusz, Szymon of Pilzno (1516-1574)
Professor of the Cracow Academy, pedagogue.

Marmontel, Jean Francois (1723-1799)
French writer, historian, and member of the French Academy.

Martini, Karl Anton (?-1800)
Austrian author and professor of law at the University of Vienna.

Martiz, Georg von der (1856-1929)
German Lieutenant General.

Maximilian I (1459-1519)
Romano-German King, 1493-1508; Holy Roman Emperor, 1508-19.

Mészáros, Lázár (1796-1858)
Hungarian officer. An excellent cavalry officer in the Imperial Army, commanded the 5th Hussars in Italy, 1845. Appointed Defense Minister of first Hungarian government by the king in 1848. With great competence and enthusiasm, set about organizing a new Hungarian Army and establishing the

Ludovika Academy. Exile in England after capitulation at Világos (Siria).

Mierosławski, Ludwik (1814-1878)
Leader of national liberation fights in Poland, Sicily, Baden, and Palatinate.

Miklós, Béla (1890-1952)
Hungarian officer. Graduated, Ludovika, 1910 as 2nd Lt. Colonel General and army commander, Aug. 1, 1943. Prime Minister, Dec. 22, 1944-Nov. 15, 1945. Remained a bourgeois party politician until his death.

Mitzler de Kolof Wawrzyniec Krzysztof (1711-1778)
Physician, publisher, and printer.

Modrzewski, Frycz Andrzej (1503-1572)
Most eminent Polish political writer of the Renaissance.

Moliére, Jean Baptiste (1622-1673)
French playwright.

Montesquieu, Charles Louis de Secondat, Baron de la Brede et de (1689-1755)
Influential French author and political theorist.

Moszyński, Fryderyck (1737-1817)
General of the Polish army, deputy commandant of the Knights' School.

Mycielski, Ignacy (1784-1831)
General of the Polish Army, Commandant of the Cadet Corps in Kalisz.

Nagy, Vilmos Nagybaczoni (1884-1976)
Hungarian officer. Graduated, Ludovika, 1905 as 2nd Lt. Colonel General and army commander, May 1, 1940. Defense Minister, Sept. 24, 1943. Imprisoned by extreme right-wing government, later persecuted by extreme left-wing government.

Biographical Index

Napoleon I (1769-1821)
Emperor of the French, 1804-1815.

Nebogatov, Nikolaj Ivanovic (1849-1922)
Russian rear admiral, surrendered the remnants of the Russian fleet after Tsushima in 1905.

Niemcewica, Julian Ursyn (1758-1841)
Poet, playwright, novelist, political, social, and cultural activist.

Nikolai I Pawlowicz (1796-1858)
Tsar of Russia, King of Poland, 1825-1855.

Novak von Arienti, Guido Freiherr von (1859-1928)
Commanding officer of the Theresian Military Academy during World War I.

Obrenović, Miloš (1780-1860)
Prince of Serbia, 1817-1839.

Olędzki, Ksawery (1790-after 1833)
Colonel of the Polish Army, commandant of Infantry Cadet School.

Otto, Wittelsbach (1815-1867)
First King of Greece, 1833-1862.

Papen, Franz von (1897-1969)
German Chancellor, diplomat.

Papp, Elemer Vary (1870-?)
Hungarian officer. Graduated, Ludovika, 1889 as cadet warrant officer. Commander, Ludovika Academy, Aug. 1, 1914—April 5, 1915. Later service at the front and on home territory. Retired after World War I.

Paprocki, Bartosz (1543-1614)
Herald, historian, moralist poet.

Paszkowski, Józef (1787-1858)
    Colonel of the Polish Army, professor of the Applied School, military writer.

Peyfuss, Max Demeter (b.1944)
    University lecturer at the Institute for East and Southeast European research in Vienna.

Pfleiderer, Krzysztof (1736-1821)
    Director of sciences in the Knights' School.

Philipp, Johannes (b.1930)
    Austrian officer. Commanding officer of the Theresian Military Academy, 1980-1984; from 1985, *Armeekommandant* of the Austrian Army.

Pestalozzi, Johann Heinrich (1746-1837)
    Swiss pedagogue.

Plutarch (c.46-c.120)
    Greek author, biographer.

Podczaski, Wincenty
    Colonel, commandant of the Cadet Corps in Kalisz.

Pope, Alexander (1688-1744)
    British poet.

Potocki, Stanislaw Kostka (1755-1821)
    Politician, writer, art theorist.

Potocki, Tomasz (1809-1861)
    Economist, publicist, participant in the November uprising.

Potocki, Wincenty (?-1825)
    General of the Polish Army.

Prądzyński, Ignacy (1792-1850)
    General of the Polish Army, military writer.

Racine, Jean (1639-1699)
    French dramatist and poet.

Radziwiłł, Karol Stanisław (1734-1790)
    Prince, the Vilnius *voivode*.

Raktivan, Manolis (1870-1931)
    Distinguished officer of the Greek Army during World War I (1916-18).

Rátz, Jenő (1882-1951)
    Hungarian officer. Graduated, Ludovika, 1904 as 2nd. Lt. Career included command of the Staff College and service as chief of the general staff. Defense Minister, April 30, 1938 as Colonel General. Later a right-wing politician. Deputy Prime Minister, March 22-June 19, 1944. After the war, given life sentence of hard labor by People's Court; died in prison.

Regulski, Józef (1773-1851)
    Colonel, Commandant of the Cadet Corps in Kalisz.

Reineck, Edward (1795-1854)
    Bavarian director of the Military Academy (1830-1840).

Reinhardt, Walther (1872-1930)
    German General.

Rej, Mikołaj (1505-1569)
    One of the most distinguished Polish authors.

Révy, Kálmán (1877-1949)
    Hungarian officer. Graduated, Ludovika, 1896, as cadet warrant officer. Prisoner of the Russians during World War I. Commander, Ludovika Academy, Aug. 28, 1919-1925. General, Jan. 1, 1924. Retired and became manager of National Officers' Club.

Rhigas Pheraios (1757-1798)
    Greek revolutionary agitator and publicist.

Roder, Vilmos (1881-1969)
: Hungarian officer. Graduated, Ludovika, 1899 as 2nd Lt. Chief of the General Staff, May 26, 1930—Jan. 16, 1935. General of Infantry, Jan. 1, 1933. Defense Minister, Oct. 12, 1936—Sept. 1937, at a time of considerable army development.

Rommel, Erwin (1891-1944)
: German officer and *Generalfeldmarschall*. In 1938-1939 commanding officer of the German war-school in the castle of Wiener Neustadt.

Roon, Albrecht, Graf von (1803-1879)
: Prussian and German Field Marshal, War Minister.

Rouget, Mikołaj (1781-1847)
: Colonel-engineer, military writer, subdirector of the Applied School of Artillery and Engineering.

Rundstedt, Gerd von (1875-1953)
: German Field Marshal.

Rydel
: Officer of the Polish Army.

Rzewuski, Ludwik
: Officer of the Polish Army.

Schleicher, Kurt von (1882-1934)
: German Lieutenant General, War Minister, Chancellor.

Sierakowski, Karol (1750-1815)
: General of the Polish Army.

Sinkó, Ervin (1898-1967)
: Leading Hungarian communist politician. In July 1919 took over guarding and reeducation of Ludovika Academy students sentenced by People's Court, showing a kind and understanding attitude and lecturing on Marxism and the essentials of communism. Emigrated after fall of the Hungarian Socialist Republic. Served as Yugoslav partisan in World War II. Pro-

fessor and head of Hungarian Department at Novi Sad University, 1959.

Sipos, Árpád (1879-1950)
Hungarian officer. Graduated, Ludovika, 1897 as cadet warrant officer. Commander, Ludovika Academy, 1925-1928.

Sokolnicki, Michał (1760-1816)
General of the Polish Army.

Sonnenfels, Joseph von (1732-1817)
Austrian political theorist, author, Aulic Councilor, and influential government consultant.

Sowiński, Józef Longin (1777-1831)
General of the Polish Army.

Speromilios, Mihocil (1800-1880)
Hero of the Greek War of Independence and Director of the Military Academy (1840-1844).

Stanisław August Poniatowski (1731-1798)
Polish King, 1764-1795.

Stein, Aurél (1862-1943)
Hungarian officer and scholar. Graduated, Ludovika, 1886 as 2nd Lt. In reserves from Jan. 1, 1887. Studied in Kesmark (Kezmarok), Vienna, Tübingen, and Leipzig. From 1888, a teacher of Sanskrit at an Indian university, later leading several expeditions to Central Asia. Returned to Hungary several times, visited the Ludovika Academy, to which he donated 600,000 crowns, in 1924; later made several subsequent gifts.

Stromfeld, Aurél (1878-1927)
Hungarian officer. Graduated, Ludovika, 1896 as cadet warrant officer. Taught tactics at the Vienna Military College. Commander, Ludovika Academy, Nov. 25, 1918—Jan. 15, 1919. Served in the Ministry of Defense during the Hungarian Socialist Republic and was charged with supervising the Ludovika. Republican chief of the general staff, 1919. After fall

of the HSR, pleaded for fair treatment for Ludovika students
and staff. Sentenced to three years' imprisonment and stripped
of rank 1920, he nevertheless remained publicly respected.

Student, Kurt (1890-1978)
Luftwaffe Colonel-General.

Sułkowski, August (1729-1786)
The Rydzyn lord of a manor, the Gniezno, Kalisz and Poznan *voivode*, vice-commandant of the Knights' School.

Széchenyi, Count István (1791-1860)
Hungarian magnate and liberal politician, leader of the Hungarian Era of Reform, 1825-1848.

Szepessy, András (1875-1916)
Hungarian officer. Graduated, Ludovika, 1894 as cadet warrant officer. Died in action as a field officer at Rarance, awarded the Order of Maria Theresa.

Szinay, Béla (1880-1948)
Hungarian officer. Graduated, Ludovika, 1899 as cadet warrant officer. Commander, Ludovika Academy, 1928—Oct. 1, 1931.

Sztyrmer, Ludwik (1809-1866)
General of the Polish Army, novelist, participicant in the November uprising.

Szurmay, Sándor (1860-1945)
Hungarian officer. Graduated, Ludovika, 1884, as 2nd Lt. Contributed much to the development of the Ludovika Academy. Commanded an army group in World War I, winning the Order of Maria Theresa for the Battle of Uzsok. Defense Minister Feb. 10, 1917—Oct. 31, 1918. General of Infantry Aug. 10, 1917.

Tarnowski, Jan (1488-1561)
Military commander and writer.

Thurheim, Granz Ludwig Graf (1710-1782)
    Austrian officer. Local commanding officer of the officer-cadet school in Wiener Neustadt, 1752-1756.

Tombor, Jenő (1880-1946)
    Hungarian officer. Graduated Ludovika, 1899, as 2nd Lt. Served at GHQ, the Hungarian Revolutionary Army, 1919. Retired, 1920. Lt. General, Jan. 6, 1945. Defense Minister, Nov. 15, 1945—July 27, 1946. Col. General, May 1, 1946.

Towarek, Rudolf (1885-1959)
    Austrian officer and Major-General. Commanding officer of the Theresian Military Academy in Wiener Neustadt, 1934-1938.

Trębicki, Stanisław (1792-1830)
    General of the Polish Army, commandant of Infantry Cadet School.

Tricoupis, Harilaos (1832-1896)
    Greek Prime Minister, 1882-1885, 1887-1890, 1892-1895.

Tyzenhaus, Antoni (1733-1785)
    Lithuanian Master of the Horse and Treasurer.

Unruh, Fritz von (1885-1970)
    German playwright, novelist, poet.

Upton, Emory (1839-1881)
    American Brigadier General and author.

Valentin d'Hauterive, Franciszek
    Colonel of the Polish Army, participant in the November uprising.

Vaugoin, Carl (1873-1949)
    Austrian War Minister, 1921, 1922-1933.

Venizelos, Eleftherios (1864-1936)
   Greek Prime Minister, 1910-1920, 1924, 1928-1932.

Verdy du Vernois, von (1832-1910)
   German General and author.

Voltaire, Francois-Marie Arouet (1694-1778)
   French author, poet, playwright; the leading writer of the Enlightenment.

Waldersee, Alfred, Graf von (1832-1904)
   German Field Marshal, Chief of Staff.

Wallenstein (or Waldstein) Wenzel von (1583-1634)
   Imperial general; commanded the Habsburg armies in the Thirty Years' War.

Waligórski, Józef
   Officer of the Polish Army.

Wasilewski, Józef (1765-1831)
   General of the Polish Army, commandant of the Cadet Corps in Kalisz.

Wasilewski, Leonard
   General of the Polish Army, writer, activist of 1848 revolution.

Wereszczyński, Józef (1530 or 1555-1598 or 1599)
   Priest, publicist.

Wierzejewski, Hilary
   Vice-commandant of the Cadet Corps in Kalisz, Captain of the Polish Army.

Witzleben, Erwin von (1881-1944)
   German Field Marshal.

Wladyslaw IV Waza (1559-1648)
   Polish King, 1632-1648.

Wysocki, Piotr (1797-1874)
    Officer of the Polish Army.

Young, Edward (1683-1765)
    British poet.

Zygmunt III Waza (1566-1632)
    Polish King, 1587-1632.

LIST OF CONTRIBUTORS

Dr. Gábor Bona
Historical Institute of the Hungarian Academy of Sciences, Budapest

Dr. Gertrud Buttlar-Elberberg
Stadtarchivdirektor, Wiener Neustadt

Doc. Dr. Jerzy Cytowski
Military History Academy, Warsaw

Professor István Deák
Institute on East Central Europe, Columbia University, New York

Professor László Deme
New College of the University of South Florida, Sarasota, Florida

Colonel Walter Scott Dillard
United States Military Academy, West Point, New York

Distinguished University Professor Stephen Fischer-Galati
University of Colorado, Boulder, Colorado

Dr. Tibor Hajdú
Historical Institute of the Hungarian Academy of Sciences, Budapest

Professor Robin Higham
Kansas State University, Manhattan, Kansas; Editor, *Military Affairs*

Mr. Kálmán Kéri
Budapest,

Professor Emeritus Béla K. Király
Brooklyn College, CUNY, New York

Major John Moncure
Assistant Professor, United States Army Military Academy,
West Point, New York

Dr. Habil. Ljudmil Petrov
Balkan Institute, Institute of Military History, Sofia

Dr. Richard Georg Plaschka
Director, Institute for Eastern and Southeastern European Studies,
University of Vienna

Professor Emeritus Theodore Ropp
Duke University, Durham, North Carolina

Professor Thanos Veremis
University of Athens

Atlantic Studies on Society in Change
WAR AND SOCIETY IN EAST CENTRAL EUROPE

Volume

I. *Special Topics and Generalizations on the Eighteenth and Nineteenth Century.* Edited by Béla K. Király and Gunther E. Rothenberg. 1979.

II. *East Central European Society and War in the Pre-Revolutionary 18th Century.* Edited by Gunther E. Rothenburg, Béla K. Király, and Peter F. Sugar. 1982.

III. *From Hunyadi to Rákóczi: War and Society in Late Medieval and Early Modern Hungary.* Edited by János M. Bak and B. K. Király. 1982.

IV. *East Central European Society and War in the Era of Revolutions: 1775-1856.* Edited by B. K. Király. 1984.

V. *Essays on World War I: Origins and Prisoners of War.* Edited by Samuel R. Williamson Jr. and Peter Pastor. 1983.

VI. *Essays on World War I: Total War and Peacemaking, A Case Study on Trianon.* Edited by B. K. Király, Peter Pastor and Ivan Sanders. 1982.

VII. *Army, Aristocracy, Monarchs: War, Society and Government in Austria, 1618-1780.* Thomas M. Baker. 1982.

VIII. *The First Serbian Uprising 1804-1813.* Edited by Wayne S. Vucinich. 1982.

IX. *The Effects of World War II:Czechoslovak Policy and the Hungarian Minority 1945-1948.* Kálmán Janics. 1982.

X. *At the Brink of War and Peace: The Tito-Stalin Split in a Historic Perspective.* Edited by Wayne S. Vucinich. 1982.

XI. *The First War Between Socialist States: The Hungarian Revolution of 1956 and Its Impact.* Edited by Béla K. Király, Barbara Lotze, Nándor Dreisziger.

XII. *The Effects of World War I, The Uprooted: Hungarian Refugees and Their Impact on Hungary's Domestic Politics.* István I. Mócsy. 1983.

XIII. *The Effects of World War I: The Class War After the Great War: The Rise of Communist Parties in East Central Europe, 1918-1921.* Edited by Ivo Banac. 1983.

XIV. *The Crucial Decade: East Central European Society and National Defense, 1859-1870.* Edited by Béla K. Király. 1984.

XVII. *Insurrections, Wars, and the Eastern Crisis in the 1870s.* Edited by B. K. Király and Gale Stokes. 1985.

XX. *Revolutions and Interventions in Hungary and Its Neighbor States, 1918-1919.* Edited by Peter Pastor.

XXII. *Essays on East Central European Society and War. 1740-1920's.* Edited by Béla K. Király and Stephen Fischer-Galati. 1988.

XXIII. *East Central European Maritime Commerce and Naval Policies, 1789-1913.* Edited by Apostolos E. Vacalopoulos, Constantinos P. Svolopoulos, Béla K. Király. 1988.

XXIV. *The East Central European Officer Corps 1740-1920s: Social Origins, Selection, Education, and Training.* Edited by Béla K. Király and Walter Scott Dillard. 1988.

XXV. *East Central European War Leaders: Civilian and Military.* Edited by Béla K. Király, Albert Nofi. 1988.

XXVI. *The Fall of the Medieval Kingdom of Hungary, Mohács 1526, — Buda 1541.* Géza Perjés. 1988.

XXVII. *The Press During the Hungarian Revolution of 1848-1849.* Domokos Kosáry. 1986.

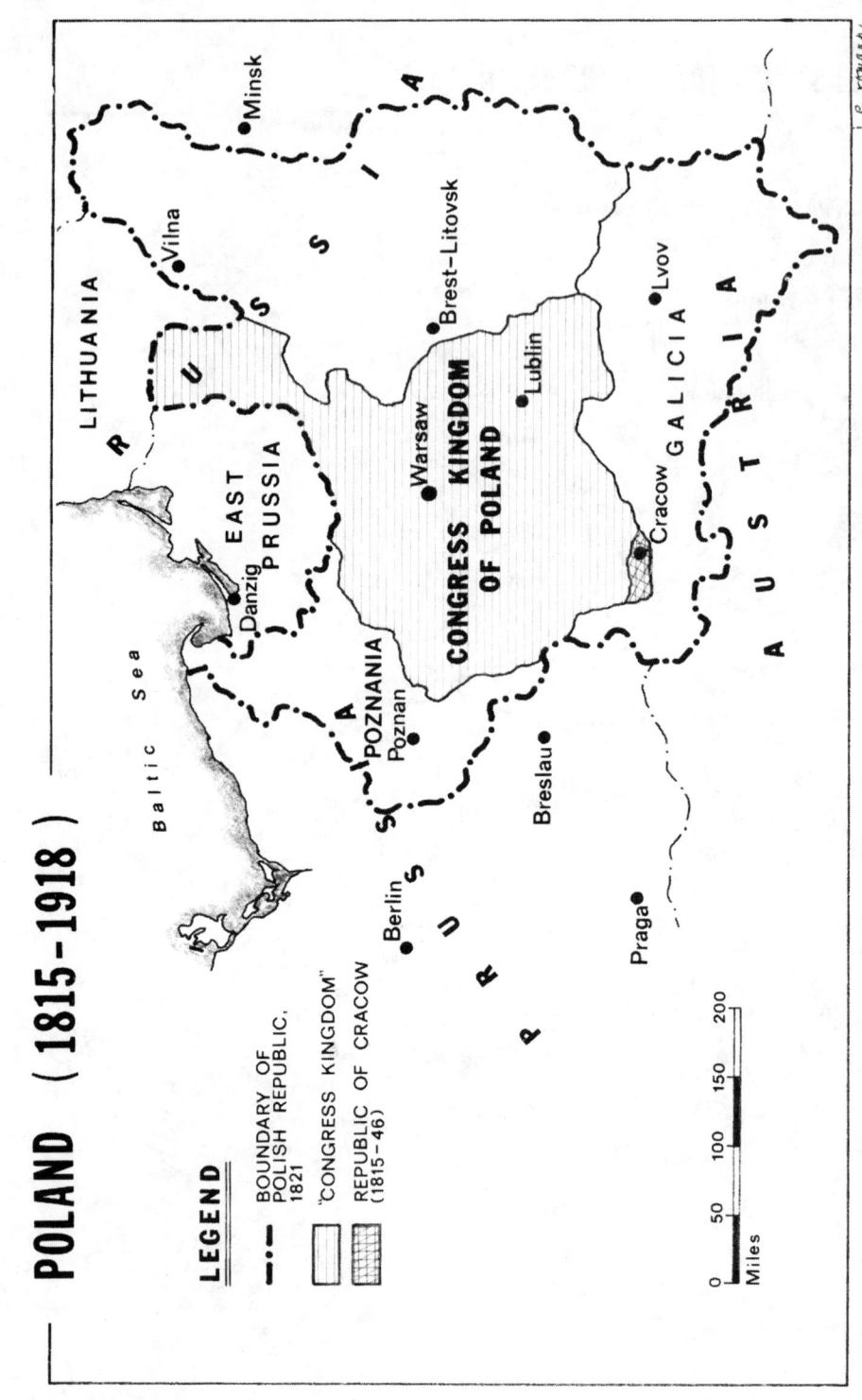

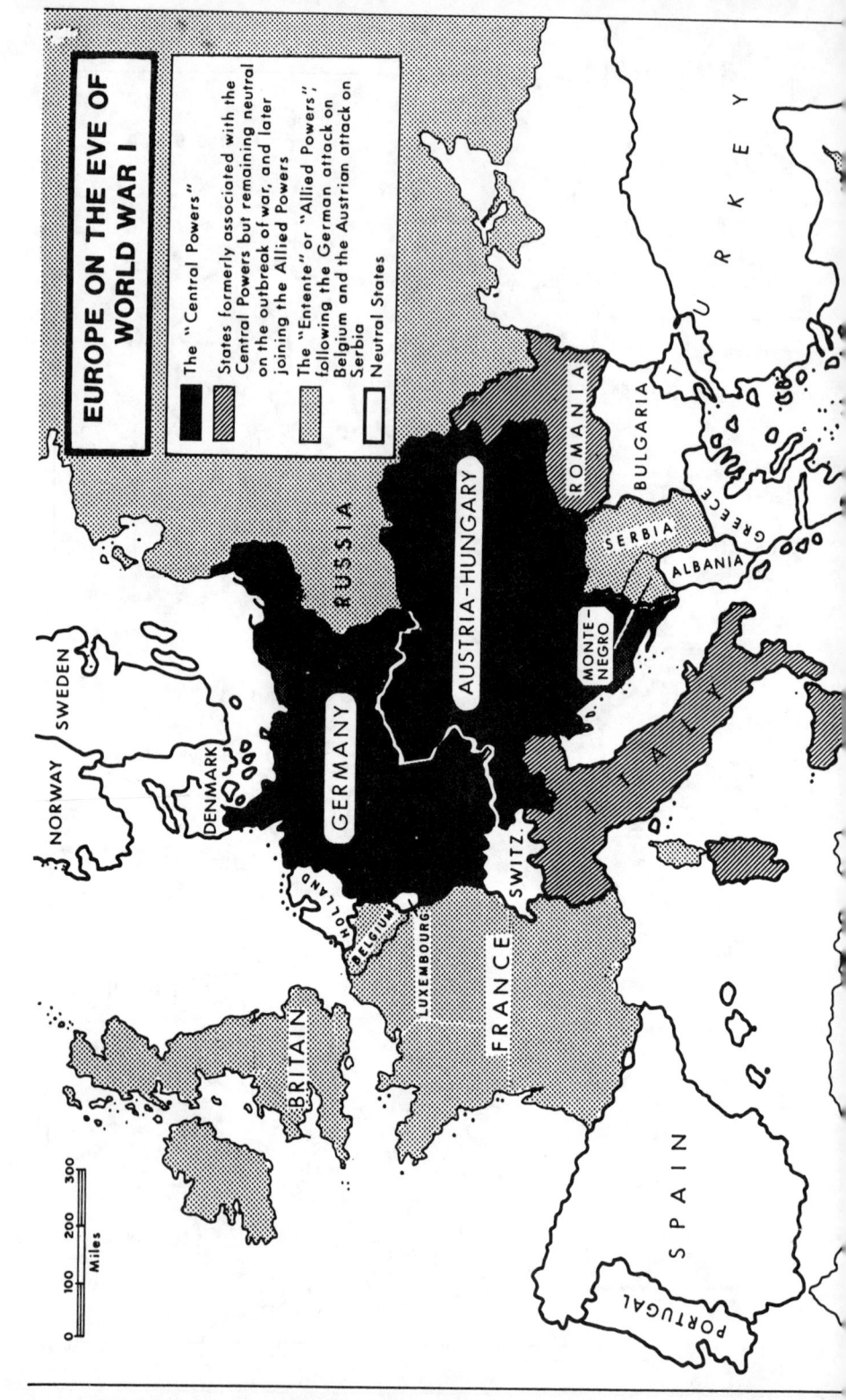

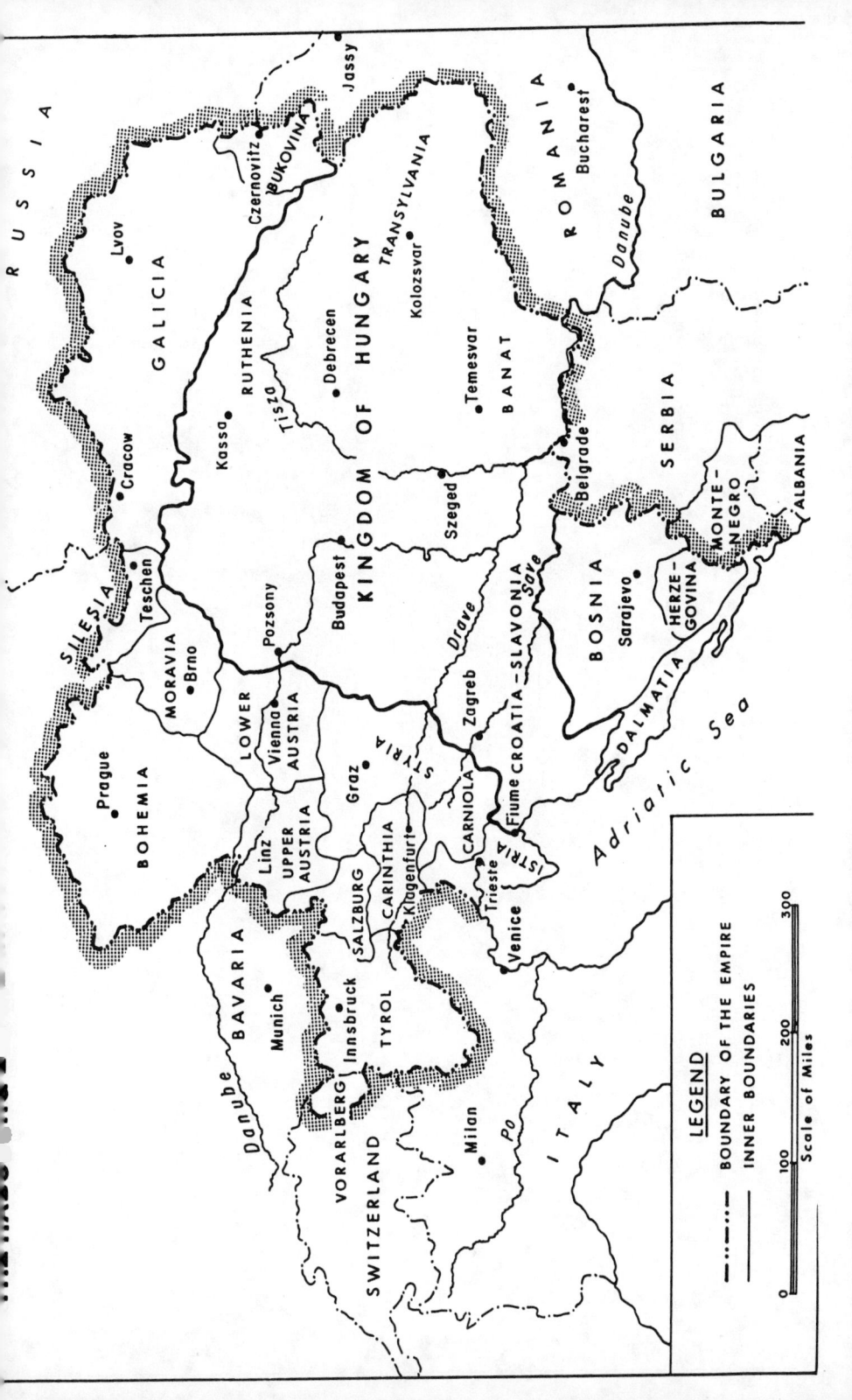